Global Terrorism

Global Terrorism

Melting Borders, Hardened Walls

PRAVIN N. SHETH

RAWAT PUBLICATIONS

Jaipur • New Delhi • Bangalore • Mumbai

ISBN 81-7033-950-2

Published by
Prem Rawat for *Rawat Publications*
Satyam Apts., Sector 3, Jawahar Nagar, Jaipur 302 004 (India)
Phone: 0141 265 1748 / 7006 Fax: 0141 265 1748
E-mail: info@rawatbooks.com
Website: www.rawatbooks.com

Delhi Office
4858/24, Ansari Road, Daryaganj, New Delhi 110 002
Phone: 011-23263290

Also at Bangalore and Mumbai

Typeset by Rawat Computers, Jaipur
Printed at Chaman Enterprises, New Delhi

To

Jayana Clerk
Noble personage; Warm, supportive comradeship

Sheela Bhatt
Excellence in Journalism; Warm Affectionate Bonding

President Bush on Terrorism: Changing Nuances

September 20, 2001: "They (the terrorists) hate our freedoms—our freedom of religion, our freedom of speech, our freedom to vote and assemble and disagree with each other...Our war will not end until every terrorist group of global reach has been found, stopped and defeated... We know that God is not neutral between freedom and fear, justice and cruelty."

May 1, 2003: "The war on terror is not over, yet it is not endless. We do not know the day of final victory, but we have seen the turning of the tide." And, on SS Cole ship, "The (Iraq) war is over. We've won."

May 13, 2003: "This incident in Saudi Arabia shows that we still have a war to fight."

June 2, 2004: "The global terrorist networks are heirs of all the murderous ideologies of the 20th century... they follow the path of Fascism, Nazism and totalitarianism...The conflict will take many turns, with setbacks on the course to victory. But we believe in Ronald Reagan's words that 'the future belongs to the free'."

August-end, 2004: "I don't think you can win this war, but you can create conditions so that those who use terror as a tool are less acceptable in parts of the world" (Bush to Matt Lauer of NBC's 'To-day' show). Next day, sensing its political implications, President repackaged his views, saying, "Make no mistake about it. We're winning and we'll win."

August-end, 2004: "We're staying on the offensive—striking terrorists abroad—so that we do not have to face them at home" (President's Acceptance Speech at Republican Convention).

October 2004: "It is unlike any conventional war we have fought in the past. It will not end with a peace treaty or by the capture of a single city or the fall of a single regime. It will be won through the steady advance of freedom, hope and opportunity."

Contents

V
Changing Scenario

VI
Theatres of Conflict

VII
Perspectives

Foreword

Terrorism as a weapon of revolutionary change has been around since at least the 19th century when the Russian terrorists fashioned it as a political tool against Czarist despotism. It has since been tried by different groups in different parts of the world and has taken different forms of struggle, new weapons of attack, new goals, and new forms of ideological justification. Long justified in political terms, it has increasingly begun to take religious form.

Although all religious groups have resorted to it sometime or other, it has now most closely associated with Islam. This raises some very difficult questions. Why have Muslims become terrorists in recent years? How do Muslim terrorists legitimize their method in religious terms, especially the phenomenon of suicide bombers, which is almost unique to them (excepting LTTE terrorists of Sri Lanka who first adopted it)? What are their goals and driving passions? Do they just want to end the American hegemony in the Middle East? Or, are they against the American global domination in general? Or, are they revolting against modernity itself? We also need to explain why Islamic terrorism has sprung up in some Muslim societies and not others, and why it has found support among some groups and not others. We also need to analyze the internal debate that it has triggered off among Muslim theologians during the last twenty years and the ways in which its religious legitimacy is discussed.

Professor Pravin Sheth's new book is a most welcome contribution to the growing literature on terrorism. It is comprehensive and covers the terrorist attack of 9/11 as well as those that preceded and followed it in different parts of the world. He is a political scientist as well as sociologist, and brings to the subject the complementary perspectives of the two disciplines. He is both an academic and an activist, and is again able to bring academic detachment and moral and political engagement to his inquiry. He has lived and continues to live in India and United States, and is thoroughly familiar with the popular and academic literature as well as the political perspectives of these two countries. He is, therefore, able to analyse terrorism from the perspective of the traumatized United States as well as the relatively detached perspectives of the rest of the world. He rightly emphasizes that although terrorism needs to be countered by military means, they are never enough. Terrorism springs from long festering grievances, and cannot be ended until these grievances are tackled by political means. Terrorism also derives its legitimacy from a particular way of looking at the world and the role of violence in it. If we are to counter it successfully, we also need to address its underlying ideology and show how alternative methods of struggle are not only available but likely to be more effective.

Professor Sheth deals with these and other questions with great skill and erudition. He has a distinct point of view but he does not allow it to intrude into his discussions of specific issues. When so much contemporary talk on terrorism is suffused with the spirit of revenge and hatred, he is a voice of wisdom and sanity. I learnt much from his valuable book and have no doubt that others will do so too.

Bhikhu Parekh
University of Westminster and House of Lords

Preface

Terrorism has pushed the world into a perilous new age of insecurity. Partly faceless but a fully focused enemy of humanity, terrorism has created such multifaceted, profound changes in the world that it needs to be comprehended from different angles and at different levels of viewing. This book is a modest attempt to contribute to the growing literature on developments around 9/11 and after, by treating terrorism as a dynamic movement, as a complex phenomenon and as a global problem.

I have tried to narrate in the book varied manifestations, forces and developments during the 44 tumultuous and transformative months after 9/11. It also recounts and documents juxtaposing mutually different viewpoints, the events and problems created by terrorism on three major theatres of conflict—USA, the Middle East, and so far, rather less focused region of South Asia.

While going through the ongoing literature on fundamentalism and terrorism, I found that important issues such as the nature and expanse of the ṣtatus quoist *umma* (Islamic world) and its relationship—actually, 'disconnect'—with America, the causal context of political Islam and the fast-forward track of anti-Americanism needs comprehensive examination. So also, the portentous presence of this menace in South Asia with

Pakistan in focus is not given proportionate attention it deserves. I have, therefore, found it imperative to delve in detail on South Asia as an India-centric region and Pakistan as a continuous patron of terrorism and the hub of the post-Taliban al Qaeda activities. Its potentiality as a conduit of nuclear terrorism is also emphasized.

Again, informed readers in the field of conflict studies will notice that, probably, for the first time, this book is designed with a framework that distinguishes it from other well-researched and rich-resourced works published so far. Chapters on cultural conflicts, globalization-'Talibanization' syndrome, Jihad-MacWorld and global-local cross-pressures are cases in point. I have also tried to distinguish this book with my exercise in last chapter at discussing major paradigms or conceptual frameworks that seek to explain and analyze terrorism as a problem and a complex phenomenon of global concern through the lens of Francis Fukuyama, Samuel Huntington, Benjamin Barber, Thomas Friedman and Mahatma Gandhi. The perspectives that develop with their perceptive paradigms help us get the insights into this highly complex psycho-political movement and religion-centric ideology. Discussed at one place, they are expected to engage us in our inquiry into the problematique and resolutique of terrorism. Sometimes as alternatives or competitive, sometimes paradoxical but mainly mutually complementary, these paradigms, together, help us develop a balanced perspective of this most challenging concern of this millennium. Instead of treating them as opposites or alternatives, it might be prudent to make them as subsuming, mutually accommodating worldviews of one another.

This book has evolved out of my first work on this subject in Gujarati language. Alongwith other intellectuals, Dr. P.J. Patel, eminent Indian sociologist and Vice-Chancellor, S.P. University, Gujarat in his 'Foreword' to it suggested that, in view of its format with documented and juxtaposed references, it should be published in English as well. In this context, and in view of the relevance of this subject as well as the ongoing concern of mankind, I got inclined to work further on this subject, update the matter and integrate new insights obtained during the 44 months of the profound change in the world after the first work was published in June 2003. Dr. Sudha Nikhil Mehta helped me in the translation of the original Gujarati text and Mahesh Vasavada, a veteran journalist, gave me the benefits of his comments on that script. I am thankful to both of them.

Meanwhile, I have changed the format, structure and content of the script that, inevitably, the dynamic nature and intimations of terrorism and the growing complexities of this phenomenon generated. Terrorist attacks spanned more areas, with more daring actions and diverse techniques; more dramatic events took place and facts unearthed that shocked the conscience of the people of America, Europe, Asia and even the Muslim world. All this is reflected in this book.

In spite of his pressing work, Lord Bhikhu Parekh, Professor of Political Theory at University of Westminister, London has spared time to go through the script and write a thoughtful "Foreword" to the book. It has enhanced the value of the book. I feel greatly gratified to him.

My wife Surbhi, with her characteristic involvement in my work, as always, prodded me to complete this work. I acknowledge, with thanks, the scholars, perceptive analysts and journalists and the media whose views I have extensively quoted here with benefit. So also, I am grateful to the dailies and magazines for the use of photo-pics from these sources.

Kailash Rawat and Pranit Rawat of Rawat Publications have taken care to make it an excellent production, as in the case of my previous books in the past. I am thankful to them, their able editing team.

However, whatever deficiencies that may be noted in interpretation or analysis of the matter in the book are entirely mine. I hope, this book will be welcomed by the social scientists, students of international relations, social activists engaged in educating people about the most formidable challenge of our security and peace, and those who work for melting the borders and removing the walls that separate man and man, religion and religion, and nation and nation.

Athens-GA USA

Pravin Sheth
pravinsheth@hotmail.com

I

The Context

1

A Turning Point of World History

[illegible]

The attacks on the World Trade Centre on September 11, 2001 came both literally and metaphorically as a bolt out of the blue. They not only came on USA, but soon rolled on other regions

1

A Turning Point in World History

> Osama bin Laden disapproves of specific U.S. policies and their attendant military, political and economic implications. His genius lies not simply in rallying Muslims for Jihad, but in articulating a consistent and convincing case that Islam is under attack of America and its allies. Al Qaeda condemns America's protection of corrupt Muslim regimes and its unqualified support of Israel, the occupation of Afghanistan and Iraq and a further litany of real world grievances.
>
> They will go to any length, not only to destroy our secular, democratic way of life, but deter what they view as specific attacks on their land, their communities, and their religion. The U.S. leaders should recognize this fact and adjust their policies accordingly. And position them accordingly abroad. Otherwise, even moderate Muslims will be oriented into supporting bin Laden's anti-Western offensive.
>
> — **Anonymous**, Head of CIA's anti-bin Laden team in *Imperial Hubris: Why the West is Losing the War on Terror* (2004)

The attacks on the World Trade Center on September 11, 2001 came both literally and metaphorically as a bolt from the blue. They not only came on USA, but soon rolled on other regions of the world too. In the process, the frontier that separated America from abroad was also to melt away.

Since 9/11, three developments became decisive worldwide. First, the war on terrorists to root out the militant *jehadis*. Second, political rise of those fundamentalists who were, so far, on the margins of religious spectrum, particularly in the Islamic world, and their networking on fast forward track. The third is the growing, widening gap between the globalized and those still unable or unwilling to be drawn into the globalization process; between the rich and the poor within and outside and across nations; between the democratic ideology and the Islamic ideology; and the deepening of perceptions of the modernist, modernizing and status quoist communities.

The ideo-political scenario, which was to change fast, threatened to undo the socio-political fabric that seemed to be shaping along local-global continuum.

The reward announced on Osama bin Laden's and Abu al Zarqawi's heads is history's most expensive manhunt. But, the psycho-civil costs were to be unquantifiable. Citizens of the world's proven democracies have begun to experience curbs on their civil liberties in 'peace time.' Civilians on airports, on trains, in gatherings in schools, hotels and theaters became the terrorists' soft targets. Shias and Sunnis were to settle their accounts violently by believers in and near mosques in Pakistan and Iraq, and between the Jews and the Palestinians in Jerusalem and Gaza. There were to be no limits to spiraling terrorist and counter-terrorist scale of violence with the breach of the boundary of civility. The boundary was even to extend to children in Jerusalem, Baghdad and Beslan. Nay, children themselves were to be suicide bombers. Teenage girls and women were to choose to be the carriers of death.

All the boundaries were to be obliterated—physical, cultural, and ideological. Only the walls of ideo-cultural divide between countries and communities were to go higher, get thicker and hardened. Boundaries melted but walls began to come up higher and higher.

* * *

September 11, 2001. Around 9.02 a.m. at Sarasota in Florida. Andy Cardenny, the Chief of Staff, leaning at his ear informed President Bush in a gentle voice, "Sir, another plane has also attacked the other tower (the World Trade Center—WTC), and it too..." The President was stunned, but he could not show such feelings, and so remained calm. The reason: he was participating in a program at a Sarasota elementary school and cameras were focusing on him from all angles! (*Newsweek*, Interview, December 4, 2001). Later on, in July 2004, Michael Moore in his controversial docu-movie showed with skillful use of a video footage that the President continued reading the story, "My Pet Dog" to the kids in that class—"with a 'listless' face for seven minutes!"

Thereafter, the Air Force One (the special plane of the President) left for Washington DC, but instead of the scheduled direct flight, it started a zigzag journey via a stop at Louisiana and other states before reaching the capital. Bush was sitting in the bowels of the White House in highly protected bunker rooms called PEOC (President's Emergency Operation Cell) at 5.30 p.m. Vice President Dick Cheney and Secretary of State Collin Powell also sat with somber face. Came the statement of the President: "We are going to what it takes to win the war." It seemed simple enough, but it inherently contained many far-reaching steps to be taken. America, a country that had earlier sent bomb missiles without any constraint on Sudan, Afghanistan, Kosovo and many other places, was stunned at this experience at home.

Twin Towers were demolished whereas the Pentagon was attacked and damaged. "Each word of WTC—'World'-'Trade'-'Center' charged with profound meaning, altogether signifying more than the sum of its parts", both symbolically and metaphorically, were to change the form, substance and the ethos of the post-9/11 world.

After the Cold War, for nearly a decade, America had enjoyed a status of being the one and only superpower and had come to be known as 'Globocop' and 'Globocorp' in the world. This event was a great and cruel shock to its psyche of superiority and immunity. A bearded man, living in caves, had been able to raze to ground, within minutes, the two sky high towers of WTC in the heart of New York City, that symbolized the great economic power of the nation, and turn them into rubble or what later came to be called as 'Ground Zero'! A few hijackers, using pin-like devices of Iron Age, had also damaged a part of the Pentagon and checkmated the proud masters of cyber age! And that too, in America, equipped as it was with the latest state-of-the-art missiles, and, again, by using America's own super jet airplanes! The hyper power that could upset the working of governments in the Middle East and Latin America through their military and intelligence networks and mediums like the CIA was itself put on the alert in the land of FBI and the Pentagon. For a couple of days, notes Craig Unger in his book, *House of Bush, House of Saud*, while ashes of the Twin Towers were still smoking and barely a plane was moving over America: "Hearts for transplant can't go by plane; Bill Clinton's in Australia and can't get home. But a 747 filled with rich Saudis including notable scions of bin Laden has no such problem. They're off to desert kingdom in the bleep of some exalted pager" (15 of the 19 among the 9/11 hijackers were Saudis). This controversy was to be raised some months thereafter, though.

Some months after, a five-color alert code was evolved. New York and Washington were to be put on orange color alert nine times by perceived terrorist attack by the third anniversary of 9/11 was marked. Orange color code was to continue for months even three years thereafter.

The telephone number 911 in America is assigned for any person in any trouble to dial and get relief and rescue missions made available at once. It is natural to recall this number when one wants an ambulance or police for help and other such services. In the psyche of people of America and the world September 11 (9/11), thus, has now turned into a metaphor as '911' indicating a universal condition of terrorism. From that very day President Bush accepted that 'we' (USA) have sent invitations (to all states of the world) to choose between 'us' (America and its allies) and 'them' (Laden, Islamic fundamentalists and their supporters) in this war against world terrorism.

As the US Secretary of State Collin Powell put it, "The shadow of terrorism has covered the entire world. But, the resolve to defeat it also was never more determined earlier; nor were the hopes of acquiring international cooperation to meet this and other broad challenges before the world as high as they are now." As President Bush has said, "From the evil of terrorism ultimately only the good would emerge. From our tears we must look for opportunities to make the world a better place for the coming generations; and this opportunity we shall seize."

In the meantime, America itself was changing fast. There is a marked change in the role and philosophy of President Bush himself. If Bush has not read world history or even American history, he is creating it! The 'time' itself gives such an imposing and momentous responsibility to a mediocre leader! Before 9/11, Bush was a 'neo-isolationist' politician who wanted to propagate modern destructive missiles system and to keep America away from international problems. But, now, he has turned into an enthusiastic internationalist. He sought to become a world leader who wants to take military steps along with humanitarian policy of providing help and try to save millions of Afghans with aid of food, medicine and reconstruction. Also, instead of scorning and ridiculing the projects of development of the backward countries, now, in Afghanistan after the Taliban, it was possible that he would himself adopt some concrete policy for ensuring sustainable stability and peace, similar to the European Marshall Plan that came after the Second World War.

Around 9/11, the personal esteem of all Americans, from ordinary to elite classes, has also nose-dived. They were used to many comforts: a large variety of ready-to-eat food; more television channels than weeks in a year; educational toys for their children; soccer camps; pizza parties, universal colleges, computer and video games and weekend picnics and long-distant tours; and many other things were woven quite naturally in their daily life to relieve them of all anxieties. However, now, the citizens in superpower state no longer take safety and security for granted; even restful sleep was questionable. Anxious thoughts would not leave their minds. The Thanksgiving Day (on November 22) that year was not celebrated at Las Vegas, Lake Tahoe or in Disney World, but by meeting local friends and people were content with 'socializing'. Consumer goods like clothes and Kleenex were sold more, but sale figures of items like shoes, socks, dog food and other such items indicate that people had turned towards savings rather than spending, after the economic pessimism and recession that followed 9/11. Doesn't all this seem uncharacteristic for a consumerist, mobile society?

On the other hand, with a scare of Anthrax, bin Laden opened another front of terrorism. In the offices of the mainstream media like the *New York Times* and leading Congressmen were received envelopes containing white powder, and this brought on a wave of real scare among the ruling circles. Even the buildings on the Capitol Hill and the sessions of the Senate had to be closed for four days! In an opinion poll conducted by the *Newsweek*, 42 percent believed that an attack with biological or chemical weapons would occur; the other 56 percent were worried about some other kind of attack. Innumerable people, suffering from mental tension, overflowed the diaries of psychiatrists and counselors asking for appointments. The chemists could not meet the rising demand for drugs for insomnia and tension, as their stocks were exhausted soon. Gas masks were sold online in thousands. Many names were put in its 'waiting list' even! An amazing rise in the number of people attending church, *Masjid* (mosque) and other religious places occurred. When a threat was received that on September 22, another attack was to take place on Boston, some 15,000 Christians in its City Hall Plaza fell to their knees for saying prayers. On the other hand, on the Thanksgiving Day that had a long holiday week, the major airports witnessed empty parking plots. From the first week of 9/11, airlines, motels and hotels, and other thriving tourist industries had begun to lose business. It stretched even to the third anniversary of 9/11, when Delta Air reported harsh financial steps resulting in the virtual shut down its operations at St. Worth airport and the U.S. Air declaring its liquidation. This had adversely affected the income of many Indians and other communities depending on tourism and hospitality industry. Without tourists, except for the business class, many seats in airplanes began to remain vacant. The hotels and motels lost their shine without tourists and coach traveler passengers. Thousands received 'lay off' notices. Owners of Day's Inn and Comfort Inn and the like said, "Now we have to reduce our staff in the motels. There is a reduction even in their salaries, which they accept." The tourist and transport industries, catering to the Americans in their economy and entertainment, have suffered badly. Certain airlines had to stop operations or put the aircrafts in hangers. Americans, insisting on saving time, and always running on wheels for achieving this aim, now had to spend more time at airports for security checks, and compromise their thoughts on individual freedom in front of the security staff etc., whether they liked it or not. *Newsweek* (October 8, 2001)'s columnist Anna Quindlen also admitted, "Finally, we have, indeed, become (in its broad sense) the 'citizen of the world'. We can now understand the suffering of the citizens in Beirut or Belfast". A friend of mine who left London to live in New York said, "The difference that existed in the acceptance of the results by the British and the proud optimism of the Americans was like the difference between the tolerance of bombings of the Nazi blitzkrieg (that the British had experienced) and the habit of the Americans to purchase war bonds; but now that difference is obliterated."

At this stage, the 'reflexive protest' usually made by the liberals and leftist intellectuals and activists against the civil or military interventions of America in other countries (Vietnam, Rwanda, Bosnia, Kuwait, Iraq-1990, etc.) was not forthcoming in a uniform or coordinated style. Of course, some of the leftist travelers of super information highway did lodge protest against the step of bombing that America took against Afghanistan; carried on a signature campaign against it in a memorandum; some professors of the Yale and Berkeley universities organized a few 'sit-in' seminars in the campus throbbing with characteristic social liberalism. A pacifist suggested, "By taking revenge for the attack by OBL (Osama bin Laden) by a stupid step of counter-attack, no one of the dead is going to return." Another pacifist advocated, "Bomb them with butter. We shall be able to turn the Afghans and other poor Muslim back from their self-annihilating activities only by satisfying them with food etc." Like the American Muslims, Carol Almond of Massachusetts also said, "We have been attacked, but we must go to the roots of why that happened." There was nothing new if the students create an atmosphere of awareness or questioning in the US.

Just as there are people who are media savvy and who make vivid statements about 'political correctness' in India, there are such people also in America. John Leo, who has named such people as 'our political chatterbox' (talkative class) said in *US News and World Report* (December 3, 2001), "This talkative class is put off even by today's war (by America) in Self-Defense; it does not matter (to them) even if America has to suffer the greatest loss of life in the history of war—and that too on its own home!"

Journalist Andrew Sullivan observes, "The intellectuals participating in programs of BBC and NPR (a popular radio service called National Public Radio) had to accept that when the Taliban were rolled back, they had remained cool over analysis!" On his website Sullivan wrote, "The pundits, editors and cable news reporters have come down two steps in the social ladder. After 9/11, their impact on stamping of views on news has diminished." This thinking class or section of the public had played a great role in making possible the resignation of President Nixon on Vietnam issue. Noting this, he points out that in today's context, thanks to their attitude, how 'disempowered' this group has become.

The well-known analyst Brush Nussbaum, in *Business Week* (October 1, 2001) says, "The Americans were used to the idea in the decade of the 90s that it is easy and natural for them to be in a situation to become rich and enjoy security, but the new reality has made the workers of security systems trotting about in uniforms as their 'new heroes'. Manual workers, who risk their own lives, such as the fire brigade men, police, etc., have found a much greater and more popular acceptance in place of bankers, moneylenders, techno-billionaires, merchants and industrialists. Those professors doing serious discussions, those who discussed matters on television shows, and shows like 'Survivor' that projected illusory values now occupied the backseat in popular psyche. When I was a student in 1969, the Berkeley Campus was the new center of opposition to Vietnam and for values of peace. The posters were seen all over declaring 'Make Love, not War". Some people always attended these 'Teach-in' and 'Sit-in' programs that kept on being organized in the Berkeley and Columbia campuses. This time, the number of people to come out for programs to oppose war was small. To see those carrying placards of anti-war slogans seemed things to be ignored altogether! One observer even said that such a class has turned into 'a bubble of unreality'."

The interesting part is that even the progressives and leftist forces are split up. In the 1960s, Todd Gitlin, now Professor of Sociology at the New York University, was the president of 'Students For A Democratic Society'. This Society had become a reflective laboratory of movements for various causes and high human values such as opposition to Vietnam, civil rights of the blacks and women, etc. But, as the *Time* magazine (October 8, 2001) writes, "Last week, the American flag was furling in the balcony of the Greenwich village apartment of Professor Gitlin against the terrorist attack (as an expression of patriotism)." Quoting Gitlin, this magazine says that "for an effective response to terrorism, use of force must be done with great discretion. The Leftist thinkers, who make a reflex protest out of sheer habit, against the military proceedings of America, are responding with a blind eye to the ground realities. That is why, this time when President Bush declared his policy against Afghanistan, the protests lodged by the Leftist/progressive groups were ignored. The online paper named *Slate* even wrote, 'The Left are Left behind!'." A pregnant pun!

In *Nation*, the leftist journalist Christopher Hutchins complained about those who protest against war that is imposed on America. Terrorists "are not supporters of a liberal and just ideal, but are supporters of a dreamland of an authoritarian leader's orthodox and extremist ideology". Hitchins aptly says, "The bombers of Manhattan are representatives of fascism with an Islamic face...They hold in contempt the values of the western countries such as freedom to women, spirit of scientific inquiry and keeping religion away from state."

The 9/11 phenomenon created a rift in the educational field of America too. Writing in Houston (Texas)'s daily, *The Chronicle*, Robert Jenson, Professor of Journalism at Austin, Texas, wrote that the terrorist attack on Manhattan was similar to 'a wide terrorist attacks' that America had earlier indulged in Vietnam and Central/Latin America. This kind of statement invited a response from that University's President Larry Falkner who too wrote a letter to *The Chronicle* against it. Reminding us of Voltaire by his method, he accepted that Jenson had a right to express his view, he wrote, "However, this belief of Jenson, which is absolutely foolish with regard to the understanding of public policy, today seems to be an unadulterated source of it." David Horowitz, so rebelliously active in the 1960s, turned extremely conservative in his opposition to Ladenism. However, Samuel Huntington, later on in his book, *Who are we? The Challenge to American National Identity* was to ask, "September 11 has brought a revival of American patriotism and a renewal of American identity. But already there are signs that this revival is fading even though the post-9/11 world, Americans face unprecedented challenges to their security."

America is an open polity that in critical times, reminds one of a cocktail of contradictory thinking. It turned out soon that during this fateful phase, President Bush and his close advisors were finalizing strategy of invading Iraq and causing the fall of President Saddam Hussein following the willing acceptance of the intelligence inputs that Saddam possessed weapons of mass destruction (WMD) and had links with al Qaeda. No one in responsible position then argued that if the US-led post-war occupation in Iraq prolongs for an indefinite period resulting in unmitigated American casualties, political uncertainty along with growing mood of anti-Americanism in the Muslim world—or, if it leads to a fear syndrome that civilians have to be drafted into military duty compulsorily, as during the Vietnam war, or if, civil war situation becomes there a reality—then the forces opposing war would get greater support from people forcing President Bush to radically think of forced, face-saving withdrawal from Iraq. Also, after capturing Afghanistan, and chasing bin Laden out of it, there were frequent references, in clearer terms, in the speeches of leaders like Bush and Powell to terms such as 'rogue nations' and the 'axis of evils' with Saddam to become the first whipping boy. The critics of Bush's America, on the other hand, were to term it as 'Evil Empire' or 'the superpower out to destroy Islam'. Bush's war on terrorism, in the process, was to take a meandering and uncharted course with the three big B's—Bush, Blair and bin Laden, the mutually checkmating adversaries—and taking the whole world as hostage, and continuously in search of ever more lethal weapons, ever more violent forms and still ever more poisonous ideologies. Historian Niall Ferguson and political scientist John Esposito, probably, are closer to figure out the present and the future world with appropriate titles of their books (2004). Ferguson has titled his book as *Colossus: The Price of America's Empire* and Esposito has aptly titled his book as *Unholy War: Terror in the Name of Islam.*

2

'Breakthrough' on All Fronts?

The policy that Washington follows would only nurture the counter-revenge of the terrorists and it will not prevent them from suspending their final goal of attacking America. All this, in the process, would only contribute to the growth of terror and weapons of mass destruction.

Due to its own shocking announcements and performance (against Afghanistan, Iraq and other similar cases) America begets such threats, and it is left with only two options. One is that attention be paid to its just and legitimate complaints and help them enter the mainstream civil society in the world; and also honour the just world order and its organizations such as the UNO.

The other option is to develop such highly sophisticated weapons capable of world destruction and thus have a monopoly of a superpower that would rule all other nations; even when the imagined threat against itself may be very remote! But even this would result in developing small yet effectively terrorizing techniques for its opponents or enemies. This process, ultimately, would generate serious fears for the people of America as well as the world.

> Those who can avert such events from happening, and can bring sufficient pressure on American authorities to make policy ensuring future security, are none other than its alert citizens.
>
> — **Noam Chomsky** (March 21, 2003)

Perhaps, the youth of America have behaved with unexpected maturity this time. It has become the 'Generation 911' now. The young people, studying in the campuses of Berkeley, Michigan, Kent, etc., have seen everything good and optimistic until now—peace, prosperity, security of employment; even as late as 1999 the 'Dot.Com' dream that would make them a millionaire and allow them to retire at the age around 30. So fulfilled would be their careers by then! But 9/11 became the turning point in their life, decidedly giving it a new direction and approach.

The opinion poll of the first week of November by *Newsweek* indicated that 83 percent young people appreciated the stand taken by President George Bush; 85 percent supported military action. Before 9/11 they had no concern with international issues and trends; but on that day their indifference evaporated. The colleges and even small 'Teach-in' (discussion) groups on topics like international relations, Middle East, Islamic studies, and biological diseases were flocked by large numbers. The clever young people, ambitious to make fortunes on the Wall Street, and earn huge profits, now began to think of joining the government, FBI and CIA etc.! At the time of Vietnam war, the students of the Michigan University were in the forefront for protesting against the then war policy. Only 28 percent of the young people were thinking of joining politics in the decade of the 90s; but now the figure has gone way up on the scale of political activism.

On certain campuses, Arab/Muslim students experienced threats or contemptuous treatment, gestures or e-mails. But most of them received consolation and support from their non-Muslim co-students. After checking out on different campuses, two journalists wrote, "Ordinarily it is understood that they are indifferent and lack political experience, but this generation has special qualities to understand the present war." Judith Rodin, the President of Training Center at University of Pennsylvania, believes, "Even more than the elders, they (the youth) understand it better that this is a clash between civilizations. This is something of an event that we have not witnessed in the last thousand years."

In any case, right from the first week of 9/11, nearly all the homes in America had a star-studded tricolor flag (white, blue, red); and in children's psyche were carved the emotions of supporting their own nation. In mid-October 2001 Halloween festival, the store managers reported that the greatest demand had been for costumes of police officers, fire fighters, Statue of Liberty, etc. The girls painted their nails with the three colors of patriotism. Indian-American women wore red-white-blue tricolor bangles or ribbons! Roger Simone, the columnist, confessed in *US News and World Report* (October 22), "Now, we understand the horrors of terrorism firsthand. Now, we are all one."

Keeping in mind the expanse and multidimensional nature of terrorism, the Bush team took quick diplomatic steps with Russia, China, India and many Arab countries, for creating an anti-terrorist alliance. Besides this 'war by diplomacy', ignoring the fact that it has a terrorist character, Pakistan was also taken into this alliance because of its geography and strategic importance in the plans of abolishing the Taliban rule from Afghanistan and capturing bin Laden and getting secret information in the field. America had some tough and threatening talks with Pakistani President Pervez Musharraf to make him work against the Taliban, a child of his own policy; and in return for his 'u-turn', the clever President played the card of demanding huge financial aid to his country, removal of sanctions etc. to come out a winner in this 'war by diplomacy'.

Shibli Telhamie, the Senior Fellow of the Think Tank Brookings Institute, says that in 1990 the alliance that America had made against Iraq was in a totally different context. In 1990, the small Gulf nations were finding Iraq a real threat. At that time, the definite mission of getting Kuwait out of the clutches of Iraq did seem appropriate. Thirdly, at that time, CNN and even the other effective media of the Middle East itself were in favor of the western nations. This made it possible to mold the Arab public opinion on their side. Iraq, on the other hand, was handicapped in this matter.

Not this time. Around 9/11, the Arab countries, their rulers and people, have not felt an immediate threat from bin Laden. The Muslim countries had doubts about when and where would this war end. There is a wide fear that beginning with the Taliban and bin Laden, this war would then gradually cover all the Arab and Muslim nations too! Besides, in the last decade, the media has developed a great deal, like satellite communication, television, etc., and even the terrorists know how to use these for the time and space of the war. Also, Al Jazeera—the Arab channel from Qatar—has become more popular for entertainment and reliable information for the people of the Muslim world, in the place of channels like CNN. In addition, in the last few years, the anti-America propaganda by media savvy Laden and others has made a great dent in its prestige with the Muslim political culture. In the pan-Muslim mind a lot of misunderstanding and even contempt has spread about America and the western culture. Bernard Lewis, the highly experienced historian and Middle East expert, explained with documents in 1990, the cultural and conscious roots and processes that caused the contempt of the Muslims for western civilization.

For such a challenging task, the Bush team meted out imaginative approach as far as possible, and used the present alliance effectively for at least Afghanistan. With multi-national diplomatic support, on October 7, 2001, with mostly the British military partnership, and from airbases of Tazakistan and Uzbekistan (the states under former Soviet Union and now under Russian influence) and of Pakistan, America began to launch missiles and air bombing on Taliban territory. For the first four weeks, it was not able to loosen the grip of Taliban or its air attacks did nothing to demoralize the opponent. In the meantime, the terrorists opened another front within America by Anthrax that left a trail of real scare of biological violence. Al Jazeera also kept on telecasting the audio tapes of Islamic leaders including bin Laden and the scenes of loss of life and material that was occurring in Afghanistan. When the power or arrogance of Taliban did not seem to be apparently affected, some grumbles began in American media and some political observers that threatened to rise to loud protests. A big power like America could not crush such a small power! There were ridiculing comments even in the Muslim and other nations. In the meantime, Musharraf, other Arab allies and India, along with others, warned President Bush to take care not to hurt the civil population in Afghanistan. Many observers reminded that Afghanistan had become military burial ground for outside armies from the time of Alexander the Great, down to the British and the Russians in recent centuries. In many countries, Muslim groups gathered in streets and sharply demonstrated their protests against America. Even the newspapers of authoritarian allies like Saudi Arabia and Egypt, continued to harp on 'ineffective' American attacks and the magic touch of bin Laden that made the Taliban invincible.

Suddenly, the scene changed dramatically. Since November 9, the retreat of the Taliban became faster. On that day its headquarters in North Afghanistan at Mazar-e-Sharif was taken over by anti-Taliban Afghan group, Northern Alliance, with America's support. Later, Herat in the west and the capital Kabul fell like ripe fruits into their hands. On 10th

November, President Bush and President Musharraf made a joint statement in New York that the forces of Northern Alliance would not enter Kabul, but would be outside it. But, in that very week, when the Taliban left their possession and suddenly went out of Kabul, the forces of Northern Alliance entered the capital. Among those imprisoned there, many were Pakistani and Arab soldiers fighting from the side of the Taliban. Musharraf did not have enough time to save these Pakistani soldiers and other spies there by sending his airplanes to lift them out. So, Musharraf who was officially lending support to fight the Taliban, but on the other hand sending trained soldiers to fight under them, was exposed for his double dealing games. *New York Times*, *San Hose Mercury News*, *Washington Post*, *San Francisco Chronicle* and such other print media, and even Rumsfeld, the Defense Secretary himself openly mentioned the double dealing of Pakistan. But, due to the pressure brought by the Secretary of State Colin Powell to ignore the whole matter, the Pakistan officers and soldiers were immediately sent back in aircrafts to Pakistan without much ado, so that not much evidence would remain of this cunning of Pakistan. Thus, maintaining all pro-America connections, America continued its work. When the Taliban had to leave Kunduz also some Pakistani and Saudi soldiers were arrested. In the last days of November the American strategy against Kandahar was successful, and all accepted this. The popularity of Bush rose went up a few notches. America's position turned stronger—rather invincible.

However, in the beginning of December, or thereafter, neither bin Laden nor Maulana Omar was captured. But now certain active forces of the Bush administration began to uphold the Action Formula to take steps against President Saddam of Iraq, who refused UNO observers to carry out inspection of his country for suspected presence of biological and chemical weapons and other weapons of mass destruction

(WMD), and who, they felt, was capable of giving such weapons to terrorists and other countries as well. All in all, by this war, America could relieve the burden of Vietnam and its failure in Somalia. In the process, the belief that the superpower would lose its prestige altogether and another kind of 9/11 would be created could also proved wrong. The illusions that the fierce Talibans would be invincible in their own country and that the 'brain' behind terrorism, bin Laden, would never lose power were also shattered by this war.

This then became not just a military victory but also a psychological and diplomatic success for America. Although Musharraf and other Arab rulers made frequent requests that during the month of Ramadan, falling late in November, the bombings and attacks by air and land must be stopped so that the Muslim public opinion is not too angry against them, America paid no attention. This nullified the tricky planning Musharraf had in mind for reinforcing his military resources and put a halt on the speedy retreat of the Talibans and get some breathing pause. It was significant that bombings continued during the Ramadan month, the forward march of Northern Alliance continued, and the charismatic leader bin Laden was put in a very awkward situation; and yet there was no repetition of the sharp demonstrations of the 7-10 October that had dotted different places from Jakarta to Karachi and Damascus! The trump card of opposition by religion community that the Muslim leaders held seemed to have lost its major value!

The most dramatic part was the change in the positions of Bush and bin Laden. As indicated in the earlier observations, on September 11, Bush was hiding in his own country; from the later days of November, it was bin Laden, Omar and al Zawahiri who had to hide in their country's caves on the run from the closely searching airplanes and spy equipments of Bush. In the last week of November, besieged in Kandahar, the

Taliban sent a signal for surrender, and requested that the Americans forget the episode 9/11. But one of the top officials of the Pentagon made a quick taunting reply, "In a short time the world would forget the Taliban itself."

Until the first week of November America was anxious that if there was no concrete result of its military attacks and if it is unable to take over important strategic land base (such as Mazar-e-Sharif air base, from where during winter the military airplanes could be used), then during the severe winter months nothing much could be accomplished and it would have to wait till next spring for any effective action. But, during such a long period, the American public would grow impatient and if war fatigue set in once, the support of the American government would go down a great deal. However, the military events of November turned into a 'psychological tonic' for Bush administration. Not only that, it also acquired a boost for forming a new forceful policy in the Middle East; and in this context, the terrorist connection and war marched ahead. (In the last week of December the dramatic change in the Israel-Palestine scene also helped this.) Laden and his open or secret supporters were put on the defensive. Thus, the equations on both sides changed for the good fortune of the world. Indeed, as Bush said, the most difficult stage of guerrilla warfare was still to be crossed. The most difficult steps are yet to follow: to uproot Laden and al Qaeda, collect billions of dollars along with the aid of allies for the reconstruction of Afghanistan; to remove the stamp of bad elements as reputation of Northern Alliance and along with it to give shape to a stable political condition.

The Karzai government, even three years after it was set up by the Americans, has its rule in reality confined to the capital city of Kabul and surrounding areas. The elements that create instability are still not under its adequate control. Even the Taliban and al Qaeda terrorists are active on the Pakistan-Afghanistan borders, if underground. With reluctant cooperation of Musharraf, America has captured the top leaders of al Qaeda; but for this he has been provided huge aid and military armaments, time and again, and a status as a non-NATO ally. America has had to adopt a policy even to displease India with its deals with Pakistan! Laden is still at large, despite intermittent protestations that the US-Pakistan forces were closing in and about to capture Laden. And, like Iraq after Saddam, even if Laden is caught or dead, the *jehadi* forces will remain aggressively violent and menacing in the new world in different theatres of conflict.

As Tim McGirk from Kabul reported (*Time*, August 9, 2004), "Since ousting the Taliban in December 2001, the U.S. struggled to hunt down al Qaeda leaders, disarm Afghanistan's warlords and shore up President Karzai against a revived Taliban-led insurgency. The renewed trade in opium has worsened those problems." Reports *Time*, Haji Juma Khan, the kingpin of a heroin-trafficking enterprise has helped al Qaeda establish a vast smuggling network that is peddling Afghan heroin out of the Pakistani port of Karachi to buyers across Middle East, Asia and Europe, and then in turn, is using the drug revenues to purchase weapons and explosives. Unloaded explosives in Karachi then are shipped overland to al Qaeda and the Taliban fighters. As Mirwais Yasini, head of the Afghan government's Counter-Narcotics Directorate, comments, "There are central linkages among Khan, Mullah Omar and bin Laden."

On the other hand, "there are visible signs of visible progress". In Kabul, the pace of reconstruction is observable and shops and markets full of goods" (*San Francisco Chronicle*, June 28, 2004). The Asia Foundation gives significant assistance to election process, to judicial reform, and to women's education. As Theodore Eliot, former US Ambassador to Afghanistan and William Fuller of Asia Foundation observed, "The progress gives us hope, but we recognize its fragility. The next few years will be decisive and the U.S. role will be indispensable.... Backing down in Afghanistan would open the way for terrorists to re-establish their bases, undermine US credibility in the Muslim world and weaken the UN and the multilateral coalition that provides support to Afghanistan's reconstruction and development...Despite the distractions in Iraq and elsewhere, there is no time for the US to divert attention from Afghanistan's security and development. Election of Hamid Karzai as the state's President in its first ever direct and comparatively free and fair election in this land of warlords and tribal loyalties will give the new government a much deserved legitimacy and an impetus to the US to cautiously promote liberal regimes in the Middle East to open up the Muslim societies with the support from within its liberal, reform-minded sections, and of other democracies."

However, the desired process got a rude jolt. On Friday, May 6, 2005 Imran Khan, a Pakistani cricket legend and strident critic of President Musharraf brandishing a copy of *Newsweek* (of May 9) read a report that US interrogators at Guantanamo prison had placed the Koran on toilet seats and even flushed one. His remarks critical of America and outraged comments of Muslim clerics were played throughout Pakistan and Afghanistan. Radical Islamic foes of the US-friendly Karzai regime quickly exploited the situation. But more significant was the spontaneous reaction in Afghanistan against the desecration of the Koran that soon turned into an organized anti-US movement. During the first four days of riots, at least 16 persons including a policeman were killed. Together with rising Taliban resistance in the east and southeastern border areas, "a political movement against the presence of US-led troops in Afghanistan is gathering pace. Given geo-cultural ties the renewed Islamic fervor could easily spread to the ethnic Pashtun belt of Pakistan, and Tajik and Uzbec regions of neighboring countries". A windfall for the terrorist forces (*Asia Times Online*, May 20, 2005)!

II

Environment

Muslim Population Dominant in 57 Countries

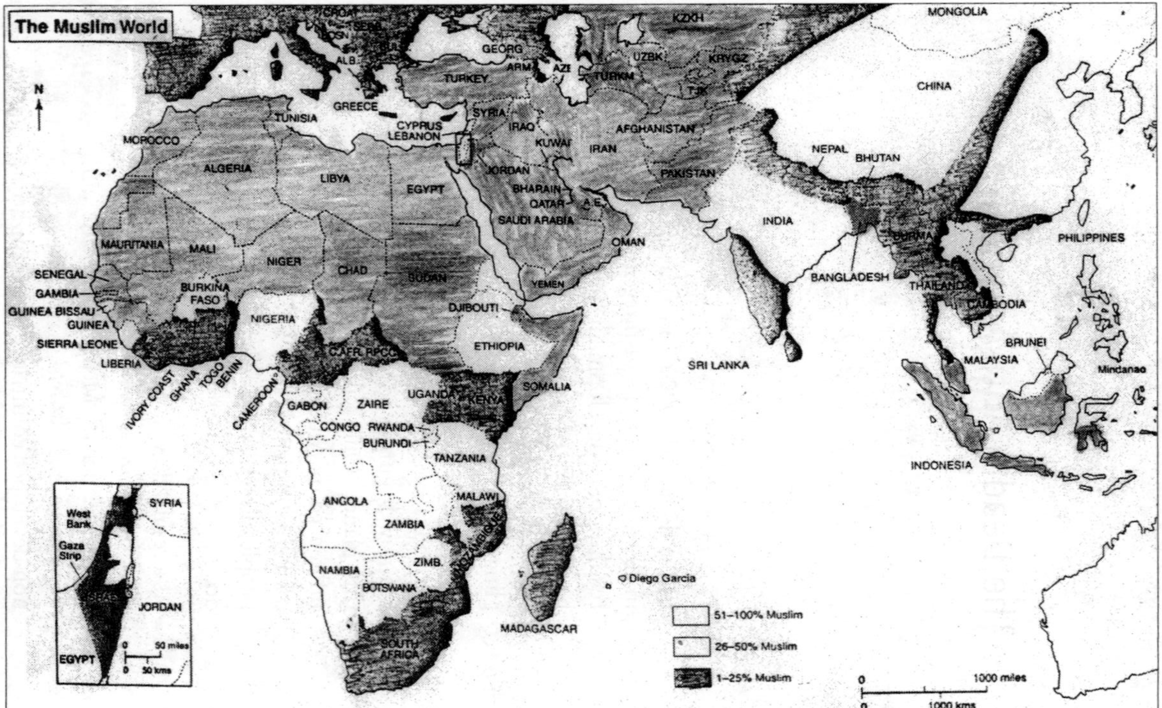

3

The Deadly Anti-American Islamic Rage

In the decade of 1990s, America quickly became very powerful in all fields. From the disintegration of the Soviet Union to the revolutionary developments in technology like the Internet—all have contributed to this phenomenon. The overall impact of this on the rest of the world is such that all countries are struggling to adjust to, accommodate their own societies with American power, domination and its socio-economic theories. Globalization has made them pervading thousand-fold, and it has now begun to touch the life in each and every country on this planet. One Pakistani diplomat told me, "We are more influenced by American culture and power, even more than our own government." That is right; we do influence the life of the people, directly or indirectly, more than their own governments do.

As a result, they have begun to blame us for their own problems now. There may even be the Seattle protest demonstrations of 1999. As Michael Mendelbaum, the author of *The Ideas that Conquered the World* says, the comparatively small and non-developed countries and organizations want to 'Gulliverise' America! Also, when America intervenes with too much action and turns into a 'Hyper Power', as a reaction to it, others unite to limit its power. The gigantic rallies etc. taken out against

> America's dealings with Iraq are an expression of this feeling only.
>
> In this context, then, it would not be surprising if the 'rogue nations', or other non-state organizations, that have nothing to lose in upsetting the world order resort to violence. The Iraq War has made all this very clear. In the meantime, the questions are always being asked; and after 9/11 the Americans ask with great surprise: 'Why do they (Muslims) hate us?' Now, this question is rejoined with our war policy with Iraq, 'But why should *everyone* hate us?'
>
> — **Thomas Friedman**

After the unbearable shock and trauma of the attacks on World Trade Center and the Pentagon, the other great shock for America was to realize how greatly America was disliked, even hated in the world! Governments and sensible people throughout the world, from Sydney to Delhi and from Manila to Rio, genuinely felt shock and grief over the despicable deed of 9/11, and their expressions of sympathy elicited instant reflexes such as, 'Oh, no!' or 'O my God!' etc.

But, at the same time, in many countries, especially in the 57 countries with Muslim populations, some people even came out on streets to cheer at the event. The 'conquest' was merrily celebrated in cities like Jakarta, Manila, Cairo, Peshawar, Bangkok, Lucknow and such Muslim/Arab nations including Palestine. When America declared its intention of air attacks on Afghanistan, many vehement demonstrations against America took place in such countries. Many members of the American elite were stunned by these reactions. Thousands of Americans, whose information was fed by the mainstream media, were also shocked when they were told about the 'Islamic rage' and the expanse and intensity of dislike and hatred nursed for America in Muslim society (*umma*) across the world. Bernard Lewis, an eminent historian of Islam, had written on the Muslim rage, as he called it, earlier in 1990, but he was not given much importance.

Even the Muslims in Western Europe expressed these sentiments! The popular media like Radio France Internationale also received angry calls, "What is so special when Americans die?", one of them said. "When millions of people died in Africa, they did not leave any (last) message on answering machines, for they were too poor to own cell-phones." On the other side of the globe, on the Chinese Internet too, sharp words appeared declaring joy for the suffering of America that was "always intervening in other people's affairs unilaterally" (*Business Week*, October 1, 2001). Abdel, a tour guide in Cairo said, "Everyone knows that there is no justice in American policy."

The anti-America sentiments differ in their reason and proportion in each country. After the end of the Cold War, America surged up as the new model for all societies in the world. Its 'honest mediation' in 1993 between Israel and PLO in search of world peace was much appreciated. But, when the negotiations went further, America turned indifferent in bringing more pressure on Israel for taking an amicable and cooperative approach and this impression lingered in the minds of Arabs and other Muslim classes. On one hand, America believes terrorist organizations like al Qaeda as 'greatly satanic'. On the other hand, many Islamist believers think that America and the West allow the cultural practices of unchecked sex, nudity, etc. and by this 'secular culture' abets sinful behavior among people. Its pornographic literature and cinema, alcohol and giving equal status to women—all such norms and forms are "corrupting religion and the culture of Islam".

Secondly, America supports and maintains some corrupt, voluptuous and authoritarian kings or rulers. In certain Muslim countries, it supports 'secular administration'. As Prof. Hans Wang says, the anti-Palestine aggressiveness of Israel is mainly rooted in America's moral and diplomatic strength continuously provided to it. In Saudi Arabia, Jordan, Egypt, Turkey etc., the US is maintaining the set up; and has also stationed its armed forces in these countries at their expense. Fareed Zakaria calls the Gulf monarchies, particularly Saudi Arabia, as 'the biggest Devil'. Along with Pakistan (till early 2002), Saudis have deflected their people's attention from their shoddy performance at home by funding religious schools/seminaries (Madrassas) and centers that spread a closed view, puritanical brand of Islam—Wahabism along half-educated, fanatical young Muslims (*Newsweek*, October 15, 2001).

Not just the American army but its politicians, diplomats and tourists also come to these countries. They bring with them their exposing and even nude dresses, songs, dances and films, pop culture etc. All these subtly deviate the elite and the youth of the Muslim nations. In spreading this and similar beliefs the conservative forces (Maulavis, Maulanas, teachers in Madrassas and others) have succeeded quite well. The organizations engaged in reviving religion say that by use of force the Americans must be removed from the 'Dar-ul-Islam', i.e., the 'sacred land of Islam', and this task must be considered as absolutely urgent. Fareed Zakaria, in his most quoted, path-finder four-piece series analysis, has given us deep insights into how the Muslim society, in general, works and reacts to the Western (read 'American') culture and its perceived dominance that corrupt them (*Newsweek*, October 15, 2001).

Pakistan and the Middle East provide fertile ground for such propaganda. But, even in the vast Muslim populations in countries like Malaysia, Bangladesh, Indonesia and the Philippines, revolutionary organizations and other international financial institutions have spread such (anti-American) beliefs.

Some sociologists have searched and found one important root of this 'Islamic rage'. The situation, with exceptions like Turkey—and probably, Malaysia—in most of the Arab/ Muslim countries (not just in the Middle East and North Africa, but even in Southeast Asia) the organizations and institutions providing social services and facilities have broken down. As Sheri Berman, a scholar at Princeton, observed,

Protest against America in Pakistan

"When state or political parties fail to provide a sense of legitimacy or purpose or basic services, other organizations have often been able to step in the void. From the Muslim Brotherhood to Hamas, and Hezbollah, they have been the alternative providers of social services. "In Islamic countries, there is a ready-made source of legitimacy in religion." The government and civil society have generally failed in nurturing and maintaining such social institutions of social welfare at schools, colleges, medical studies and health care institutions, empowering youth and women, etc. As the economies of these countries are also broken or breaking up youth suffer from unemployment. To fill such huge vacuum Islamic institutions such as Madrassas, welfare centers and hospitals, run on religious lines, have replaced 'secular' institutions. As Mark Brown, the head of the UNDP notes, "When secular, liberal models failed with these people, they shifted their loyalty and inclination towards Islamic belief."

In Asian countries formerly the Republics under the Soviet Union, such as Kyrgyzstan, Uzbekistan and Tajikistan, the pace of economic reform seemed too slow down for the American aid to flow in the decade of 1990s. But, a weak economy has had an adverse effect on of society. Cathleen Collins, researching in this region since last three years,

The Muslim-Majority West, Central and South Asia

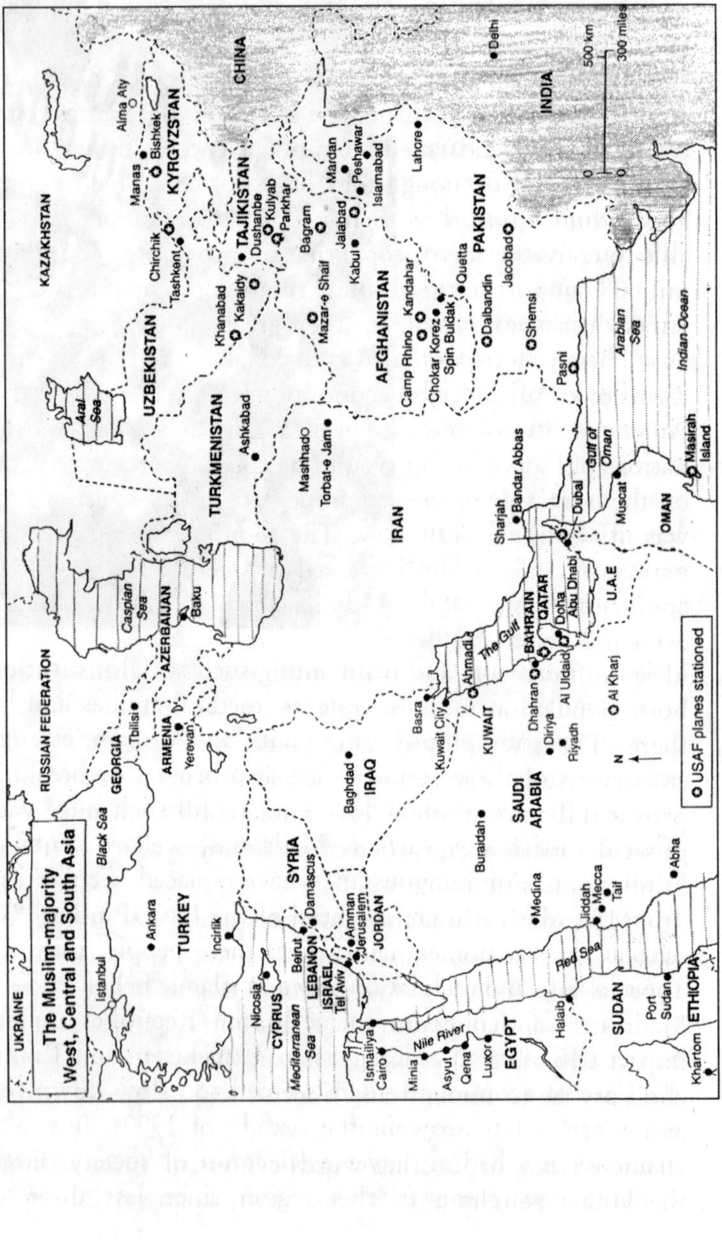

believes, "As its social effect, the disappointed Muslim population here is now leaning towards Islamic fundamentalism."

The 'failed states' of Saudi Arabia, Egypt, Pakistan and Afghanistan skillfully turned the blame on to America for their totally corrupt and failed attempts at good administration or strong economy. Though they have not been able to give any good administration to their people, their leaders have been able to convince their people that by providing economic and military support to the absolute rulers and religious rulers, it is America that responsible for their great sufferings.

These rulers have failed even to take advantage of the new forces of globalization of economy in 1990s. In this decade, the American economy crossed into new horizons; and some nations of East Asia and even India could record some progress on these lines. But, the economic progress of Muslim nations was, if anything, very slow. The economic progress of Arab nations in this decade increased by mere 0.7 percent! Their countries, rich with petro-dollars, proved short-sighted, and even indifferent in developing infrastructures or improving lifestyle for progress of their own people. In the meantime, both population and unemployment continued to increase there. The unemployed and directionless youth joined the conservative Islamic institutions and terrorist armies, for they provided them, if nothing else, food and drink, and in absence of secular ideals the purpose of maintaining religion was being fulfilled, and still doing so.

Madrassas became the centers for education in place of the schools that had come up during the British imperialism. Here, a special reference to Pakistan would not be out of place. The Madrassas in that country are not just ordinary centers to impart education of orthodox Islam; these are centers to train child psyche to implant and nourish a prejudice against India and thereby creating youth psyche with orthodox Islamic characteristics, or in other words centers of 'brainwashing' of the young generations of their own country. The Central

Bureau of Investigation of India, in its report of 2000, has provided many details of their existence in the border areas too. In *US News and World Report* (October 20, 2001), as its Editor-in-Chief Zuckerman comments, such Madrassas "do not open windows of Muslim children and youth for enlightening them, but they have become shutters to close their minds off".

Similarly, the countries such as Saudi Arabia, Pakistan, Iraq, Iran, Egypt, Syria, Afghanistan, etc., also have not played the part of any 'secular' state; they have behaved like states dominated by religion. Instead of state keeping religion away from worldly subjects or matter, this approach has resulted in religion shaping certain public policies of the state. The politics also supports religion; instead of the state and administration, Masjids (mosques) shape the public opinion on many public matters. At the time of *namaz* prayers on Friday, thousands are given sermons not just on religious tenets of orthodox Islam, but provoking lectures are also delivered regarding non-Muslim societies and countries. This time also, many anti-American riots have taken place after such Friday *namaz* or collective prayers. The demonstrations with posters of photographs of bin Laden that occurred from Malegaon and Kashmir to Cairo and Manila prove that the time of 'prayers' is used for spreading poison in the minds of the Muslims against the *kafirs* or non-Muslims.

The 'brainwashing' and training of *Mujahidins* (martyrs for religion) is also done in such a way through Madrassas and Masjids. A son of poor parents said, "In our hands should be books and pen, but we are being given to hold machine guns. Now, the conditions are such that we can earn our living only by using rifles and Kalashnikovs." In a survey by journalist Cheevors of *The New York Times*, it was revealed in a school at Kunduz after the removal of the Taliban, the students could name only five occupations: shepherd, shopkeeper, doctor, teacher and... *Mujahidin* (holy warriors)! One smart girl, keeping Cheevors with his camera in mind, added: 'journalist'! Even more saddening is that the people have a deep-rooted conviction in spite of such wandering life of soldiers and ordinary incomes that by turning a *fidayeen* (martyr) they would enjoy the pleasures of heaven after death. The purpose of opposing the western culture and becoming a *fidayeen* while doing this has turned the main purpose for them to become terrorists. That is why, the number of 'suicide bombs', 'suicide car bombs' etc. are on the increase. Naturally, the responding steps by America, Israel, and India too would turn as violent and fierce.

In the Middle East and elsewhere, the Palestinians are quite responsible for raising anti-American sentiments among Muslims and also for making the non-Muslim liberal class to voice them. In the Israel-Palestine conflicts, mostly America has sided with Israel. The pro-Jew lobby has remained very powerful in American politics, it is well-known. In the last decade, American presidents have attempted, sometimes initiated, efforts to carve out a separate state of Palestine from region under control of Israel, and to end the conflicts of the two peoples at war and offered to people with bipolarized cultures treaties like Camp David etc. But, so far, no success is discerned in the attempts to get official acceptance by Arab countries for Israel, and its establishment as a separate and sovereign state remains unaccomplished. Also, since the violent attacks of Palestinian terrorists on Israel that are continuation of the protests of *Intefada* (Palestinians' violent uprising against Israelis occupying their areas) in the last decade, even the Egypt of Anwar Sadat and Hosni Mubarak is also displeased. At the time of attack of America on Iraq in December 1990, Egypt, Jordan, Saudi Arabia, and UAE and the Gulf countries were on the side of America. But, when America put sanctions on Iraq, which led to severe shortage of food grain etc., and five million children died due to hunger, then the blame was squarely laid at the door of America. Due to clever propaganda of fundamentalists, even the moderate Arab states openly or secretly turned into critics of America. A case in point is that in Kuwait that was saved by America from attack of Saddam Hussein in 1990, there were anti-American demonstrations on September 12. Den Shirgi, political scientist of American University at Cairo says, "Arabs seem to have begun to believe that America would not only view them with contempt, but even seem to believe that they hold them somewhat below human race" (also see, Edward Said's *Orientalism*). Thus, the deadly combination of the highbrow attitude of the Americans, inferiority complex of the Muslims and backward conditions of most of Arab countries, the radical Islam-centric forces have created an explosive and poisonous mixture very effectively. With its smouldering 'anger', Islamic fundamentalism became a medium of protests and a convenient catharsis against America.

4

Fundamentalism: Nature and Development

> The roots of Islamic fundamentalism lie in an oppressive past constructed by the West to colonise the body and mind, and an equally oppressive present where deadly missiles are fired at Palestinians, Iraqis and Afghans. The past is repeatedly invoked in the context of the events in erstwhile Yugoslavia, Sudan, Chechnya, Palestine, Iraq, Kosovo and Afghanistan.... Doubtless, the perspectives of the Islamic fundamentalists are often distorted. Doubtless, their emphasis on *taqlid* (strict emphasis to the letter of the Islamic law) stifles internal dissent, dims the chances of innovation and interpretation (*jehad*), and impedes the emancipation of women. At the same time, they are not the rustic Bedouins to be herded by a Lawrence of Arabia, but skilled, sophisticated, urbanised professionals.
>
> The U.S. appears to have lost round one of the battle. Victory in the second round depends on how best American policy makers can combine their military and political strategies to recognise the desire for change and progress in Muslim countries.
>
> — **Mushirul Hasan** (*Indian Express*, December 12, 2001)

Fundamentalism is an ideology of the extremists, a feeling of self-righteousness, and moral correctness of one's cause and one's objective. It convinces the believer that others and their causes are wrong, and they should be corrected, even by resorting to coercion, and they should be defeated or converted, and if need be, even eradicated (Ehsan Ahrari, *Asia Times.com*, October 9, 2004). It stifles the spirit of inquiry even in an otherwise intelligent person, and arrests the potentiality of a community to reinterpret its basic tenets and modify them in light of advances that other societies have convincingly demonstrated. Fundamentalism, in this way, keeps the believers in the static and stifled state of a myopic religious belief system. All the religions, more or less, have patches of fundamentalist upsurge.

The post-9/11 America, Britain and the world called upon to take a serious look at and understand Muslim countries and Islamic society in depth. There are as many as 57 countries with Muslim majority or with considerable Muslim population. Almost one-fifth of the world population (1.2 billion) is Muslim as compared to 1.06 billion catholics. "Islam has replaced Catholicism as the world's biggest faith" (World Christian Encyclopedia). The more disturbing concern for America is that in the last decade one religious group of its population that has increased at the fastest rate is that of the Muslims. They are the second largest minority in Italy. They are growing in number at faster rate than other immigrant minorities in France and Germany. Upon what would be the inclinations and worldview of the Muslim society largely depends the status of the environment of peace and security in these countries and the entire world.

When bin Laden said that he had launched a religious war or *jehad* against America, millions of his co-religionists all over the world believed him. In the 12th century many regions of Europe and (present) West Asia had witnessed the 'crusades' or religious clashes between the holders of the Cross and the Crescent with their ups and downs. However, before few years, the hate or anti-American sentiment was not so widespread. Countries with very large Muslim populations such as Turkey, Indonesia, then India, Pakistan, Bangladesh were not known to have anti-American sentiments at all. In 1920s, Kamal Ata Turk was the one to usher in modernization in Turkey with predominantly Sunni Muslim population. It ranks sixth among countries with large Muslim population, and is a member of NATO. A democratic rule, even if somewhat defective, prevails there.

However, in the Middle East (or from India's viewpoint, the West Asia), we can see sentiments of anti-Americanism and fundamental nature of Islam in all its murky colors quite clearly. An extremist feeling of anti-America is prevalent in all these countries: Iran, Iraq, Syria, Saudi Arabia, Palestine occupied by Israel, Lebanon, Jordan, Egypt, and small sheikhdoms of the little Persian Gulf. Here, Islamic fundamentalism is flowing speedily like mental lava all over. We find in these regions suicide bombers in large number, and people who burn the effigies of Bush and the American national flag. Mullahs, with Koran in hand, pour out the poison of *jehad* in their sermons. Laden compels us to recall Afghanistan first; but ironically, in 9/11 phenomenon, no Afghan was involved among the terrorists who made those gruesome attacks! Most belonged to Saudi Arabia—America's close ally in the Middle East. Even then, Afghanistan is undoubtedly a center for training and a hiding camp for terrorists from where they had made their attacks on America. (Iraq has emerged as a new training ground for Islamist terrorists). These terrorists are trained with financial help from Saudi Arabia and the highly competent intelligence set up of Pakistan—the ISI. Considerable elements from these also infiltrate into Kashmir and Nepal.

It was possible in the 19th century to think of reformation in Islam from within. As late as the 1960s also, no one could imagine that America and the Arab world would get involved in a kind of cultural conflict. The colonial flags of Britain and France had stopped flying there. After the tripartite invasion of Suez its memories had turned more negative for the Arabs. When the Islamic people wanted to remain away from the powerful Soviet Union due to its atheist and communist philosophy, the prosperous America, like the other countries of the Third World, had become the nation of glamor for the Arabs/Muslims as well. To the elite and higher middle class it meant pacy cars, Coca Cola, hotels, scientific inventions, equipments for comforts and luxuries, and gigantic corporations that refined the crude oil from their oil wells right at home and turned it into petro-dollars for them!

The rulers of Egypt desired to make their country modern, but their faulty thinking and administration failed to boost their economy; and so for the rest of the Arab countries they appeared to be rays of a false dawn. Israel defeated them very badly in the wars of 1948, 1967 and 1973. As America sided with Israel in these wars, they began to have sore feeling towards it. After two decades, Saddam Hussein wiped out what little remained of the idea of an Arab-centered political scene.

The downfall of Nasser's Republican Egypt, the promoter and model of modernization, was graphic. The figure of unemployment rose to 25 percent. Once a brain behind the Arab progress, Egypt now produces only 375 books per year, while Israel publishes 4,000 books every year. In the last decade Egypt has shown efficiency only in one thing: to crush out any disagreements with the government, and to suppress the growth in civil society!

The performance of the other Arab neighbors is even weaker. Syria has turned into the world's greatest oppressive police nation. After Nasser, and three decades ago, Iraq used to be one of the most progressive and secular Arab nations. Women there went to work out of home, there was freedom for artists for their creative work, and journalists could perform well in their profession. But, Saddam wanted to become the center and leader of Muslim world. His 'megalomania' resulted in turning Iraq into a militarist and authoritarian state, besides closing of its own society. Other Arab nations also became victims of dictatorial rulers, kings, sheikhs and pashas.

After Nasser, the prosperity due to its oil reserves had brought another period of optimism for the Arabs. But, due to the lack of foresighted leadership, the tremendous earnings from that source were not diverted to improve infrastructures and progress for the general public; but a new kind of elites was created instead. These influential and ruling elites became West-oriented and modern on the surface. They invested the petro-dollars for selfish reasons into American banks and industries. They adopted new methods for pleasures and luxuries. But the deprived Arab people and western nations also turned into their critics. Fareed Zakaria, the editor-in-chief of prestigious *Newsweek*, and himself of Indian origin (and son of the great scholar of Islamic culture, Dr. Rafiq Zakaria) observes: If you take a look at the papers of Egypt, Jordan and Syria, how insultingly are the cartoons depict the Sheikhs of the Gulf countries! (They project) their life as full of luxuries, corruption and weakness! And, America had fought the Gulf War "not to save Kuwait, but to save the rulers of such Sheikhdoms and Saudi authoritarian rule". Thus, the ordinary public connects sufferings, oppressive rulers and America in one link.

At yet another level also, there is a problem in Muslim society—that is, at the level of thinking. Once, it was the Muslim civilization that initiated new thinking, made inventions of Mariner's compass, and in the fields of ammunition, astronomy, printing and many others, and thus contributed significantly to the progress of the world, and which had established principles of equality and brotherhood, are now full of hate nearly all the elements of western culture, especially modernism. Muslim nations ignore the powerful economic progress achieved by their rival neighboring state of Israel, by promoting modern education, by adopting imaginative and new techniques of water usage for growth of agriculture (despite scarcity of water) and management abilities put to get good result for their people. Instead of following the prestigious and successful model of Israel, which has created a high-tech society, is living full and enjoyable cultural life and is nurturing of a healthy democratic way of life, the Muslim countries totally ignore it. As a result, their per capita income, except for a country like Kuwait, is merely 5 to 10 percent of that of Israel; and although one-fourth of the populations of these countries are young, they remain unemployed and are compelled to join the Islamic institutions and terrorist training centers to get some income rather than none.

There is one more level at which these countries oppose the West, and that is at the level of freedom and status of women in society. They cannot stomach the principles and practice of the western society at all. Bernard Lewis gives us the proper perspective of what is in store for the deep psychological conflict the West has to face against the Arab world. He explains with great clarity the humiliation that the Muslims have had to suffer in the last three centuries. The Islamic world had held itself, with reasons, the most superior and powerful in intellectual and cultural fields; but in the age of imperialism, it experienced the spread of alien (western) laws, thoughts, and lifestyle etc. in its own areas...and finally, the social liberalism of giving freedom to women and children would result so that within their own homes "man would find his position as the master of the house under attack". Thus, the social fluidity that we call freedom means, to them, an unpalatable impact from outside. In his memorable speech on September 20th he gave before Congress, President Bush had observed, "(The Islamic fundamentalists) hate our freedoms, our religious freedoms and even the freedom to disagree with each other..." They believe America to be the leader of the Crusaders or non-believers (*kafirs*) of religion, and infiltrators who have entered the Islamic religious places and Muslim regions. The Islamic fundamentalists aim to drive off all such forces. There is a big class of Islamic orthodox people and their religious leaders are not impressed by anything of the West—even when Singapore, South Korea, Hong Kong and China etc. have made tremendous economic progress following modernization, liberalization or globalization initiated by the West. This is because they firmly and unflinchingly believe that Islam is the greatest culture of the world; that "we do not want to turn into 'Islamic areas' of the West". Their aversion is so great that they do not even consider the fact that these eastern countries have adopted the western model only after changing it to suit their own cultures and special needs. At the heart of the Muslim problem this type of one-sided evaluation and myopic/partial understanding of the West has played a significant part.

After the First World War there was some hope that in countries like Turkey, Egypt and Lebanon, and after the Second World War in Iran under Reza Shah, their elite class would open the doors to liberalism and modernity. But this hope proved only a flicker that died soon. Like some people of the Third World believe, the elite of the Muslim society considers modernization to be a blind imitation—nay a replication—of westernization to replace the eastern culture and lifestyles. They think of westernization as Americanization, equate modernity with modernism—a belief that represents a highly distorted cultural, social and economic process.

Also, modernization in West Asia remained confined to oil refining and its trade and commerce (rather than spread to principles of discipline in work, thrift, productive investment, management of human and material resources, etc.). Can the few modern, material facilities like the television shows, fast food and drinking of coke or importing, with the help of petrodollars, of fashionable cars like Lexus and Mercedes, or eateries like McDonald, grand buildings and roads, and fashionable capitals, be keys to basic social reformation and development, ever?

But, could anyone import such things as open markets, democratic system, political parties, rule of law and responsible government, etc., which are the basic elements of modernization? Instead of making politics modern and people-oriented, the Arab rulers distributed their new-found wealth as if in charity for basic necessities. They gave a few modern showpieces. But, in return, they bought a silence among the people for their corrupt and authoritarian administration. In American Revolution, the basic principle was diametrically opposite: "No Taxation without Representation (in the British Parliament)!"

It is this America that is at the heart of the New Age. Even if the orthodox Arab thinkers and fundamentalists try to stop America by closing off their borders, then it would come to them through television and mail. If you censor the mail, it would come in the form of the fast food and jeans. If you put a stop to production of such things, they would enter by the backdoor through satellite television in drawing rooms of the people.

All young people feel a dilemma or confusion about old and new thinking and practices, and struggle to search for a simple alternative. Fundamentalism is such a simple way of thinking. Islamic fundamentalism has found this out and offers a simple alternative. The extremists were looking for such people who are discovered now universally in backward/ deprived societies. We may even say that there is globalization of even fundamentalism! Twenty years ago, Indonesian Muslims could not pinpoint Palestine on world map. Now, they consider the problem of Palestine as their own. In India, we find some posters on the walls of some areas with the slogan: "Become a Saddam". People in London, Manila and Karachi have come out on the streets when America launches attacks on Afghanistan and Iraq and burn the cardboard figures of President Bush.

A serious matter is that in most of the Muslim countries, more than half the population is below 25 years of age. They leave their little villages and crowd into bigger metros like Beirut, Cairo or Kuwait. They can see there the big chasm between classes with regard to income and wealth. They see women roaming freely, without wearing the *burqa*, laughing and eating in restaurants, and even working with them as well. But, there are no ways, or any atmosphere, to help them adjust to or overcome this 'culture shock'.

Such a large disgruntled and frustrated young section of population then lends its support, through the medium of religion, to new political movement of opposition and protest. Even Muhammad Atta who lived in Germany, studied engineering at Hamburg, but, yet, keeping the West (its ethos) at a distance, led the attack on the first tower of WTC personally. As Terry McDermott's insightful study of 9/11 hijackers, (*Perfect Soldiers*, 2005) reveals: "It's a story about the dangerous power of ideas wrongly wielded." Laden turns into a supporter and symbol of opposition to the age of America-inspired globalization and modernization trends. His personality, his clear words—all make him into a charismatic leader.

Rafiq, Laden and Omar made an amazing use of religion for a society that was cocooned, confused, disappointed and forlorn in a new environment of religious, cultural and modern global dimensions to come out of its depression. The entire conditions are such that they easily gave a call for fighting a holy war between Islam and western world. Terrorists like Unabomber (Columbia), Aum Shintokyo (Japan) and Baruch Goldstein (Hebron) became isolated due to lack of social support, whereas in the call for holy war against America bin Laden received great support from millions of his co-religionists from all over the world, and they acclaimed the 9/11 as well. Comfortable only in global capitalism and consumerist culture, the Americans had to experience the sudden quake of 9/11 to realize how powerful and revolutionary such forces of political Islam are.

A section of the western media has reacted strongly to Islamic fundamentalism. For example, Oriana Fallaci, an Italian journalist, wrote in her books, *The Rage and Pride* and *The Force of Reason*, "Our military might or victory in war would not be solving the question of Islamic terrorism. Instead, it would aggravate the itch to inflict more terror. This is the bitter truth..."

In her acidic language, Fallaci adds, "Fundamentalists do not believe in apology. They take pride in killing people. This is a religious war for Islamic fundamentalists. They want to conquer your soul rather than any territory. They want to end your independence. These people do not hesitate in killing in the name of Allah.

The fanatic Islamic Jihadis(t) are ungrateful creatures. They take the best training in your countries. They are not just reading Koran in caves of Pakistan or Iran or Afghanistan...They come in droves to our countries (of Europe and America) for earning. They get jobs in our cities, our universities and our business companies.

They even purchase our churches. They take control of our banks. They listen to our television, radio and read our newspapers. They also learn our technology; and then, with our own 747 airplanes hijacked, break up our towers."

The limit is crossed when in a democratic Italy, at a conference in Rome, one Muslim leader says, "Taking advantage of your democracy, we shall attack you and dominate you." Fallaci's ideas received a widespread welcome. Millions of copies of her books were sold in the Western Europe. The word 'Eurabia' that she coined for the 'unhealthy spread' of the growing Muslim population and their way of living in France, Germany, and other developed nations in Europe, struck a resonance chord among the cultural fundamentalists in these countries.

But, other thinkers strike a sober note for this phenomenon. As Fareed Zakaria points out, the queer mixture of religion and politics made this even more explosive and of worldwide imports and impact. No religion is so closely knit with politics, as is Islam. It's political Islam. In 1954, President Nasser imprisoned his opponents who were fundamentalists going by the name of 'Muslim brotherhood'. One of those was Sayyid Qutub, a frail man, with a burning pen, who wrote a book, when in prison entitled, *Signposts on the Road*. In some ways, this book "marks the beginnings of modern political Islam or what is often called Islamic fundamentalism" (Zakaria, *Newsweek,* October 15, 2001). Qutub declared Nasser as an unholy non-Muslim who held modern views; and he praised the modern political Islam that later came to be called Islamic fundamentalism. The Arab countries after Nasser gradually began to slide into oppressive rule and that led to gradual increase in the backwardness of Muslim society; such thinking was on increase and it provided the Muslims with new philosophy and new meaning for life. Faud Azmi, the well-known Egyptian scholar, writes in his thought-provoking work, *The Arab Predicament*, "Before this, people were like audiences in the making of policies and episodes that took place. From such a political culture, persons like bin Laden have now made it possible for them to participate in them. Now well-known, that mass politics of coming out on streets by the Arabs has become real, and it has provided them with a powerful language to express their opposition to their sorry plight."

Fareed Zakaria says, "The Arab and some of the other Muslim countries are like a political desert. There are no political parties in their true meaning, no institutional channel for opposition, no independent press, and no royal roads for expressing any disagreement. But, this space is filled by the Masjid, where one can discuss politics. In the Namaz prayers of Friday, more than the interpretation of the Koran, the Mullahs' suggestions on political affairs are more important."

Besides, adds Zakaria, where the state does not perform its duties, those social services are provided by the Muslim Brotherhood, Hamas, Hezbollah and other such extremist bellicose organizations. They run religious schools, provide medical services and temporary homes. Those who have high regard for civil society in the Middle East, are feeling uneasy and troubled that these forces (like Masjid-Hezbollah) that remain away from civil values are turning into civil society themselves. Princeton scholar Sherri Berman, recalling the fascist parties' parallel role of providing social services, observes, "Whenever the state and political parties fail to achieve the basic objectives of popular acceptance or social services and facilities, then such outside organizations come forward to fill the vacuum. In the Islamic countries religion has turned into a ready source of popular acceptance. In fact, the state itself supports such organizations in order to divert the discontent of the people to some other objective! For this region, Islamic fundamentalism is characteristic. Yet, its basic trends are similar to those that gave rise to Nazism-Fascism" (In democracies like India, one is reminded of some issues or structures such as rise of Shiv Sena or party of Lalu Prasad Yadav; or some organizations that provided social service and then entered the political arena, such as RSS and SIMI, etc.).

In addition, when a society is divided by differences and sectionalism, positive forces like education and technology also sometimes nurture such troublesome episodes. In 1979, Ayatollah Khomeini, a fundamentalist Shia leader, had used effectively the technology of audio-cassettes in overthrowing the Shah of Iran. Similarly, while residing in a cave secretly, bin Laden continued to move his entire network by modern tele-technique; and the West made full use of its media (television, video etc.) to propagate its own side in the world. In mid-November, Kabul had fallen. The Taliban were on the retreat and he himself was in hiding in south Afghanistan moving from one place to another. One story of Prophet Muhammad is that he made his *hizrat* or moving away from Mecca to Medina along with his friend Abu Bakr and lived in a cave called Althaur during this period. In mid-November, Laden made bold to give an interview to the Pakistani journalist Mir sitting at the mouth of that very cave! Laden cleverly compared his own furtive movements and state of living in a cave to this story, thereby capturing the Muslim imagination. He did this also through media, explains Professor Dewitt Pinostey, an authority on Islamic symbols and violence.

Relevant here is a sober observation of Dr. Najd Hussain, an American Muslim of Indian origin: "Jihad, or as it has been invoked falsely, is, just one excuse and an outlet of that frustration...Jihad of the 6th century helped build the Muslim community in the Arabia and beyond. Without that there would have been no Islam. But another misnomered *jehad*—the act of extremism—threatens the tenets and adherents of Islam. Indian Muslims, who have so far done remarkably well following the guidelines of the Prophet in waging their internal *jehad*, must take the lead and show the world that consistent with our times today can have the understanding of the 21st century and yet the power of 6th century." General Zinni, c-in-c of the US Central Command in the Middle East (1997-2000) says it well: "There is nothing in this part of the world (the Middle East) that makes it an inevitable clash of civilizations, incapable of the kind of political and social reforms that they need to go through."

The development of Islamic fundamentalism has taken place from a large variety and interaction of factors and forces. To bring those large sections of Muslim society affected by the fundamentalist thinking back into the fold of mainstream or parallel to it, the thinkers and leaders of Muslim society as well as those of the world would have to show the foresight appropriate for great statesmen and social engineers.

5
Churning in of Muslim Society

> It is time that misguided terrorists do some introspection. Thanks to their recent suicidal actions, a wave of ill-will and contempt against the Muslims has spread in the whole world. They have come to be considered everywhere and in all fields as doubtful and untrustworthy people. An impression is created as if Islam itself is a savage and inhuman religion.
>
> Someone has said, "Not all Muslims are terrorists; but all terrorists seem to be Muslims." This statement, in essence, is the counter-approach of non-Muslims for the Muslims.
>
> The terrorists and those who support them must stop a while and think if really their Jihad has achieved what its objective was? The sad outcome of the actions of Jihadis is that the non-Muslims of the entire world have been alienated from the Muslims.
>
> — **Rafiq Zakaria** (*Times of India*, January 8, 2001)

It is significant that in spite of receiving huge aid from America for years, some of the Arab countries, instead of any introspection, have tried to turn the Islamic rage of their Muslim population against their own patron country. For example, the editor Ibrahim Nefi, in the semi-official daily of Egypt, *Al*

Ahram, wrote in the first week of November, 2001, "In the places where the Americans are throwing food packets in Afghanistan, it is done purposefully, for those places are full of mines they have thrown earlier! Similarly, according to reports, the Americans distribute 'biologically processed' food packets in its humanist gesture of aid, and thus endanger the health of the Afghan people." The administration appointed by Hosni Mubarak himself writes such things. Till mid-September, Palestine media also spewed poison against America. However, noting the displeasure of America about it, Yasser Arafat stopped it. In this context, the perceptive columnist of *The New York Times*, Thomas Friedman questions the links of the Arab rulers and their media, "Would then it be a surprise at all if the people, to express their hate, come out into the streets of Cairo and Mecca?" (the term 'Arab Street' is used in Europe and America for protest demonstrations in streets in the Middle East.) The net result of all such process has been the spread of Ladenism.

The Arab/Muslim rulers have failed to provide their subjects free political system, socially modern or liberal life and basic needs. America, by merely sustaining such rulers and elite, must suffer the anger of the people. "Those young people who have migrated to America and other western countries have prospered, but most of the youth have not been able to do this. They have turned to Masjid and Islam to evince their opposition. The Muslim political set-ups also, in order to cover up their failures, have helped with financial and other aid to the fundamentalists, the terrorists and other Islamic institutions, allowed them space to operate according to their misguided ideals, and diverted the public anger through media towards America."

Above all, America itself has confirmed its own impression as an aggressive nation, arrogant with great power it wields, by taking military steps in such Muslim countries as Sudan, Iraq, Libya, Iran and others; and risked becoming unpopular. About the question of Palestine, the Arab-Muslim and non-Muslim intellectuals (including many from the Third

World countries like India) firmly believe that America has connived at Israel's aggressive or violent steps against Palestine and not taken similar steps to keep it under control; and there is logic in this belief.

However, making America as the main culprit for the backwardness or the problems of the Muslim society, and making it the target of its rage and hate may become the mental 'catharsis' for the Muslims; but their main problem still remains. Unfortunately, it is the impression that the educated, thinking and modern class of the *Umma* community also not enthusiastic about openly voicing their viewpoints and thoughts. No leading Muslim or well-known leader has appeared or even phoned in to Al Jazeera (the popular television channel in the Middle East like the CNN in USA) to say that the step of bin Laden of hijacking Islamic symbols, in order to kill the innocents in the 9/11, was totally wrong and un-Islamic. "No leading Islamic thinkers dial up the Mideast's equivalent of CNN and demand airtime to assail bin Laden's hijacking of Islamic symbols to justify mass murder" (Trudy Rubin, a columnist for *Philadelphia Inquirer*, cited in *Mercury News*, October 16, 2001). In reality, the Muslims themselves should come forward to fight against violence, fanaticism and fundamentalism; and the groups of intellectuals and thinkers must come forward in such a critical moment to take this fight among the believers in Islam, Maulavis and religious preachers, for debate and discussion with great goodwill. For example:

- How can leaders like bin Laden spread their influence without any protest or discussion in the large Muslim society that is spread in a number of countries and have their own regional traditions as well? Why have not the Muslim scholars become active and try to balance, with their own understanding, the sermons of the Muslim Maulavis are belching out their teachings in Masjids?
- Laden wants to uproot the present Arab and Muslim administrations, and replace them with those of Taliban style, fundamentalist and orthodox Islamic states. The

moderate or middle-path Muslims should have risen against this. It is true that most of the Arab/Muslim states are authoritarian and backward, but the Taliban type of state would have made the Muslim people even more anachronistic. On this issue, why have the wise Muslim intellectuals turned out to be mute, weak and insipid?

- It is also true that in his interviews bin Laden constantly and cleverly fused Islamic fundamentalism and his own opposition to an America that was using force against Muslim and non-Islamic states in order to keep its political superiority intact. America is unpopular among Muslims; America has been supporting Israel; it has laid down sanctions on Iraq that caused killing of thousands of its children; it keeps military camps and base in Saudi Arabia and elsewhere and controls them indirectly. There is widespread dissatisfaction about all these among the Muslims. Taking these as his justifying points, it is difficult to criticize Laden, these intellectuals argue.
- However, the Muslim society itself has not been able to change such authoritarian rule that cannot fulfil their basic needs. Is that to be blamed on America or on the people of the relevant country? If in place of Saddam, the state is re-formed to bring in the rule as imagined by Laden, would it be a democratic or liberal set-up? If the sanctions were lifted on Saddam's state, would the threats or possibilities have gone away that he would use, as he did earlier—say his use of poisonous gas against the Kurds?

Thus, for their own failures or backward conditions, would one blame America or any other nation/s only to a certain extent or, would they prefer as a better alternative to fundamentalism and terrorism or Ladenism, taking them back to the Middle Ages? The people and more so the genuine thinkers among them, who maintain total silence on these serious issues, come into a defensive position.

This also applies to such Muslim society of democratic India and the world. Many Muslims in India had criticized events of 9/11; and yet, very few Muslims have come forward in India or in America to publicly and explicitly condemn the terrorist act of bin Laden. From San Jose's daily *Mercury News* down to many well-known American magazines took a survey of their opinion, may have said that the attack on the WTC was wrong, but in that very breathe they also observed that "however, the foreign policy of America is also responsible for it!" Agha Sayeed, Professor of Ethnic Studies at University of California, Berkeley denies the logic of bin Laden and then immediately asks, "But whose product is bin Laden? Only of America that fought the proxy war in Afghanistan against Russia, isn't it?" Omar Mohamud, the President of the Council for American-Islamic Relations (CAIR), gave his support to Bush's war against terrorism, but he also added that it was necessary to get more proof that only bin Laden was behind the attacks of 9/11. Professor Stephen Cohen, expert on South Asia region, notes, "It does not seem that there is any special concern or discussion here, after this fateful day about the responsibility of Muslims as a community. There were many among the terrorists who had lived in American Muslim community earlier." As far back as January 1999, the spiritual leader of the Masjid of Mountain View in Silicon Valley, and head of Islamic Supreme Council of America, Washington, and Sheikh Hasam Kabbani had said in one forum that many Masjids of America are controlled by people of religious thinking that can only be termed as extremist and fanatic. But most of the Muslims do not agree with them. Kabbani was criticized for such observation at that time not only by the other Muslim institutions but also the CAIR of America. Indeed, after 9/11, Kabbani says, their statements were softer in tone.

However, let alone the thinking of reforms and liberalism, the Masjids propagate in sharp tongue and tone only the orthodox thinking. Even when many Muslims share moderate thinking, there is no space for any open-minded and quiet discussion at all. Even in such a loaded atmosphere, in a classic example of bold reaction, Shabana Azmi, celebrated Bollywood star, made such a graphic suggestion that Imam Bukhari (who openly came out in support of the Talibans in the late 2001) be air-lifted from New Delhi and dropped in Kandhar to live there. She asked the Imam to join the Taliban, "and leave the Indian Muslims alone". The cryptic remark of a Muslim woman put the head of the biggest (Juma) Masjid of India, Imam Bukhari on the defensive. Only in a socially liberal democratic country like India such an attitude is possible. However, we do hear some clear voices of disagreement against the approach of fundamentalism and Ladenism from the Muslim world, we must take note. Samri Farid, the Egyptian film critic of *Al Hayat* in London wrote in early November, "I am ashamed by the matter that is published in the press of Egypt and other countries (against the bombings by America). Most of what I read proves that the poison of non-democratic military rule has entered the blood of the elite. They do not believe that such destruction (as 9/11) is a matter of shame. How inauspicious seems the future of these regions?"

In one of the programs telecast by the Al Jazeera television was of debate between Shafiq Dhabara, the liberal political scientist from Kuwait, one Islamist and another extremist Arab nationalist. When the last two defended bin Laden, Shafiq responded, "The civil war of Lebanon was not a plot of the Americans! Nor was the war between Iran and Iraq (in 1980s) a conspiracy of the Americans. All these are our own products. We must come out of the mentality of blaming others for our problems." Dr. Ansari, the Dean of Law Faculty of the Qatar University, wrote in *Al Raya*, "How could the terrorist turn into our 'Hero'? Why are our Islamic scholars silent? We must solve this problem from the root. The key to it is general and liberal education only."

Palestine leader from Jerusalem, Seri Nusaibeh boldly and clearly stated his view. Criticizing the strategy of Palestine, he said in October 2001, "We challenge the Israelis that we want to kick you out of our nation. Okay, we want our land in West Bank and Gaza, and freedom, liberty, etc. But then to send that message properly to the Israelis, our young people go to discos and restaurants, and blow up everyone by suicidal bombs. The whole matter is not only mad and ill-conceived, but even works against the expected result also. The real way is to make the Israelis understand (the problem) by peaceful process."

The American leadership also will have to adopt a genuine bridge of trust and impartial relationship with the Muslim society. America must show the Muslims/Arabs that it does not need to have military camps or armies stationed there. Can it convince Saudi Arabia or Afghanistan that it does not want to camp out there for long? The American leaders, including President Bush, as well as the UNO must make the Muslim rulers understand: "Look here, we desire that your society gets to know the world trends and thoughts; we want it to open its mind and turn liberal, so that you can hear the voice of those among you who aspire for an alternative Muslim future or a future of any other type."

America, Russia, Britain, India and others in the world would deal with bin Laden. But, the responsibility of removal of the greater problem of 'bin Ladenism' that stares in their face remains with the Muslim scholars, thinkers and the entire *Umma* community. We do come across certain dim rays of consciousness on this issue. The Lebanese Shia leader Sheikh Muhammad Fadalallah was involved in the terrorist bombing of 1983 when 241 Americans were killed; but in November, 2001 he told the magazine *Al Moharar*, "Laden is not a world leader; he does not represent Islam...Laden is merely taking advantage of the oppression in the Arab world!" Yet, unfortunately, the experiments and campaigns for opening up of new opportunities in the fields of weak political capacity, possibilities of oil-based development, and opening up of culture etc. have, on the whole, been unproductive in those Muslim countries.

Today, many former schools of thought have disappeared. The pan-Arab nationalism, a powerful concept of Nasser that was popular in 1950-70, is shattered in the winds of change. The dream of great intellectuals of Syria, Egypt and other countries for reconstruction of Muslim society and economy on the norms of socialist-communist theories and principles of equality also has proved unattainable.

Instead, the concept of mixing politics and Islam for rejuvenating the Muslim society is being circulated since last two-and-a-half decades. In 1978-79, Ayatollah Khomeini had kindled a hope by ending monarchy by his Iranian Revolution. The Mullahs tried to achieve economic prosperity; but now, the young Iranians in very large number seem to prefer more modern system and liberalization.

The worldview of Laden is focused on a totally opposite direction. He has made 'political Islam' even more one-sided, and by loading it with extremism, has turned it highly intolerant and violent. Its unethical content is already exposed. Everyone who watched videotape of attack on Indian Parliament (December 13, 2001 or 12/13) in which great pleasure is seen on his face as he talked of the destruction of WTC, is convinced of his satanic mind.

The other countries can, at the most, conduct discussions on the problem and encourage thoughts; but the arguments of introspection can come only from the Muslims of various nations only—and that, too, from within the *Umma*. As the Muslims of America, UK, India and West Europe are brought up in democratic system, and as they have sufficient space for carrying on discussions of this type, they can take a transparent initiative in the matter. The first indications of liberalism, though, are also coming from the other Muslim society, when we noted Fadalallah condemning terrorism.

In the historic-cultural context of the Islamic fundamentalism, it seems that the status of these Arab nations in the economic and political areas has remained quite low in the world. Floating on the oil of the Iranian Gulf, not only the prosperous nations but even a small country like Yemen also has remained at the lowest rungs of modernity related to economic, political and social structures. In the ranking allotted by the World Bank, Freedom House and UNO for annual increase of GDP (1965-99), and civil liberty system, among the 162 countries so graded, Syria stands at 97th, Lebanon 65th, Jordan 88th, Morocco 112th, Algeria 100th, Tunisia 98th and Libya 59th in rank. Among the bigger countries, Saudi Arabia has 67th, Iran 90th and Egypt 105th position; there is no information on Iraq. Among the small Gulf countries, Kuwait has 43rd, Bahrain 40th, Qatar 48th, and UAE 45th position. Yemen comes on 133rd position; and with regard to the freedom of press, in most of these nations, it is negligible, or absent. Except for the Gulf countries, the youth population under 25 years of age is very large—between 50 and 68 percent! Backward conditions and such a large young population—these two Indicators actually point out the dissatisfying and explosive situation, as Thomas Friedman has emphasized so often. Incidentally, India also has occupied the 130th position in another report, i.e., Human Development Report, but its indicators are different. Also, it is high on civil liberties. Again, in terms of employment and other economic and political indicators, the Arab societies lack modernity. Is it then a wonder that the fundamentalist religious leaders would fill in the vacuum! "If bin Laden's variant of political Islam were debated on its merits, its hollowness and immortality would be apparent. But this is a debate that the United States can only encourage. The real arguments must take place among Muslims themselves" (Trudy Rubin). Comments Asra Q. Nomani, author of *Standing Alone in Mecca*, "The dilemma facing most Muslims is that this war (on terrorism) pits us against ourselves...Like Prophet Muhammad faced off against his own tribe worshiping false idols in 7th century, modern Muslims are pitted against people worshiping false idols of hatred, violence and intolerance."

Heinous massacre of school children in Beslan by the Chechen guerillas has brought to surface the undercurrents of the latent moderate opinion within this stereotyped *Umma*.

At Beslan an arcade of shattered lives competes for media attention. Here, the freelance Ronins of the Arab world teamed with reigning Chechen guerrilla Samil Basayev and spilled many thousand liters of blood. In inexplicable times, where the moral high ground is determined by the age of the newly dead, Beslan is right up there on the charts. A place where a Chechen clone of the al Qaeda debated briefly the pros and cons of shooting children and decided that killing kids was an Islam-endorsed pursuit. Half of the 326 hostages killed in Beslan were children.

Fuelled by their demented vision of Islam, the goons, even in their most heinous discharge of fanaticism, perhaps, did us one favour. They provided space for Muslim moderates to speak out. In an environment where Arabs criticizing terrorism often delegitimize themselves, the outpouring over Beslan was unique. A few samples. Strident criticism came from Abdel Al-Rahman Al-Rashed, ex-editor of London daily *Al-Sharq Al-Awsat* and general manager, Al-Arabiya satellite TV network: "Obviously, not all Muslims are terrorists but, regrettably, the majority of terrorists in the world are Muslims. The kidnappers of the students in Ossetia are Muslims. The killers of the Nepalese workers and cooks are also Muslims. Those who rape and murder in Darfour are Muslims, and their victims are Muslims as well. Osama bin Laden is a Muslim and Al-Houthi (the head of a terrorist group in Yemen) is a Muslim. The majority of those who carried out suicide operations against buses, schools, houses, and buildings around the world in the last 10 years were also Muslims."

"What a terrible record," he then laments. "Does this not say something about us, about our society and our culture? If we put all of these pictures together in one day, we will see that these pictures are difficult, embarrassing and humiliating for us. However, instead of avoiding them and justifying them, it is incumbent upon us first of all to recognize their authenticity rather than to compose eloquent articles and speeches proclaiming our innocence...."

The test here is for building of a new 21st century Muslim community, based on the principles Islam gave us in the 7th century. "Reform is inevitable, but it won't come easy" (*Time Online*, September 7, 2004). And let it be underlined: "Reform must come from within; it must be their brand, their way to bring forward into the future the traditions that will shape their form of democracy, their form of market economy, and their social change."

III

International Dynamics

6

America: New Precincts of Foreign Policy

> The belief that we (America) are retreating from the war with the Taliban has proved illusory. But another belief is circulating that even after its defeat, America is losing the propaganda war against bin Ladenism.
>
> Indeed there is still a lot of anti-American sentiment prevailing in the Arab-Muslim world. But, on the whole, a careful thought has to be given to the diplomatic and war strategies so that the Muslim sensitivity is not hurt.
>
> The positive results of this policy by America also are already evident. For example, after years, the position of America has become strong among the leading classes of those countries. Our victory has made this possible. Now, we must insist that these rulers oppose the extremism within their own jurisdictions. They should encourage the media that has been opposing America and Israel for this purpose; and also should see that the inferiority complex and a feeling of weakness that prevails in their subjects are lessened.
>
> — **Fareed Zakaria** (*Newsweek*, November 26, 2001)

During the campaigns for the presidential elections of 2000, George Bush appeared to be nearly indifferent or even illiterate for foreign policy issues. America was aiming to make progress in the trends of globalization keeping itself and its interests in its center. America has had an indifferent approach in the proposals that came up in the international fora trying to stop the use of biological and chemical weapons and to apply other such regulations as well as to appoint international observers for any misdemeanors. In the pre-9/11 phase of Bush presidency, the US sought to practice 'unilateral' foreign policy in many areas of international cooperation. Even though endorsed by the predecessor President Clinton, Bush administration was not ready to accept the resolution of the Kyoto Conference that each country observes the rules for better environment and give guarantee as to its performance in order to save the world from global warming and from increase in the production of poisonous gases. It also decided to pull out of the membership of the International Criminal Court and abandon the 1972 Anti-Ballistic Missile Treaty. America also wanted to be indifferent to help solve the problems of the world such as poverty, unemployment, education, health etc. or to contribute at its own level some other kinds of contributions too. The new ruling sections of prosperous America were aiming to remain away not only from the political-environmental-economic-human problems of the world, they were also inclined to adopt a new isolationist foreign policy. While American armies could invade any country from Vietnam to Nicaragua and Bosnia, Kuwait and even Kosovo, but America itself, growing into one superpower, with two great oceans of the world protecting its borders, was supposedly free of any attack from outside. However, such America was shocked on 9/11 morning by the attack on it, at center of if its power and pride, and later, by the scare of disease and death through Anthrax that entered America in envelopes! These dramatic scenario prompted America to resume links with the outside world. With the anti-American protest demonstrations all over the world, from Manila to Khartoum, by crowds of thousands of people, came a remarkable shift in its worldview. After consultations with his advisors, President Bush has reshaped his foreign policy that is extrovert. It is the basis for the aim of fighting a worldwide war against terrorism.

Britain has been a traditionally close ally of America. Western Europe also tends to lend its support to America. India itself has been suffering at the hands of terrorism and is aware of the consequent losses since long. Significantly, America received support of Russia this time—a country traditionally suspicious of American moves. China has also given diplomatic support to some extent. South America, Southeast Asia, regional organizations of Africa and the Security Council (UNO) also have given unanimous support to America in this. Unexpected, if partial, support came from Iran. Russia (Chechnya), China (Zinkiang) and Iran have experiences of Islamic fanatics, fundamentalists and terrorists in their own territories. Russia and China lend it their support, as it is also their own problem. Uzbekistan and Tazakistan on the borders of Afghanistan that were republics of erstwhile Soviet Union and are free countries now, also face the problem of terrorist activities. So, besides their natural friends of Central Asia, these countries were also roped in by America for joining hands in this war against terrorism. These countries are situated in the west, north and northeast borders of Afghanistan.

Strategically important areas where Afghanistan can be attacked are its eastern and southern borders that touch Pakistan. However, Pakistan considered the continuation of Taliban rule as its own interest. If America is known to be the father of Taliban, then Pakistan can be considered its midwife. In the new context, Collin Powell, the Secretary of the State, twisting the arm of President Musharraf, said that if the latter would not join in the US strategy for capture of Laden, then America would have to give a thought to ending the camps of the terrorists within Pakistan.

Musharraf took a calculated risk in dealing with this uncertain situation. He offered that he would provide bases on Pakistan soil for bomber aircrafts and other related military maneuvers. In return he quickly outlined a financial aid that would be a great relief in critical economic condition Pakistan faced.

However, characteristically, America gave greater importance to use of the soil of Uzbekistan and Tazakistan as strategic bases for attacks on Afghanistan. From here the land army of the Northern Alliance (that came to be called United Front of Afghanistan since October 2001) advanced against the Taliban military camps. The Northern Alliance provided the various tribes of Afghanistan to be integrated as one body in their effort to remove the Taliban rule.

On November 9, replying to the insistence of Musharraf, President Bush declared that when Northern Alliance enters Kabul, American forces would not enter there. In mid-November, the troops of Northern Alliance marched victoriously into Kabul, and there were reports that there were talks between America and Pakistan in tense atmospherics. Pakistan wanted that it should continue to play some role in Afghanistan and calculated that if the capital still remained with the Taliban, it would be able to play a greater role in the new government after their fall. Pakistan was therefore bringing pressure on America not to enter Kabul, but America did not comply with the idea.

After October 7, America has not displayed any significant achievement in military field, and so the punditocracy of Bush administration began to predict negatively that the policy of Bush is bound to fail, etc. There was an overall agreement in the media and people of the Middle East and Pakistan regarding 'limitless mysterious' power of bin Laden. However, after the fall of Mazar-e-Sharif, the war scenario quickly changed in favor of America. Not only the military officers but also the intelligence organizations of Pakistan were helping the Taliban in Afghanistan. There were 6,000 such alleged Pakistanis who might be captured from Kabul, Kunduz and Mazar-e-Sharif. Pakistan needed time for lifting them away back to Pakistan so that no proof of its involvement could be found. *US News and*

World Report (November 19, 2001) stated that there were 25 to 35 percent Pakistanis in Taliban troops. For this reason and to regain popularity with other Muslim nations, Musharraf sought to bring pressure on America to refrain from war activities and bombing during the month of Ramadan (beginning November 19, 2001). If this did not happen, the Muslim people would come out on the streets and America would face even greater opposition. His calculation was that if he succeeds in halting the speedily advancing American forces, he could get enough time to reinforce Pakistan's sagging standing in that region. America coolly ignored his tactics. However, while it did not stop the progress of its armies, considering the value of the geo-political and strategic compulsions of having Pakistan on its side, America made Musharraf its ally. Ignored and sidelined during Clinton administration, Pakistan now received new recognition and economic support of America.

Although there are documented presentations in the US Congress every year in the hearings of South Asia matters and the reports of the CIA about terrorist incidents in Jammu & Kashmir, and about Pakistani connection with the Taliban and Kashmir terrorists, etc., due to its own strategic compulsions, America has not found it pragmatic to declare Pakistan a 'terrorist state' so far. President Clinton had himself commented on the soil of Pakistan in March 2000 on the 'cross-border terrorism' that prevailed in Kashmir. However, after 9/11, Pakistan has become, instead of a possible 'terrorist state', a 'frontline state'. The patron and fertile ground of terrorism, it has been awarded the status of a non-NATO ally of USA!

In spite of the frequent presentation to the Bush administration, India has had to face diplomatic disappointments. At the same time, America has been soothing gestures to India that in its overall and long-term anti-terrorist policy it has included the terrorism in Kashmir, but in view of the 'real politick', or practicality of the present situation, America could have formulated a foreign policy in tune with its stated objectives of war on terrorism on all fronts worldwide including India. On December 13 that year, the terrorists attacked Indian Parliament itself as a step of their plans, and India provided America and other countries all the definite proofs of the attack and its origins too. Even after that, Collin Powell softly recommended India (as well as Pakistan) to keep its anguish under control. Powell even instigated that organizations like Lashkar-e-Toiba (LeT) want the two countries to go to war! Thus, on the whole, some of the political analysts of India have even felt that it has become difficult to distinguish between America's 'real politick' and 'hypocritical politics'. On December 26, the Indian Foreign Minister Jaswant Singh even commented in his telephonic talk with Collin Powell about the use of certain statements that separated 9/11 and 12/13 (the day of terrorist attack on Indian Parliament) and at least verbally, Powell had to accept that America does not make such distinctions.

The declaration of Powell that "India and Pakistan must fight together against their common enemy, terrorism", indicates the degree of 'principled' foreign policy.

In the first week of December, Afghanistan was liberated from the hands of the Taliban. By that time suggestions were pouring forth in one section of the White House as to whether the war must be extended to Iraq under President Saddam Hussein, putting forward the fear about its possession and possible use of biological and chemical weapons of mass destruction. It went out of American 'memory' at that time, that in the last decade 30,000 or more people had lost lives from terrorist acts and very recent episode of cruel bomb attack on Kashmir Assembly was also not noted. This made it very clear that 'terrorism' is only such when it touches America or its interests, not otherwise. The definition, understanding and policy in this regard are entirely centered on America and America only. This has become totally clear. In reality, an Indian analyst called America as '*double standard Inc.*'.

So then, for its own strategic policy calculations, America can ignore activities of Pakistan; it can ignore the actual experience and consequences of Kashmir and Delhi; and it can even declare that it has a policy that considers the two countries on par and that it follows parallel policies for them! By the most recent events, it stands exposed on its 'double speak'. In its foreign policy America considers human rights and terrorism as central, but its this argument and stand also have been exposed after the problems of Kosovo and Yugoslavia, and more so in the important and shocking stage of dealings with terrorism.

Relevant here is to refer to observations of the Columbia University Professor Mahmood Mamdani in *Good Muslim, Bad Muslim* (with sub-title, *America, the Cold War, and the Roots of Terror*). He explains the early history behind various happenings of *jehad*, which is closer to the western sense of the "just war" than the crusader's sense of "holy war". He says that from Nixon to Vice President Dick Cheney and Defense

New York on Orange Alert, July 2004

Secretary Donald Rumsfeld drew lessons that America's wars should not be fought by American soldiers in the main. So began a series of "proxy wars". In Africa, in Mozambique and Angola to begin with. Refining techniques in Nicaragua before the last proxy war against Soviet Union through the Pak-supported Taliban, the US followed "the most cynical exercise of all" in the Iraq-Iran war when it helped build up Saddam Hussein in early 1980s. Here, the sub-title of Mamdani's book becomes significant. He shows how, with the support of Israel and South Africa (under Apartheid), the US virtually created its future enemies; supplied them with weapons, trained, funded and directed them; and taught them the tactics of terrorism, including kidnapping (more than 5,000 Contras alone!). "That is just for starters." Mamdani states, "The Reagan administration took two initiatives that were to have lasting impacts on US foreign policy. The first was to turn to drug trade for an illicit source of funds (as in Latin America and Afghanistan); the second was to turn to religious right to implement those foreign policy objectives that Congress ruled against, thus beginning a trend toward privatizing war." To the usual anti-communist ideology, the CIA harnessed and helped refine an Islamic component—to up the battlefield fervor and attract funding from the Islamic world. He adds, "The blueprint for the Afghan *jehad* was worked out by the CIA, in collaboration with the ISI (Inter Service Intelligence) of Pakistan." Its strategy extended to roping in intelligence structures of Saudi Arabia, Egypt, Israel, Britain, and China. For leading this 'crusade', finally, "it settled for the son of an illustrious family closely connected to the Saudi royal house".

That was Osama bin Laden, who began by building a large CIA-funded project in 1986—a tunnel complex under the mountains near Pakistan with the latter's benign eyes. That led to formation of the history's most influential nucleas-cum-channel, al Qaeda, in 1989. That US-patronized tunnel turned out to symbolize the complex nexus between al Qaeda, Afghanistan and Pakistan!

After a relatively swift and casualty-free (for the American military) war in Afghanistan, and thereafter in Iraq (March 2003), the US has experienced that war can be won with a far superior military technology and prowess. But winning peace—even consolidating the occupation regime—is a mirage in these desert-like countries. As Fareed Zakaria perceptively stated, "The belief that we (America) are retreating from the war with the Taliban has proved illusory. But another belief is circulating that even after its defeat, America is losing the propaganda war against him." Zakaria hoped for another dimensions of the US foreign policy. "The positive results of the policy by America also are already evident. For example, after years, the position of America has become strong among the leading classes of those countries. Our victory (in Afghanistan) has made this possible. Now, we must insist that these rulers oppose the extremism within their own jurisdictions. They should encourage the media that has been opposing America and Israel for this purpose; and also should see that the inferiority complex and a feeling of weakness that prevails in their subjects are lessened" (*Newsweek*, November 26, 2001).

America's Iraq war has washed off the instant sympathy and support it had received in the wake of 9/11. It did not merely provoke the conventional 'Arab street' but what Thomas Friedman terms the vast 'world street'. On February 15, 2003, millions of people were on roads in cities the world over. London saw a record of million marching against the impending Iraq war. Again, during the five weeks since March 15, 2003, 60 million people were estimated to have protested against the war. 100,000 plus protested in cities across Germany including 30,000 who held hands in 31-mile chain between two cities in this state (*Guardian Unlimited*, March 29, 2003). In the US itself 8,000 to 12,000 gathered on the steps of Capitol building on Pennsylvania Avenue in Washington D.C. Black-robed women in Sana'a, Yemen held the banner with words "The U.S. and Britain are the Axis of Evil". In Caracas, Chile one protestor held a banner stating, "That wretched gang decided to leapfrog the U.N.'s authority." About 15,000 protested in Athens. Fergal Keane wrote in *The Independent*, London (March 29, 2003), "The cradle of (Babylonian) civilization is destroyed by the 'so-called civilized' leaders of the West."

America has landed itself in a no-win situation in Iraq. Living there for longer period as well as leaving it in the near future complicates its predicament. Now, "its decision to go to war in Iraq is a second guess, but the principle of considering the considerable opportunity cost of war is vital and should be paramount in our nation's foreign policy debate" (John Podesta and Deborah Rappaport, *Atlanta Journal-Constitution*, September 15, 2004). Iraq made the 2004 presidential election a truly foreign-policy election.

Indeed, there is still a lot of anti-American sentiment prevailing in the Arab/Muslim world. But, on the whole, a careful thought need to be given to the diplomatic and war strategies so that the Muslim sensitivity is not hurt. As Mamdani concludes, "Caught in a situation where both adversaries in the war on terror claim to be fighting terror with the weapons of terror, nothing less than a global movement for peace will save the humanity." To 'peace' it may be added, poverty alleviation and liberal cultural education, imaginatively promoted, also need to be on our agenda.

Viewed in the above perspective, two points emerge. One, the plight of America is even worse than it was in Vietnam in late 1960s. There it had an escape hatch which helped it to use as a face-saving get out in 1973. But, as the Mid-East expert Stephen P. Cohen states, "We have no way to stay in Iraq and no way to get out. All options there are bad...Bush's whole focus is on America whose role in the world is to negate the negation of the terrorists. But, America has always been about the affirmation of something positive. That is missing today. Beyond Afghanistan, they've been much better at destruction than construction." Second, Mamdani's ending note is terse and timely. "America cannot occupy the world. It has to live in it."

7

India: Challenge and Response

> General Musharraf and his colleagues have been claiming that Kashmir is the central issue in the Indo-Pak Agenda. In this situation, it should be proved with facts that their real agenda is to destabilize the democratic, secular and pluralistic India.
>
> If Musharraf does not punish those who carried out the terrible attack on Indian Parliament and keeps on supporting terrorism, then we shall have to use our suitable and internationally justifiable surgical military alternative for which there is a strategic scope in the matter.
>
> And the time and place for this would be only our choice.
>
> — **G. Parthasarathy**
> (former Indian High Commissioner to Pakistan)

After America's direct experience of terrorism on 9/11, India expected a positive response of America and the implications of ending the problems of terrorism within the structure of 'the clash of two civilizations' that would lead to its favoring India, and not Pakistan. It was to prove wrong. The reality of the US' 'politics of pragmatism' thus put India in a big quandary. After the horrendous attack on Indian Parliament on December 13, 2001, it was neither practical nor logical and not even proper for India to sustain an uneasy of peace but continuing to suffer the decade long undeclared war that was being fought at low levels with a focus on Kashmir and was absolutely imposed on India by Pakistan without provocation. However, had the government of Vajpayee understood the real character of present terrorism? L.K. Advani, the then Home Minister, made a statement after this attack that India has been a victim of terrorism since last 20 years and has been combating it as well! In fact, in the 1980s and early 1990s, the violence that had spread in Punjab and Kashmir was due to the faulty political behavior of the Indian leaders at the center and the states concerned. The exploitation of our security forces that was out of proportion also contributed to it. On the other hand, the violent events that have occurred in the last 4-5 years have taken the character of extremist or *jehadi*(st) terrorism inspired by fanatic religious forces. *Kashmiriyat*, the unique character of Kashmiri people, is now lost in the wilderness of Islamic *jehad* type of struggle.

The Indian system of dispensing justice is also unique. Those arrested for violent and terrorist acts during the administrations from Narasimha Rao down to Vajpayee, only one person was convicted under the terrorist laws! The known terrorists Azhar Masud and Omar Sheikh arrested much before the IC-814's hijack incident in December 1999, had been languishing in prisons for full five years without any court proceedings or sentence! Thus, in whatever alert and effective steps needed to be taken at various levels in order to manage terrorism, the successive governments of Congress, Janata Dal and the NDA coalition led by BJP were all failures.

In December 1999, terrorists inspired by Pakistan hijacked the plane of Indian Airlines, IC-814, flying from Kathmandu in Nepal to New Delhi. They were successful in taking the plane on to Kandahar. In order to save the lives of Indian passengers, the Vajpayee government agreed to the daunting demand of hijackers and freed four terrorists imprisoned in Tihar Jail, including Muhammad Azhar. Just a decade ago, terrorists in

Kashmir had kidnapped Rubiya, the daughter of Muhammad Mufti, the then Home Minister in the central government led by V.P. Singh. A questionable precedent was then set when the demands of terrorists were agreed to for the safety of their prisoner. That same terrorist, Azhar had been in forefront then, and he was also the mastermind behind the attack on Indian Parliament. After all these experiences and quietly suffering for so long, and adopting a liberal and soft policy for dealing with it, India showed clear indications to Pakistan that for its undeclared war by proxy it is imposing on India in the form of terrorist activities, it would have to pay very heavy price.

In July 1999, the widespread infiltrations in Kargil by Pakistan were met by heavy air attacks by India, when it destroyed the terrorist camps and bunkers set up by the enemy within Indian borders; but India also showed a wise restraint by not crossing over the LoC (Line of Control) between the two countries. The combined experience of the hijacking of IC-184 and Kargil had made the Indian public opinion very aggressive and was likely to bring real pressure on the government to start taking military action against Pakistan at a risk of full-fledged war. Earlier, when on October 1 that year, the plan to destroy Kashmir Vidhan Sabha (Assembly) in Srinagar by car bombs and suicidal squads was executed, and 38 persons lost their lives in the incident, America did not bring sufficient pressure on Pakistan at that time (because of its own need to have Pakistan on their side in the matter of Afghanistan), and Musharraf did not take steps to stop repetition of such incidents either. As a result of this, the opinion of people, government, most political parties and media in India was that effective pressure could have been brought on Pakistan by direct diplomatic policy of India and also by America.

Although it was logical and justified that India could have taken retaliatory military steps as soon as the attack on Kashmir Assembly occurred, but India did not do so only because America explained that its position in Afghanistan would suffer a setback if Pakistan is alienated. Even then, all the efforts to placate Pakistan have proved ineffective. On the contrary, a cynical plan to destroy the symbolic base of Indian democracy—Parliament House in New Delhi—was made so that its democracy and political leadership structure would collapse, and was actually carried out by the attack of December 13. At this defiance, any self-respecting and sovereign nation would not be talking of continuing a policy of peace and patience.

In the years following 1989, many Kashmiris had been carrying on, from within Kashmir, an armed opposition to India for a separatist dream. But, after 1994, this brigade came under the great influence of Pakistan-inspired Kashmiris and Pakistani fundamentalists. Now, the Taliban Afghans and Arabs have also joined hands. Thus, the local armed rebel terrorist activities, instead of remaining 'homegrown', were also hijacked. Secondly, in the early years, the victims of armed attacks were the officers and soldiers of the Border Security Forces (BSF) and innocent citizens of Jammu & Kashmir. But, the attack on the State Assembly was definitely aimed to damage our civil democratic representatives and was not just a military or armed attack. Thus, in the plans of terrorists also, we can see a qualitative change.

After the events of hijacking at Kandahar, Kargil conflict and attack on the Kashmir Assembly the public opinion was swelling in favor of taking strong steps against Pakistan. Even pacifists like Prabhu Chawla, the managing editor of *India Today*, and the former Prime Minister V.P. Singh who advocated earlier that only peaceful talks could solve the problem between the two nations, began to now recommend coercive diplomacy against Pakistan. Most of the political parties (except for CPM), including the Congress, criticized the present policy of the government in this matter and wanted to take strong diplomatic steps, and later, even military steps if needed. The parties and the media also changed their soft stance to a hard one.

On the other hand, Air Commodore Jasjit Singh, Brahma Chelani, Uday Bhaskar, Subrhamanyam and other members of Indian 'Think Tank', and the former Army Chief Malik etc. warned that India would not be able to achieve its main objective by any military action. Thus, on such an important question of the country, if a variety of opinions, complementary and even opposing idea, logic and sentiments are possible to express, it is a compliment to India's democratic set-up, and it could be advantageous to it also!

The Vajpayee government had to form a clear policy and a quick decision based on all such complex set of views, colored opinions, ideas, and facts. According to H. Kaushal, one approach was to try for a limited objective. It meant a limited military attack on terrorist camps located within Pak-occupied Kashmir (PoK), although Pakistan was not likely to view it as a 'limited' maneuver. It was more likely, in fact, that as a reaction, Pakistan would indulge in a full-fledged war. (As it was, by the time Indian government was considering the attack, these camps had been folded up and had now disappeared, to be set up elsewhere.) Also, most of such 150 camps were located in Pakistan, and so any attempt to destroy them would naturally attract reaction by Pakistan with declaring of war. Thus, 'limited military action' did not seem prudent for the Indian objective in mind. Besides, the terrorist camps and bases are never permanent in location. Also, even after having destroyed most of them, Pakistan can replace them with the terrorists who have migrated to Pakistan in large numbers from Afghanistan. In addition, the Madrassas have played the role of churning out trained potential terrorists *en masse* so that they can be easily and speedily prepared for any violent and damaging actions in future, anywhere. It is true, therefore, that destroying these camps would mean much less terrorism for India and Kashmir, but that would be a temporary relief only. That is why, Vajpayee and Advani declared that now India aims to destroy nothing less than terrorism itself!

Secondly, looking at its political culture and history of its dealings with Pakistan (1948, 1965, 1971) so far, while India has a much better equipped and more powerful position for war, if it chooses the second option of war, but in case of such a war if Pakistan suffers retreat or defeat, which is more likely, it cannot be ruled out that it would resort to atomic weapons. Indian leadership and strategists know it well that Pakistan has not given any 'No First Use' guarantee. And, the most sobering fact is that use of nuclear bombs would entail unbearable human destruction, suffering and torture for both sides. This total destruction must be avoided at all costs.

Under the circumstances, if the focus were on strong diplomatic steps, as strong as possible, it would only indicate political wisdom and a sense of responsibility. However, when the basic condition for them is effectiveness, the dilemma of India is quite understandable.

In such a scenario of international relations, the role of America became greatly important. President Clinton had identified Kashmir as the 'most dangerous region' of the world. While referring to India and Pakistan, the rulers and media in America never forget to mention that they are two nuclear powers opposed to each other. Thus, America needs Pakistan for dealing with Afghanistan and capture of bin Laden, and also has a vested interest in establishing peace between these two neighboring adversaries.

On 22nd December, on the highly popular San Francisco center of the National Broadcasting Radio's "Talk of the Nation" program, a telephonic discussion was held between the 'Think Tank' experts of South Asia in America and analysts of *New York Times* at Islamabad and New Delhi. The genuine anxiety felt in the US about the possible use of nuclear weapons for war was expressed then. The points/steps considered by America to avoid such a development were also discussed. In late October it was feared that if the Laden's forces marginalized Musharraf and Pakistan slipped into the hands of more extremist *jehadi* forces, the new rulers would turn highly dangerous for America, India and all the nearby countries. That is why, under the pressure of Bush-Rumsfeld, the nuclear establishments were sought to be shifted to more secure places. Those who are experts on this issue believe that the American strategists are in the know about their location, and that American leaders are in a position to persuade Musharraf to their way of thinking. Also, the nuclear weapons and power centers have been hidden at separate places. It would need some hours to coordinate them, so that there is no nuclear explosion by accident. The former Chief of Air Staff, Sarin, in an interview given to *Indian Express* (January 5, 2002), clearly said that in terms of air force and nuclear power, India has a definitely superior position than Pakistan, and so he also advocates an offensive and speedy initiative of attack by India.

Four decades ago, when the Cold War was at its zenith with the Cuba crisis in 1962, the Soviet leader Khrushchev had placed missile in the backyard of America. At that time, President Kennedy showed determination in declaring himself ready to use American missiles against it. This war of nerves between the two great world powers lasted for 13 anxious days. After the 12/13 episode in 2001, within 15 days, the armies of both India and Pakistan occupied the combat position with even readied missiles on the borders and in Kashmir. Two nuclear powers of South Asia were in the grip of war fever, with aggressive statements and gun attacks at the borders. The war of nerves reached an unprecedented high! At this time India remembered the experience it had two-and-a-half years ago.

That was in May 1999, when Pakistan had supported guerilla forces and bombarded the Kashmir region under Indian control for weeks, and the situation was delicate to the point of leading to war. At this time, America had brought diplomatic pressure on Pakistan to change its posture, and India also had really displayed its capacity of a determined power. For these two reasons, Pakistan had to recall its guerilla forces back to base.

Even in the winter 2001 crisis, India has patiently yet effectively displayed its capacity and power for determined military policy. In the second fortnight of December 2001, America continued its pressure on both the nations for exercising self-control, though Bush advised Pakistan also 'to end terrorism' itself. They also increased the pressure in the year-end for arrests of terrorists as demanded by India, and disperse the terrorist organizations that had mushroomed in Pakistan. However, both the nations had readied their forces at the borders in unusually large numbers, and this brought forth a comment by Evo Daltor, a member of the 'Think Tank' like Brookings Institute, "Is South Asia turning into a potential center for explosion of a nuclear war?"

Merely for the purpose of initiating attack so as to destroy a few terrorist centers, India cannot risk a nuclear war. Suppose, such a step yields only a limited advantage? For decades India has proved its superiority over Pakistan in traditional war apparatus (infantry—tanks, air force and navy, missiles, etc.) Indian 'jawans' and officers of all sections of the army are ranked among the top in terms of training and military preparedness. However, since the nuclear tests of May 1998, it has lost this edge over Pakistan, as has been made clear by Cohen and Denis Kuks, as well as the details in the studies of Jasjit Singh.

In the third week of December an alternative had been suggested that Bush administration might mediate between the two countries, and if a war does take place, they might be made to agree to use conventional weapons only rather than nuclear ones. Otherwise, America would think of taking steps that were not made clear yet, to implement its undefined crisis plan. The other more risky and bold plan was also under discussion: India would make a lightening pre-emptive air attacks to destroy Pakistan's atomic capacity, and simultaneously India would declare that it would not use any nuclear weapon. Both these alternatives of early action would perhaps limit the possibility of total destruction by nuclear war in South Asia. There have been some public agreements and other treaties between India and Israel for cooperation. It was reported that the experts of this field in India are taking cue from Israel's bitter experiences of suicide attacks even when it is also a better equipped, capable and experienced nation, facing since long from the challenge of terrorizing violence.

Thus, to remove the terrorist threat as much as possible, and to teach an effective lesson to its great patron Pakistan also, such considerations are going on since mid-2002. However, the situation is so complex, and its international implications so serious besides being harmful for India as well, that it took the government a long time for evaluation of each possible move. In this context, some journalists like Tavleen Singh and other columnists ridiculed Vajpayee as 'Hot Talk, Cold Feet', or 'Hot Pursuit, Cold Feet'. One journalist even wrote, "We should retaliate to Pakistan by hot pursuit, not hot words."

For one thing, the dilemma that Indian government (and it may be of any combination of political parties) has to face in taking such decisions must be fully understood. On one hand, the extreme and constant armed attacks on security forces, collective experience of violent episodes, the terrorist attacks on heart centers like Delhi and Srinagar besides civil institutions—all have brought India to the limit of patience. Now, it was strongly felt that Pakistan, for its proxy war or constant conflicts at lower levels, would have to be taught a real lesson so that it would have to suffer untold destruction and loss (of men, material and resources). But, on the other hand, once a war-like step is actually taken, it could not be determined or predicted as to the extension in the scope of ensuing war. It might not be possible even by the computers to know the map, picture or scenario of next developments or whether it would envelope most of Pakistan as well as India, once it turns into a missile war. In any case, the suggestion of the experts and the media that we might remain self-controlled regarding Pakistan's 'nuclear blackmail' but must not feel anxious or terrorized by it, seems to have been carefully woven in the Indian government policy now. In this context, India chose to use the path of diplomatic pressure first and only if then found inevitable, to take the path of actual war. It was decided to gradually increase diplomatic pressure on Pakistan, by measured and increasingly strong steps. At the same time, it was felt necessary to bring pressure on America, to create a favorable international public opinion, and thereby create a favorable environment for its steps in this matter. Preparations for war also must be seriously undertaken, and arrangements be quickly made for the security of India's strategic and important infrastructures against possible attacks by Pakistan in the meantime. Also, care was to be taken not to announce in public what were the plans for this by the Vajpayee government, but it was declared that to implement any step, India would make the choice of time and place (Editorial by Vir Sanghavi in *Hindustan Times*).

During all this, the Vajpayee government began to take the steps in the first stage of the plan of bringing diplomatic pressures on Pakistan. It was declared that 'Samjhauta Express' and 'Lahore Bus Services' would be suspended from 31st January, 2002. Also, Indian High Commissioner Nambiar at Islamabad, was recalled although, in response High Commissioner Jahangir Kazi of Pakistan to New Delhi was not recalled to Islamabad at once. One secretary of the Indian government said that the reason behind this was that half the office staff of the Pakistani High Commissioner is involved in some kind of spying activity in India. So how could the 'cunning President of Pakistan', Musharraf, think of recalling them! According to G. Parthasarathy, the former High Commissioner for India to Pakistan, 80 percent of the staff was appointed by the ISI itself! Also, as the next step, the Pakistan Airlines were stopped from operating in the Indian skies. The flight of their airplanes to East Asia was also forbidden. Within that week, India reduced its staff of the office of the High Commissioner to half its former strength. Experts were even advising closure of all facilities of trade and commerce allotted to Pakistan by India (although, as Indian exports to Pakistan were higher, such a step would be disadvantageous to India only). Going even further, a treaty between Nehru and Liyakat Ali in 1958 that allowed the waters of Sutlej to continue flowing into Pakistan, but now the government was advised to even stop this water supply. This would highly damage the crops of wheat, cotton etc. of the Pakistan farmers. The idea behind this suggestion was that the farmers and the general public would blame their President and his policies for such losses and their dissatisfaction would increase against him. Also, if Musharraf did not budge by the diplomatic pressures and did not take concrete steps to meet demands of India, then only such extreme steps also must be taken.

Thus, when India flexed its military muscles, clearly indicated to America and Pakistan of its determination, and began to take diplomatic steps, and due to this when America's pressure also increased on Pakistan, then only that country began to respond in a positive manner. One may not go into too many details, but must note that it banned the activities of terrorist organizations like Lashkar-e-Toiba (LeT) and Jaish-e-Muhammad (JeM), and in response to the demand of India, also arrested 50 terrorists and jailed them for a definite period. In the list provided by India was also the name of Masud Azhar and Tiger Memon who had triggered the terrorist bombings in Mumbai on 12th March, 1993, and of Chhota Shakil besides Dawood Ibrahim (Dawood was later named as having links with al Qaeda by CIA). However, these persons were not arrested. It would have been better if they were to be handed over to India or deported from Pakistan as well. It is also significant that at about this time Musharraf began to criticize Islamic fundamentalists and *jehadi* extremists who were responsible in keeping Pakistan backward and poor. India appreciated this new stance, but it was not a sufficient gesture for it. Besides, one is not convinced that this is a permanent change; India explained this point to America, Britain, France, and Germany that had called for its self-control. In the meantime, reports began to come that China has begun military maneuvers on the borders of the Himalayas just to indicate its favoring of Pakistan. In any case, the strategy of 'war by diplomacy' earlier used by Pakistan was used by India too. Shekhar Gupta, the chief editor of *Indian Express*, appreciated that Indian government's military and diplomatic steps in this conflict were taken after great deliberations, and were not revealed at wrong moments either.

In early days of January 2002, at the SAARC conference that held at Kathmandu, Vajpayee avoided meeting Musharraf, which was suggestive of the change in Vajpayee who earlier had been so eager at Agra for talks.

The CNN broke news on January 1, 2000 about two developments. One, Musharraf claimed that there was not enough evidence about 30 of the names submitted by India as terrorists that must be arrested by him for their terrorist activities in India, and so he refused to arrest them; and second, he was inclined to sign a memorandum of understanding with India that both the countries would refrain from aiming at each others' nuclear installations!

It is natural to confuse and surprise Indians that while on one hand Pakistan refused to comply with India's demand for arresting fully known terrorists (including Dawood Ibrahim) who were involved in killing innocent citizens of Mumbai and other anti-India terrorist activities for years, but on the other hand, it is ready to sign a treaty for mutual security of nuclear power plants with India! But, perhaps, the analysis in the preceding paragraphs may explain this contradictory attitude. Pakistan was in a difficult situation at that moment. On and off, America was also putting pressure on it. So, there was likelihood, however small, that India might take pre-emptive steps of shattering its nuclear power plants even before any diplomatic maneuvers are fully gone into. Besides, an undeclared and prolonged war by India would be a fitting response to Pakistan's own unbearable policy of inflicting terrorist tactics, and would be a lesson for it as a last resort.

Musharraf seemed to have developed a doubt then if his threats and 'nuclear blackmail' policy would be effective in dealing with India any longer. Therefore, he must have got ready to save its lifeline of nuclear power plants somehow, and wait for a more suitable opportunity to resort to his familiar 'war by diplomacy' later. Also, by this understanding, instead of a nuclear war, the probability of a traditional war remains. In such a war, it feels that it is superior, India can better deal with Pakistan at that level, while its own nuclear power plants also remain secure. All in all, the guess was that both the countries were thinking of future based on their own calculations.

On 2nd January, in another bomb explosion outside the building of Jammu & Kashmir Assembly, 22 people were hurt and one policeman died. On that same day, *The Dawn* gave a news item that provided hope for breaking ice between the two countries. Pakistan that had been feeling reluctant about it, now declared the ban on terrorist organizations like LeT and JeM. It was also admitted that these organizations had their hand in nearly 70 percent of the terrorist activities that had occurred in the last three years in India. The western countries welcomed this step of Musharraf: "This is the most courageous step of the President to diffuse the dangerous tension that had gripped the (Indian) subcontinent since the attack on the Parliament." Appreciating this move, *The Dawn* wrote, "Musharraf has killed two birds with one stone by this step: one, the war with India would be avoided; and second, it would be easier to deal with terrorism at domestic level also." On the other hand, the Indian Prime Minister has not ruled out the possibility of use of nuclear weapons in case of war with Pakistan; and in the SAARC conference (4th January) he definitely rejected any meeting with Pakistan's President. There were indications of Pakistan bending against this firm approach of India but India continued to be strictly firm on its stand. The situation thus was very flux, complex and full of tension at the beginning of the year.

When Musharraf went to attend SAARC conference at Kathmandu, he traveled there via Beijing. It was significant that this was his second visit there within a fortnight. The spokesperson of the Pakistan government declared that China was ready to support Pakistan in 'all types of situations' in the present context. However, the report of BBC poured cold water over such dubious claims.

On 5th January, at Kathmandu, Vajpayee shook hands with Musharraf to make the delegates view his gesture, but the next day in his interview with *The Telegraph*, he said, "It was a handshake of extended hands that were folded into fists." And India's Foreign Minister Jaswant Singh thus on such gestures of Musharraf, "The problems between two nations are not 'an exercise of public relations'." In his speech at SAARC Vajpayee made it clear: Instead of making symbolic gestures, Pakistan must take "real and concrete steps to curb terrorism". At that moment, the entire world could see the crestfallen face of Musharraf on their televisions. The successful PR politician of Agra in 2000 received symbolic comments that marked an audiovisual response by Vajpayee at Kathmandu. At that time, although Collin Powell talked to Vajpayee for ten minutes on telephone, Vajpayee did not meet Musharraf.

In the meantime, Powell made it public that when Musharraf returns from Kathmandu, he would be announcing a number of steps his government is planning to come down on the terrorists. Reports were given in *San Jose Mercury News*, *New York Times* and even in Pakistan media that Madrassas and centers of religious training within Pakistan would be brought under control. Thus, the pressure brought by America on Pakistan seemed to be working slowly. Jaswant Singh had commented at Kathmandu, "Pakistan would not listen to suggestions from India. But it definitely accepts them when they come from America!" This statement says a lot about the situation.

The declaration passed unanimously at SAARC against terrorism was like an acceptance of India's argument. All seven members of SAARC accepted 'Resolution 1373' of the UN Security Council that was passed after September 11 (in which it clearly orders all nations and organizations to dissuade from use of violent force and fight all types of terrorism) and declared, "We shall have to continue to fight constantly against terrorism in all its forms and practices."

From such highly complex situations and events that may be at times even contradictory, India has learnt a lesson: to bring effective diplomatic pressure on Pakistan to curb terrorism as far as possible, but at the same time, if it becomes inevitable, it also must be prepared to take careful military steps; and to demonstrate its own political will with help of symbols and gestures, at the same time, on the ground level, keep its military forces in continuously prepared conditions and even taking certain basic, measured steps to reinforce its stand in this issue.

India also learnt that it must try hard to get other nations' (mainly America) help for curbing terrorism in its internal jurisdiction. But, on this important front, it has mostly to fight alone for itself, by itself. Keeping this in mind, India would have to give shape to its short- and long-term policies. In the meantime, relations with USA and Russia must be strengthened. It must strive to see that international goodwill grows in favor of India and curb extremist public opinion, to keep a balanced judgment in all situations and to continue its own firm stand.

In summer 2002, India mobilized about a million strong troops on its border with Pakistan and along LoC in Kashmir to which Pakistan responded in similar ways. The military confrontation reached a flash point with the prognosis of an impending nuclear war between the South Asian twins. However, the US intervened assuring India about "Musharraf's resolve to stop cross-border infiltration and reigning in terrorist activities on Pakistan's land". So also unfathomable implications—military, economic and human—for India also weighed down on New Delhi. Meanwhile, infiltration seemed to have been on decline. In this context, India silently withdrew its forces from the hot border. Months of massive army mobilization without substantive results cost India a huge financial loss and embarrassment. In the fall of that year, people of J&K participated in the State Assembly poll despite the threat of the Kashmiri militants and protestations of Pakistan. Foreign observers also praised the overall peaceful and fair elections that underlined the democratic traditions of India.

It was in this environs that during his visit of Kashmir valley, Prime Minister Vajpayee made its historic announcement of resuming a dialogue with Pakistan. Pakistan's response was instant and positive. Both agreed to evolve what they called 'a composite dialogue'. It was welcomed by the people and media of both the countries infested by the conflict syndrome since years. Even a seasoned expert Fareed Zakaria observed: "India and Pakistan took the decision to compose their differences and start the contours of composite dialogue for peace. This they did within 10 days that they could not during the last 10 years" (*Newsweek*, January 19, 2004). "Both leaders have evolved." However, slow and halted developments on negotiation front marked by Pakistan's 'double speak' on Kashmir issue and increased cross-border infiltration and training camps in PoK vitiated the atmosphere conducive to confidence-building measures. In early September, when foreign ministers of India and Pakistan, Singh and Kasuri, respectively, met in New Delhi, India explicitly brought the cases of infiltration, etc., to which Kasuri responded with indifference. Pakistan insisted to decide a timeframe within which the Kashmir problem be solved. In view of its complexities, India would not be definitive on the timeframe. Both agreed to "to have more talk about talks". Time and patience are running out on both sides. The stalemate suits the hardliners and extremists in the Pakistani establishment.

8

Pakistan: War by Diplomacy

Under the administration of Musharraf, the control of active terrorist forces is often neglected either due to weakness of the President or as a deliberate connivance; and yet Bush administration also has not taken this seriously. Due to such reluctance or limitations in the name of 'strategic policy', the infrastructure of terrorism has not been destroyed so far. In fact, effectiveness of anti-terrorist steps seems to be receding. The attack on Iraq and its occupation by USA and Britain has, on the contrary, increased the anger of Islamic world.

On the other hand, in certain military, strategic and economic matters, India-America-Israel have come closer to each other. The relations of India and Israel would turn very close, according to a statement made by Brijesh Mishra, the Adviser to Indian National Security to the 'Think Tank' at Washington DC. That is why if al Qaeda and such forces, in their traditional enmity with the Jews and Christians, now add India as well, it would be no surprise.

— From *Outlook India* online

In the four months following September 11, besides Bush and bin Laden, one, who captured attention of media to a great extent, is President Musharraf. In the newspapers of America and England, India and Pakistan and the whole Muslim world, and television interviews, no other head of the state or his background has been reported for so long a period. The reason behind this is the geo-political importance of Pakistan and the shrewd diplomacy of its President. First, the turn-around with the Taliban, and then about the attacks on Kashmir-New Delhi what he has to say in the matter have been at the center of psyche of people.

Of course, most interest has flowed from his controversial background. In 1979, Soviet Russia established a regime in Afghanistan that was influenced by communism. America took the help of the then Pakistan President General Zia-ul-Haq against this development. With gigantic funds and most modern weapons provided by America, Zia handed over some portion to the Taliban, but most of it was kept for his own country. At the same time, encouraging the religious fanatics, he tried to make his own political future stronger.

With the aid from America camps and bunkers were established in Pakistan and Baluchistan region to train the Islamic fundamentalists and terrorists. Finally, since 1989, the Soviet influence began to abate in Afghanistan. In that very year, in the elections of the J&K Assembly, when the party of Sheikh Abdullah manipulated the poll procedure, the people there expressed their anger and anguish by raising the flag of separatist demands against New Delhi. Gradually, the rulers of Pakistan continued to increase financial aid and provision of weapons and ammunition as well as diplomatic help to this local section. In 1995, Afghanistan came completely under the Taliban rule. This gave Pakistan an opportunity to enter within the borders of its western neighbor for strategic purposes. Besides, now, the Pakistan government began to help in a greater proportion the Pakistani and Afghan *jehadis* (with encouragement from ISI) to indulge in more violence in Kashmir. Thus, with the help of such dubious elements, Pakistan was successful in hijacking the home-grown movement of Kashmir for its anti-India strategy. In his book,

Converted Kashmir: Memorable Mistakes, Narendra Sehgal has shown how in early times the population in Kashmir was converted to Islam at the point of a sword, and then in the present times, how terrorism has spread here with the rise of religious fanaticism. In her latest book, Victoria Sconfield has shown that in the last decades, due to the political trends, organized *jehadi* propaganda, oppressive steps by the Indian security forces on the people of Jammu & Kashmir and on the whole some faulty policies of governments at New Delhi and Srinagar, a large part of the population of Kashmir valley now is inclined to create a state for itself that is neither under India nor under Pakistan, but independent of both the neighbors.

In the years between 1990 and 2001, the figure of people killed in Jammu & Kashmir touched from 30,000 to 60,000, as one estimate goes. Among them, the Muslims (inhabitant citizens of J&K) have lost their lives to the largest extent. Next are the 'jawans' and officers of Indian security forces and then the last category is of the Hindus/Sikhs. (As the valley has the largest population of Muslims in it, they are the largest number of victims in the armed attacks of the terrorists and their armed clashes with the security forces. Hindus figure lower even in total population and so this low figure.) For years, the section to lose their lives the most had been the security forces; but since last few months in 2002 when the Indian forces decided to take very strong steps, the terrorist assailants have suffered more casualties. In 2001, the top extremists gunned down in Kashmir were 2,020, including 134 of armed terrorists. This is the biggest figure of the last decade, though the figure of the civilians' death has also touched the highest so far (919).

By a successful chicanery of harassing its neighbor that is much larger not only in size but also more powerful in economy, military power, men and material resources besides rate of progress, Pakistan has forced it into a situation of fighting for years against Kashmiri and non-Kashmiri terrorists in a proxy war. In this situation, India has had the experience of terrorism in South Asia of a war that is not war but low level war-like activities much before America's shocking experience of 9/11. But, in spite of frequent presentations by India on this matter to America and other nations, the US remained unconcerned to India's plight. Even the reports of CIA, structures of foreign policy making in America, and the reports and studies submitted by experts at annual hearings of the Congressional South Asia Committees regarding Pakistan's role in fomenting militant activities in J&K also were disregarded altogether. Finally, the experience of 9/11 rudely shocked them into consciousness of reality of the danger from the ghost of terrorism within an hour that morning!

At that moment the possibility was high that America would increase the pressure on Pakistan and it would stand along with the whole world with India in the fight against terrorism. However, due to the US' unethical, cynical and very pragmatic politics, India could not get that immediate or

The Most Explosive Region

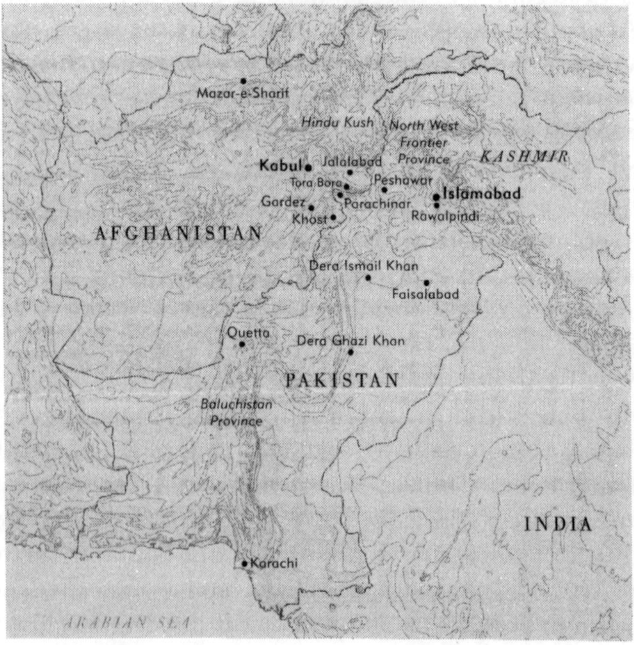

sufficient advantage from it. "If America was the father of the Taliban, Pakistan was its mother." Under the threat and temptations of America, Musharraf declared that Pakistan would join the US-led alliance with the world against terrorism. On 14th September his address on the CNN and other television channels became a turning point in the history of terrorist policies. The foxy general took the famous 'u-turn' in his approach with the Taliban matter, but at the same time, he also threatened India to 'lay off' its hands in Kashmir problem!

During the few hours spent by President Clinton on the Pakistani land in March 2000, Clinton used the term 'cross-border terrorism' and advised the General Musharraf that it be stopped. However, due to its geo-political importance, his successor President Bush needed Pakistan for his objective of capturing bin Laden; so he conveniently ignored and remained indifferent to the Pakistan-inspired terrorism that India had been suffering since long.

After his famous 'u-turn', Musharraf has successfully convinced his own people that his is a 'Pakistan first' principle. He demanded and received huge financial aid and removal of sanctions that were imposed by America after Pakistan's nuclear explosion. The reason forwarded was that Pakistan should not face a retaliation of serious challenges against his army, administration and people after his dangerous 'u-turn' policy declaration. Here, coincidentally, a significant matter came up. On the very day when the very serious bomb attack on Indian Parliament took place, Paris Club rearranged the repayment schedule of Pakistan with very generous terms for its enormous debt of $12.2 billion. Within the week, America dispatched the first installment of financial aid too! Air Commodore Jasjit Singh, former Director of the prestigious Indian 'Think Tank', the Institute of Defense Analysis, observes, "This matter indicates that Pakistan has developed greater confidence for making its international position stronger; on the other hand, America and its allies find that it is in their interest to have such closer relations. Yet, there are indications that Pakistan's dependence on the western nations will continue."

However, there was another example of a much more cynical, if undeclared, foreign policy in the form of 'understanding', if not a 'treaty', between them. This was to become public within a short period. The mainstream dailies like *New York Times, Washington Post*, and *Los Angeles Times*, published reports from their alert correspondents on Afghanistan fronts that revealed certain shocking details. For example, Tunku Varadrajan of *The Wall Street Journal* asked from the editorial section, giving illustrations, "Yes, Pakistan evacuated (its) men from Kunduz. Why did the US let them?"

They mentioned how, when the Northern Alliance surrounded Kunduz, the Pakistani Air Force helicopters could land in Kunduz and lift Pakistan army officers and two Brigadiers out of Kunduz and helped them escape safely to Pakistan. After 23rd November, under the benign care of Powell, many such successful rescue missions were being carried out right before the eyes of Northern Alliance. Without the knowledge and consent of America, no such serious occurrences could have taken place. "In saving such soldiers fighting on behalf of the Taliban and al Qaeda, Pakistan is no doubt guilty. These army men were not some hot-headed hired soldiers trained by some religious fanatic training centers; they were holders of appointments within the Pakistan armed forces, with claims to pensions and disciplined professional soldiers." And yet, the American rulers allowed them to be saved! On 24th November *New York Times* published a report of similar pattern: "The allies of the Taliban were then transported safely from the arena of war." Two reporters of the *Times* narrated the scene that they themselves witnessed. After verifying his facts with a high diplomat in the area, Tunku wrote, "The reason behind the pleas of General Musharraf to delay air raids on Afghanistan for such a long time was that even after his 'u-turn' a large number of Pakistan's army units were still fighting on behalf of the Taliban. In order to remove any evidence of this and to shift his units, he needed time." On November 9, President Bush gave a public assurance that even when the armies of Northern Alliance reached Kabul, they will not occupy the capital; and for this also Pakistan's aim was to gain time so that its army units could be removed from there. Thus, by Powell's support, the very armies against whom America was fighting were saved. However, during all this time, sufficient number of Pakistani soldiers had been arrested fighting for the Taliban to prove its involvement. The American, Indian and other agencies have taken sufficient note of such a deceitful and opportunist alliance of the two nations in this entire affair.

About Musharraf, his double-faced game, and his open support to terrorism in matters of Kashmir and India, Tunku writes, "One day when the war comes to an end in this region, a lot of things would come to light." He then goes on to warn, "In the meantime, we have begun to learn a lesson. If you choose allies who play a double-faced game, you would sink up to your knees, along with them into a bog—and what else can I say?—it would be an experience to be bogged down into a smelly matter that could be full of only excreta."

A Protester Chants Anti-U.S. Slogans at a Rally in Lahore, Pakistan, on the Third Anniversary of the Terrorist Attacks on the United States

In *The Washington Post* (October 3) Jim Hoagland in his column "An Ally's Terrorism" (this 'ally' being Pakistan) writing under that suggestive title, raised a question about the basic intention of the powers that be in including as allies such nations that practiced terrorism or abetted it. He also equated the attack on Indian Parliament as symbolically the same as an attack on the Pentagon and WTC; and reiterated that when there are such indications of terrorism spreading in South Asia, touching Musharraf with 'kid-gloves' by America indicates the lack of farsightedness.

The fact of reality of Pakistan-supported terrorism in Kashmir and other parts of India; pressure from India that both America and Pakistan should take steps against it; and the ploys of America to avoid, or delay, as much as possible any action in this matter—the series continued in the usual fashion in the meantime. For example, after the 1st October attack on J&K Assembly also, in order to avoid displeasing Musharraf, America observed silence at first on the event and on earlier such violent actions of JeM—a terrorist set-up from Pakistan. So much so that only after the attack on Indian Parliament occurred, it 'froze' the financial aid to Pakistan. Even after the proofs submitted by India, Pakistan tried to hide behind some pretexts; but finally, when India indicated its political determination and arrayed 5,00,000 of its troops on the borders, and after America also brought effective pressure, did Pakistan declare a ban on terrorist organizations like LeT, JeM, etc., on 13th January. Similarly, after much delaying tactics, and now knowing that it could not be postponed any longer, did Collin Powell, this time in the interest of America only, bring pressure on Musharraf. It was then that the Pakistan government put curbs on the religious training centers and Madrassas, imprisoned some 2,000 fanatics or fundamentalists and brought under lock and key hundreds of offices of terrorist organizations. However, the terrorists named by India as its 'most wanted', and persons like Dawood Ibrahim and Tiger Memon, who directed the bombings of March 12, 1993 in Mumbai, and who are basically of Indian origin, were not handed over to India as demanded, on one pretext or other.

During the visit of Powell to Islamabad on January 16, 2002 also this issue remained controversial. However, in the meantime, the J&K police and security forces have coordinated well and this has led to the elimination of nearly 2,020 terrorists, of whom 134 were most fierce and even heavily armed. This is the highest figure for the last decade. In 2001 Indians have confiscated their arms and ammunition, besides explosive materials also in huge amounts. No doubt, it is also a sad truth that the number of loss of civilians' lives also has gone up, for 919 citizens were killed and 2,120 injured in such clashes of 2001. The figure of police officers to lose their lives in the encounters was also larger than in 2000, though in comparison, the figure for special police officers was lesser in 2001 than in the year 2000.

Pakistan's extremely powerful intelligence agency, ISI, possessing huge resources, has greatly advanced the activity of pushing terrorists and dangerous armaments into Kashmir and India's other cities like Hyderabad, Delhi, Mumbai and Kutch, etc. The former chief of ISI, Hamid Gul has himself admitted that his agency has joined the network of bin Laden, used its training centers for terrorists, and through them, have trained their own rebels for their mission of violent activities against their traditional enemy—India. How ISI and some of the top officers of armed forces of Pakistan are also fundamentalists has been exposed in details provided by the Islamabad-based journalist Michael Scoffer in his *US News and World Report* (November 12, 2001).

Finally, India demonstrated its firm political resolve in the first fortnight of 2002. It sealed the long borders with Pakistan and positioned its troops with great readiness, thus creating a context for America to bring pressure on Pakistan. Musharraf, a clever man, came to understood well the 'no nonsense' attitude of India.

On January 12, 2002, Musharraf made a landmark Statement of Policy, but not before he had taken into confidence his supporter, Collin Powell. Not only this, on January

10, a group of American Senators had made a public statement in Islamabad that the President would be making a speech that would usher in great changes in Pak policy!! No nation would allow or show so publicly that it is influenced by an outside power, or accept it even indirectly, but Musharraf did it! (On the other hand, on January 17, Collin Powell informed the journalists in New Delhi that "whatever steps Musharraf is taking for arresting terrorists, would be evaluated by India on its own".) Of course, for his statement to indicate his readiness for the re-construction of the political and social systems of Pakistan, the General received 'instant' applause from America and western countries. Without doubt, indeed, such a Statement of Policy from him opens an important and welcome chapter in the history of Pakistan.

Especially the statements and opinions like "there is no place for terrorism and religious fanaticism in Pakistan", "the religious fundamentalism has kept Pakistan in a state of poverty, illiteracy and backwardness", etc., are indeed the 'alleged' new guidelines for Pakistan, if honestly pursued.

In order to indicate that he is aiming to strive constantly for the 'new path', and take steps against militant forces, Musharraf declared a ban on five terrorist organizations including Lakshar-e-Tioba and Jaish-e-Muhamad. He imprisoned more than 2,000 fighting extremists. But, at the same time, he declared that he would continue to give 'moral, political and diplomatic' support to the Kashmiri movement as well.

As a President of Pakistan, he emphasized the need to make it 'modern, tolerant and dynamic'; and as the Chief of the Army, he declared that he would fittingly retaliate against any military move of India. He also called upon India for solving the mutual problems including the question of Kashmir, through talks and negotiations!

Thus, having acquired a 'shining image' as a high-profile PR man for his country in the post-9/11 political scenario, Mushrraf now obtained support both from his own domestic 'constituency' and from international community. By 'openly' challenging the fundamentalists of his own country, he has been welcomed as a brave ruler and even as Pakistan's own 'Ata Turk'.

However, a scholarly officer, B. Raman has asserted by citing an orderly sequence of proofs, ranging from the Simla Agreement of 1971 down to the Lahore Agreement, how Pakistan has constantly broken or gone back on its commitments given in such treaties and agreements with India. When, after the agreement with the then Prime Minister of Pakistan, Nawaz Sharif, India's Prime Minister Vajpayee was traveling in a bus to Lahore, at that very moment, Musharraf, the then chief of the army, was involved in secretly infiltrating his dangerous men and machines into Kargil on the LoC on Indian soil and building there bunkers. India had to kill that ploy by bombarding the surreptious hidings of Pakistani troops. The deceitful deeds of the Pak government then were laid bare with graphic proofs by India before the world. Thereafter, Indian rulers, people or media could never connive at such developments. That is why, instead of warmly welcoming this statement of Musharraf, unlike many other nations, India gave it a cold shoulder response.

Manoj Soni, a perceptive analyst of international trends, made a comment in *Times of India* (January 14, 2002): In such an important statement, Musharraf has avoided any mention of the basis of the consent that had developed in the Indo-Pakistan relations in Simla Agreement and Lahore Agreement. He has decided to put a stop to terrorist activities within Pakistan, but has not declared his readiness to put a stop to it in the PoK or Azad Kashmir. It can be assumed though that he would want the new ISI-managed or other such movements in Kashmir to be read as 'home-grown' rather than hijacked ones!

Besides, he names the terrorist and religious fundamentalist forces as 'state within state' after the lapse of such a long time; but, in fact, right from the time of President Zia, and in his time too, methodical encouragement has been provided to these forces to develop. He did not utter one word in this statement about the terrorist attacks on Srinagar Assembly and Indian Parliament that are the core centers of Indian democracy! He talks one thing as a President and assumes a different 'posture' as a chief of army!! Tavleen Singh and some other Indian journalists have called him 'General Janus'. It seems a very apt title for him indeed.

Yet, it was indeed a memorable speech in Pakistan history that Musharraf made with strong criticism against religious fundamentalism of his country and his determination of suppressing it. Similarly, his steps to curb Pakistan-based terrorist organizations have been welcomed by all the countries except those of the Arab world. He has shown an inclination to build Pakistan as a modern and tolerant state. A very significant take-off point! However, this is going to be a long-drawnout process; and for India it is only like a 'post-dated check'.

India worries that after changing their name/title also, what if the Islamic organizations, even with their new infra-structure, continue their activities in Kashmir? The game that Musharraf is playing with India about the extradition of such terrorists and criminals as Dawood Ibrahim (officially named as 'the most wanted terrorist' by the US) and other anti-national criminals (Muslims and Sikhs) raises real doubts about the intentions of the President to be transparent or sincere. That is why, the Indian rulers are more keen on assessing his deeds rather than his words. Time and again, they emphasized this attitude and insisted in diplomatic language to America, Russia, Britain and such other nations to see that his word is put into action at the earliest.

Some analysts like B. Raman point out that some of the terrorist organizations like Harqat-ul-Mujahidin and Al Badr that are active in Kashmir have not been banned. The five such organizations working in the rest of India except Kashmir have been banned. By declaring emphatically support for 'Kashmir cause' and stating that "Kashmir is in our blood", Musharraf has indeed displayed for all to see his 'Janus-like' two faces for the world. He garnered support of domestic constituency and appreciation of international politicians and media, but has not bowed to complaints and demands of India even when these were realistic, but cleverly posing as if he is giving into them. B. Raman (*Outlook*, January 11, 2002) comments, "This is only a change of posture (by Musharraf), not his mental make-up." Thus, there are no signs to indicate any determination of Musharraf to curb Pakistan-inspired terrorism against India in anyway.

That shows that it was comparatively less difficult for Musharraf to pull back his support for the Taliban; but not so easy for him to pull out from association with Kashmir separatists, militant fundamentalists and *jehadi* terrorists. For probably, this may jeopardize his own political position in Pakistan. The reason is that for decades the Pakistan army, political leaders, politics and media have deeply involved the heart of Pakistani people in the Kashmir as an emotive issue.

For India, it is difficult to fulfill all the conditions Musharraf has set about Kashmir. He reiterates that this issue is central for the resolution conflict of the two nations. The difference of opinion must be resolved by peaceful methods and negotiations. The people of Pakistan must also accept the solutions offered. One of the important solutions suggested is that both the nations accept the present international LoC of J&K as their borders. However, since Powell was conducting diplomatic talks in South Asia in mid-January, Musharraf rejected any such solution as acceptable.

However, following Prime Minister Vajpayee's fresh offer of dialogue for peace in April 2003, Musharraf has given positive response. Vajpayee's successor, Prime Minister Manmohan Singh has carried the peace process further. During the historic meet of the two leaders in New Delhi on April 16-17, 2005, both committed to a determined effort for resolution of conflict including Kashmir.

This time, Musharraf has not insisted on a definitive time-frame for a solution of the Kashmir dispute—though 'a core issue'—but stressed, it should be seriously discussed and sorted out in 'reasonable time'. He, however, ruled out the use of military means of 'coercive diplomacy' to resolve it or any other dispute facing the two countries.

He reminded India that the pursuit of peace and confidence building measures (CBMs) should not lead to pushing Kashmir dispute under carpet. Significantly, soon after his New Delhi meet, the General stated to the 58th Formation Commanders' Conference on April 25 that "The era of conflict management is over and conflict resolution has to be done with sincerity. CBMs and dispute resolution would have to be in tandem." It was for the first time that he used these phrases!

IV

Polar Processes

9

Clash of Civilizations?

'Mandir-Masjid-Manav Mandir'

Raze down all the religious buildings,
Temples, Mosques, Gurudwaras and Churches,
Burn all their bricks to ashes,
Now.

Let on the mounds of those ashes,
Grow aromatic n' beautiful flower gardens;
Build nurseries for children and rooms
For studies in those places,
Now.

Let the places of worship work for Man's welfare,
Change them into Hospitals, orphanages and
Turn them into schools and universities,
Now.

Alter them into places for Art Academies,
Centers of Art and Alters of Science;
Let them turn into a golden hue of Dawn,
Playing glad games on undulating rice-fields,
Now.

Rename Religion
As Humanity,
Now.

— **Taslima Nasreen** (from poems in *Mukti Gaan*)

Suddenly, the habitual readers began to call the episode 9/11 as 'a clash of civilizations'. In 1993, Prof. Samuel Huntington, the well-known political scientist from Harvard University, had written in the prestigious journal *Foreign Affairs* an article with an exciting title of 'A Clash of Civilizations' which had come under great discussion since 1990. Within three years he published a book expanding on this theme and providing illustrations for his position. It had the title: *The Clash of Civilizations and Remaking of the World Order*. In this work, he submitted, "The central and most dangerous dimension of the global politics shaping up now would be that it would be clashes of groups with different cultures."

Presenting his thesis in this book, Huntington observes, "The socio-political differences and divisions that prevailed during the Cold War do not seem to prevail in this multi-polarized and multi-cultured world." However, he also describes the widely spread Muslim society, and their preferences of status quo, anti-progress and no-change ideals. "This would diminish gradually the friendship of Muslim countries and their government with the West, and clashes of low intensity or sometime of greater intensity would continue to occur between them time and again." According to one interpretation, Huntington is reluctant to say so openly, but when he refers to 'West', his actual mental image is in reality that of 'Christian societies'.

Western society has accepted cultural and ethnical variations, and adopted the idea of 'multi-culturism' too. It supports 'secularism' for state and social norms, and thus has kept Caesar and Christ, or 'Crown' and 'Cross' separate from each other, and even follows this ideal in practice. Most of all, 'modernity' or 'modernism' is an important characteristic of western world. That there is room for change and improvement in its lifestyle, institutionalized orders and other aspects of life are not just beliefs, but also put into practice. Indian society too is a multi-ethnic and multi-cultural one by its nature. Like the western societies, it also adopts tolerance as a standard of social behavior and keeps an open mind about modernity too.

On the other hand, the Muslim society has kept up a preference for 'status quo'. There is no encouragement for re-interpretation and reform in Islamic religion. The Maulavis and other religious order persons interpret and decide the thought and practice of life, based on Islam as explained by the Koran. State and religion are not separate from each other; in fact, they are intertwined here, and so in many countries have shown preference for religious states. Islam's learned men and priests like Alims, Maulavis, Maulanas, etc., insist on standards and norms of social and other fields of life as prescribed in the Koran only, and they are absolutely indifferent to changes in these standards of life and practices with time and place. They believe modernity to be an 'evil', and therefore the western countries that are equivalent to modernity are also considered 'evil' and so we do not find any positive attitude for them in the Islamic society in the whole world. Also, the nine Crusades that were fought between the followers of Islam and Christianity in the 11th and 12th centuries are also not relegated out of memory. Both Saladan for the Crescent and Richard the Lion for the Cross are always recalled as symbolic warriors in this context.

Osama bin Laden had made a special claim that his fight is against the Jews and the Christians. At the same time, somewhere in the statements of al Qaeda mention has also been made of their fight being against the Hindus as well. The taped messages of bin Laden and in an interview on videotape, his determination to destroy the West, and specially its leader America, is shown. Citing an important source, Huntington had said, "The Muslim nationalism is becoming more and more aggressive. It does not take into consideration the national feelings of others at all. It seems to have become a personal possession, a privilege and political weapon of the newly influential Muslim nations...Islamic fundamentalism has now grown more and more decisive factor in finalizing what are the interests of Muslim nations."

Brizinski, supporting the thesis of Huntington, also recalls the polarization of the western democratic systems and dictatorships or authoritarian systems that presently prevail in the Muslim countries: "While in America and other western nations, besides in India, Israel, South and Central Europe, and in regions of East Asia, democracy is growing stronger, in that very period Islamic movements turned increasingly effective in the Muslim nations." Huntington calls it as 'Islamic resurgence'. This phenomenon is turning into a re-establishment of Islamic form of society and state in these countries.

The Soviet-Afghan war (1979-1989) gave a new boost to Islamic fundamentalism. This war was fought, and won, on the basis of Islamic principles against Soviet communism. During, and after it, Saudi Arabia contributed 955 million dollars to al Qaeda and Taliban administration. "If the Islamic resurgence moves forward, the very security of the west would be endangered."

Islamic attack would expand or march forward due to a state with Islam at its heart or center of action, a state, with financial resources, military strength, organization skills and Islamic identity and readiness, the most necessary element for providing social and political leadership to Muslim society. Saudi Arabia, Pakistan and Iraq were considered such states. The political irony is that the first two states that were supporting patrons of terrorism, conveniently turned partners in America's war against terrorism. And, of course, America has also taken them into its own fold for its foreign policy that is without scruples or mercy for others. No doubt, this approach is cutely named as 'a pragmatic approach'. Since Britain and America touch Pakistan, the prime mover of terrorism in Kashmir and other parts of India, with 'silken gloves', they have obliterated cultural polarization!

Even then, these nations have fulfilled their role as forces that feed Islamic fundamentalism in their own ways. Harvard University Professor Daniel Pipes, in his work *The Path of God: Islam and Political Power*, emphasizes, "The immeasurable wealth from oil that the Islamic states obtained in the 1970s helped provide enough finance for encouraging religious extremes." Giving examples of Saudi Arabia and Gulf Emirates, he shows how they have financed countries like Pakistan for carrying on armed terrorism for this purpose. By this trick, the Arab rulers were successful in diverting the dissatisfaction of their peoples away from their authoritarian rule that was ineffective in terms of any progress for them; and they also were able to divert their minds by changing the target of orthodox forces against modernity and countries like, and specially, America that embodied modernity. However, Pipes has also shown that in time the income from oil would reduce for Saudi and Libya, etc., and with that, he predicts, a limit would be reached about their ambitions to impose Islamic conditions on the world. At such a point of time, either they would have to make an adjustment with reality and compromise with westernization, or to remain in a defensive position due to their poverty and backwardness.

This is not to say that there is no truth in the thesis of Islam vs. West; this is only to say that it is a half-truth, not the whole truth. Laden, and earlier Ramza Yusuf, arrested in 1993 in trying to blow up that same World Trade Center, called in peppery language, the Americans as 'butchers, liars and pretenders', and condemned the love of modernity of the West as a global pollution.

In the last two decades, the class of people that used to advocate imitating the West, has come under the influence of the fundamentalists. After the revolution against Reza Shah, the modernist ruler of Iran, bin Laden has made the picture even blacker than ever. And, ironically, he has succeeded in painting the West as black in the eyes of his followers.

Talking about 'Islam and West', Prof. Bernard Lewis says, "The followers of Islam used to consider Islam way high in its stature in comparison to other cultures. But in modern times, this is a thing of past". In his *The Roots of Islam Rage*, he had predicted (in 1990): "We shall have to take great care to avoid an age of religion-centered wars arising from ancient differences of opinions and prejudices until the Muslims themselves clean up their thoughts in this matter."

Not agreeing with Lewis, his own (former) brilliant student, Professor ... says, "Lewis considers Islam as a bundle of religious thoughts and values within the frame of Islamic culture...but today a number of scholars in this field consider Islam as a flowing movement between innumerable cultures."

Prof. Edward Said, who is the biggest critic of Lewis, is a scholar of Muslim studies. This Palestinian, settled in USA, considers Lewis as a primary historian for eastern cultures in his widely acclaimed book *Orientalism*, in which the European imperialism has been justified. In his series 'Suicidal Ignorance' ('Counter Punch', 18 November 2001) Said tries to counter the viewpoints of Lewis, Thomas Friedman and Faud Ajami (Azmi): "According to 'Our' interpretation, 'we' are against the Muslim terrorism and Islamic Rage." He shows that bin Laden is not (equivalent to) Islam. Claiming that the Bush administration has failed in understanding what is Palestine fighting against, and why, and what provocative role of Israel has been in the Middle East, he goes on to show why the Islamic rage has been pitted against the Christians and Jews. At the same time, he says that we must also remember that extremist thinkers like him only have given an edge to the thinking of the terrorists and to the conflict against the West. As al Qaeda has declared, "Islamists are to aim anywhere in the world where Americans and Jews live...Wherever the Muslims live, have to be prepared for Jihad. With the grace of Allah, victory would be only with the Muslims." They consider the Christians as people who had fought the 'Crusades', and in the same breath also put the Jews in the same line as the Whites. Laden has time and again employed a language that make all the 'eager to work religious defenders' the orthodox Muslim *jehadis* fall into his plans.

On the other side, soon after 9/11, President Bush also declared the war against terrorism as a 'Crusade'. But, when this was criticized as a vision or statement that would divide the world into two camps of West vs. Islam, he has renounced with good discretion to avoid such statement or even a vision; and thus displayed an attitude that befits a superpower.

In the dictionary of the religious fanatics, however, the term 'Crusade' is a dirty word, reminding them of the conflicts of 11th and 12th centuries. The similar Islamic term for the western world is '*jehad*'. Not only Laden but other Islamic fundamentalists also say that ultimately Bush has reached the White House only with the help of Evangelist vote; and that his main politically supporting vote base is not secular. When in the last presidential election campaigns, in December 1999, Bush was asked at Dais Moins (Iowa), "Which political philosopher has had the greatest impact on you?" He had replied at once, "The philosophy of (Jesus) Christ; for He has transformed my heart." (We must remember here that the question had been about political philosopher!) Among his colleagues, Attorney General Ashcroft, an orthodox Christian, is noteworthy. (Ashcroft is busy at present in harsh court proceedings against the plane hijacker *jehadis* who attacked New York and Washington).

Political scientist Huntington presented his thesis with empirical perspective of cultural bipolarism. But much before this, Princeton Professor Bernard Lewis in his prophetic-like work entitled *In the Roots of Muslim Rage* (1991) had warned the western world including America that the Muslims, after decline of their proud superior cultural world position, blame the West for their present weak and backward conditions. After 9/11 Lewis has been seen often in the prestigious media of America and Britain presenting his views; and readership of his work has multiplied. Lewis evaluates the progress of the Islamic nations with classic liberal value standards. (Though, some radical intellectuals in his own university do not agree with this, and opine that any particular culture has to be evaluated in the context of time and place only.) Towards the chaotic and status quo conditions prevailing in the Middle East, America adopts the view of a 'patron'—for example, of 'pity'—and uses different and lower standards for examining its progress; and therefore expects not much from them about matters like economic welfare and political freedom. As a result, it remains tolerant of the weak yet authoritarian Arab nations, argues Lewis. He also says that the reason behind this is the self-interest of America with regard to its need for oil. But, "the Arabs hate this cultural superiority attitude of America".

In the context of this discussion it would be relevant to refer to an Iranian lady (author of a book with the suggestive title of *Reading Lolita in Tehran*) named Azar Nafisi, who surmises, "I am an admirer of Said, and I was a critic of Lewis from the beginning; but after reading the works of Lewis I have come to understand that the Muslims were their own greatest critics until mid-19th century rather than any oriental scholar." In the present context, Nafisi recommends Muslims to once more turn to introspection. To get away from the bipolar perspective of the world if we want to find any common ground, it would be indeed a necessity to do so.

The Muslim Brotherhood—the Egyptian fundamentalist organization—itself has published the work of Lewis. In the Introduction, the translator says, "I do not know who this man (Lewis) is, but one thing is very clear: either he is a sincere friend, or an honest enemy who does not want to lie."

In such a significant issue as clash of civilizations, from the above high level intellectual discussion, the reader can himself make his own conclusions.

When we turn the focus of the camera of history on the entire politico-cultural trends, what can we read?

The Muslim world hates the western world. This may be out of jealousy, or out of experience (this feeling is highly seen in the broad lower strata population that is illiterate or educated in Madrassas). They find the western ways of life alien and uncivilized even. They resent the prosperity of the West. They have a general belief that America and its cultural allies are prosperous due to their exploitation of the oil-rich Muslim countries. As we had noted, in the Middle East, America favored Israel over Palestine question and in the Arab-Israel wars; it also put sanctions against Iraq after a war with it. This made America a villain and an enemy in the eyes of the orthodox Muslims. They had been fighting to make an orthodox Islam of their understanding win in the Muslim countries. For this purpose, they have been helping in fighting non-Muslims to Muslim groups in Saudi Arabia, Iran and certain Gulf countries. We can see traces of its footprints as far as Philippines and Indonesia too.

In two-thirds of the wars fought in the last one-and-a-half decade in the world, Muslims or Muslim nations have been involved. In a decade-long conflict between Iraq and Iran, five lakh people lost their lives. In 1990s, several small and big conflicts have taken place between Muslims and non-Muslims. These were in Bosnia and Macedonia in Europe, in Chechenya, Azarbaijan, Tazikistan and Kosovo in West Asia, and even Philippines and Indonesia. Pakistan and Iran saw conflicts between Shia and Sunni sects, and in Pakistan the victims have been Shia Ahmediya and Muhajirs. For years conflicts have taken place at low or greater ferocity again and again in Kashmir (India), West Asia and Chechenya. Thus, the last decades of the 20th century saw conflicts among Muslims, whereas in the opening years of the 21st century, the conflicts saw one side as America and the other as Islamic *jehadi* leaders in the forefront.

A new and highly dangerous element that seems to be developing in these wars is terrorism. After their victory against Russia, the Afghan Mujahidins and terrorist Islamic groups that had no alternative expertise than making war now were out of job; their countries (Afghanistan and Pakistan) had neither any capacity nor any resources to absorb them into their economy. Such elements then turned to making rebel movements or armed attacks on the Muslim population of Kashmir, Chechenya and even China's Sikiang region. To them Taliban and Pakistani ruling powers have been providing aid and encouragement, financial, material and arms and ammunition. As pointed out in *The Economist* (London), from 1993 to 2000, the number of terrorist episodes has been 16, out of which for 13 episodes, Muslims have been responsible. In the list of nations supporting terrorism also Muslim countries figure prominently. (Of course, America has conveniently left out the names of Pakistan and Saudi Arabia from this 'list', as these can be put in the other list of 'additional Muslim nations'!)

It would be appropriate here to refer to an illusory line of difference. Among the Islamic states, a difference is made between pro-West and anti-West. President Bush had declared in his chastising policy that America would not make any distinction among the nations who shelter the terrorists and the terrorists themselves. But soon after such a declaration even, Pakistan that was the mother of Taliban and inspirer and abettor of armed violent terrorist attacks in Kashmir against India became a valuable member of the camp of the western powers! Rogue countries like Jordan and Syria, and nearly all the countries of the Middle East made a beeline to join this camp. Yasser Arafat donated blood for the 'cause' and was a television show! Thus, Musharraf and Arafat put to shame even the classic character of a Pretender Tutuff as portrayed by Molliere in this game! Thus international politics made the issue turbid beyond recognition!

Currently, Islam is dripping with religious fanaticism and war-like spirit. Although not the entire Muslim society of the world carry these emotions, yet certain facts cannot be ignored. One, in most of wars and inter-state violent activities, Muslims or Muslim states are deeply involved. We also find that they are dominant in the smuggling of intoxicating drugs and illegal provision of arms and ammunition all over the world.

In *New York Times*, Thomas Friedman writes, "The terrorists who attacked America reflect in much greater proportion than we can think the mood of their native people...99 percent Arabs or Muslims are not terrorists, we should note. But the parallel truth also is that 100 percent of those terrorists who are threatening us at present are Muslims and Arabs. ...And they do not merely inhabit in the caves of Afghanistan, but they also live in New Jersey, Florida and Ontario, etc., too."

If we look at the problem from this viewpoint, we feel that the Middle Ages mentality is at work between the Muslim fundamentalists and Christian-West in separating them and keeping them separate. Such a bipolar separatist attitude (specially of violent variety) was not felt even at the height of the Cold War. That is why, the early years of a new cultural age seem to be under the nightmare of such cultural clashes. Is this clash of civilizations taking shape between commercial-minded West's Christian world and 'a new fanatic Khilafat'? In any cases, "the 'fault-lines' (geo-political cracks) have spread in the vast land of Afro-Asia from the English alphabet 'A' (Afghanistan) to 'U' (Uzbekistan)."

Huntington believes that "in the clash of civilizations, America and Britain will have to hang together or separately". However, when he says that they are not fighting Islam, not even Afghanistan, but against terrorism, then deep down, they are not against bin Laden or not even terrorism, but against only the thinking and values upheld by Islam.

Where does India stand in this scenario of thought and practice? India is with the West in principles of pluralism, secularism, multi-cultural societal set-up, and to a certain extent, modernity and changeability. For India's own perception and preferences, the Islamists consider India as non-Islamic and followers of different faiths. Organizations like

Lashkar-e-Toiba consider even democracy as a western set-up. For, according to Islam, sovereignty lies with Allah—a principle that western political thought or democracy does not accept. That is why, Islamic fundamentalists think that success of democracy in India is subverting its Muslim population and adversely affects the people of Pakistan. This mentality had evidently prompted the terrorists to attack the buildings of the Legislative Assembly in Kashmir and the Indian Parliament.

In BBC's video providing information, 'The Unfinished War', one Muslim fanatic leader says, "The enemies of Islam are Hindus. Reward for a Muslim soldier is to die in Kashmir in the name of Allah." In the literature of al Qaeda Hindus are also sometimes mentioned with scathing contempt along with Christians and Jews. Especially the forces inspired and supported with arms and other provocations by Pakistan and Taliban in Kashmir and other parts of India have placed India in the camp opposite Islam.

Even then, like China, due to its own cultural essence and heritage, India possesses a more ancient and better culture. David Fowley, the great scholar of Indology and Director of American Institute of Vedic Studies, New Maxico, in his latest book, *Hinduism and the Clash of Civilizations*, explains that the western monoculture in the name of bringing up the standard of life and improving eco-technology would separate the multi-cultures and civilizations of the world from their individual forms, essence and tradition. He recommends that India should remain away from such bipolar 'clash of civilizations' as much as possible. He says, "The processes of globalization, through mediums of education, media and entertainment, on their own terms, enjoy dominance over the whole world as 'Western-European-American Culture'; and aim to eliminate or subjugate all the other cultures."

Having referred to this thought also, we can say that on the whole, in context of multiple cultures and acceptance of their existence, secularism and tolerance, India is very near to them, even when not exactly with the West, but in its own way and different from Islamic thinking. This situation and condition of India has come to light in connection with the continued experiences of Islamic *jehad* in Kashmir and elsewhere. Broadly speaking, India has great faith in cultural co-existence.

Secondly, it must be noted that in India also one section has begun to cling to Hindu fundamentalism or fanaticism and certain forces are active in trying to make them dominant. In this context, the views of the Professor at Berkeley University and a scholar of Indian Studies, Marc Jurgenmeyer, in his latest work *Terror in the Mind of God: The Global Rise of Violence* (2001), are highly relevant to the global scenario after 9/11. Jurgenmeyer makes a critical study of the trends of violence that range from America to North Ireland, from Chechenya and Middle East to South Asia and Japan, and shows that these are symptoms of the increasing conflicts among forces that began with the rise of secular state since 18th century and that had removed religious system from public life. In the last decade of the 20th century it was a historical event when the Berlin Wall of Thought crumbled down. However, the wall that is built due to Islamic mentality is psycho-political and cultural one. Even the forces of globalization, technology and modern communication facilities of the modern age find it difficult to remove. On the other hand, the wall (of secularism) between Church and state that has been built by the democracies in the West and India has not crumbled, but its foundations are surely being shaken. For example, Jurgenmeyer draws our attention to the communal or extremist 'mines' in the path of secularism in India. He discusses the small yet well-organized minority groups (such as Sikhs, Hindus and Muslims etc.) and their roles. He associates Hizbullaha and Hindutva brigades with Hamas and sectarian separatists of North Ireland, and Christian identity movements protesting against abortion and modernity, and Babbar Khalsa and Bajrang Dal, all along with Islamic fanaticism. The reason is that all these fundamentalist elements have a common enemy, viz., secular modernity, and therefore they attack the equipments of it. The organizations like Hamas and Hindutva brigades (VHP and Bajrang Dal etc.), Hizbullah and such other Islamic *jehadi* groups put their own interpretation of their religion with nationalism. This point makes them anti-peace elements within their own states for followers of other faiths, and also for other nations.

Of course, there are some basic differences among these groups; for example, Hindutva groups are intolerant towards narrow traditionalism or minorities, but their fundamentalism is nowhere similar to violent terrorism of Hizbullah or al Qaeda, not even like the religious *jehadis* spread by Taliban, Musharraf or bin Laden. And, therefore, these groups cannot be clubbed as an integral part of terrorist problem that worries the present times.

In *The Evolution of Civilizations: An Introduction to Historical Analysis*, Carol Kwigley opines that the 'New Cultures' of India and China would in time prove healthier and fresher than those of West or Islam. As far as possible, India must keep itself separated from the conflicts of the cultures of Islam and West (so highly connected with Christianity). The conflict is between them—Islam and West—and let them fight it out; India should not get too involved.

We may conclude the discussion with the vision of Huntington (though we may reserve the right to agree or disagree with him): If Islamic resurgence would continue to increase, it would endanger the very existence and security of the West. As Kwigley believes, the cultures of India and China, with new energies, would replace the western and conservative cultures. He makes an interesting if controversial observation: "In the bipolar clashes of cultures, those that remain aloof or away, would be benefited the most from it all. The western world, Russia, China and Japan would be more or less destroyed; and if during these episodes, India—which is going to participate—is saved from this consequence, then it would be able to try and reconstruct the world on the basis of Hindu approach (tolerant, acceptance of multi-culturism and co-existence)."

The Canada's political personality, Lester Pearson, understands this phenomenon a little differently. "Humanity is being dragged in such an age where it would be necessary to learn peaceful multi-cultural exchange. People would have to study each others' histories and ideals and enrich each others' lives." Ultimately, of course, only by replacing the 'clash of civilizations' with 'communication among cultures', can the world hope to progress on the path of peace and development.

10

Globalization vs. Talibanization

In the Third World, especially in the eyes of Muslim societies, 'modernity' is interwoven with the West; and westernization is also considered another name for Americanization; and on the other hand, the Muslim fundamentalists are actually 'globalizing' terrorism!

At another level, countries like India that aim to achieve modern and democratic system and live in a multi-cultural society, have serious differences of opinion on significant issues such as globalization and rights to intellectual properties with a country like America that also possesses democratic system and multi-culture society, and yet they too have been made victims of Islamic fundamentalism and Pakistan-inspired state terrorism.

However, in a total perspective, we must remember that globalization with its tools of corporate capitalism and consumer goods and facilities from MacWorld's, CocaCola or McDonald, down to entertainment, media and other consumer facilities and comforts are likely to 'de-culture' India and the other countries of the Third World (that is to say, remove them from their own individual traditional cultures). The reason is that such 'de-cultured' societies can be more easily trained into the great flow of globalization than those who posses very deeply rooted indigenous highly traditional cultures. Thus, if a conflict is avoided between the countries aiming for globalization (the West) and the other countries (the Rest), not much space could be available for the spread of terrorism.

For Indian, neither the new Islamic paradigm nor the path of West-centered globalization is advisable to follow. It is our cultural obligation to remain away from both these worldviews; for, both Islamization and Americanization aim to 'de-culture' the countries they come in close contact. This is entirely in opposition to, and dangerous for, India's own peculiar and enormously rich cultural paradigm of '*Vishvaneedam*' or '*Vasudhaiv Kutumbakam*', meaning "the whole world is a home of humans"; or "the entire world is one family".

The trend of globalization is able to enrich us only on the surface or periphery of life (in terms of material well-being); but could it bring about a worldview that does nothing to remove the regional and local cultural roots? Would it remove our own roots; or, to bring under the western economic-techno-cultural influence mould all into one-typecast, would it turn a destroying force for the other societies in cultural, environmental and political spheres?

On the answer of this question the balance, resourcefulness and progressive conditions of the new world order and the entire mankind would depend.

— Extracted from seminar papers

If we want to study the world of terrorism in more simple bipolar conditions, instead of the 'clash of civilizations' theory, it would be more pragmatic to view it as the opposing thought infrastructures of globalization and Talibanization, it is so suggested by Thomas Friedman, Vandana Shiva and other such scholars.

What are the roots of the philosophy of terrorism? What are the forces for its encouragement? What kinds of policies give it an impetus and carry it forward? What are its expressive and conducting aspects? The scholars mentioned above, like Bernard Lewis and Samuel Huntington, in order to understand the 'ecology' of terrorism, raise these, and other such questions, but their 'thesis' turns out to be very different from them.

After having met a large number of citizens of different levels all over the world, in one of his five works that has attracted attention all over the world, *The Lexus and the Olive Tree*, Friedman says that people like Ramzi Yusuf who was aiming to bomb the World Trade Center in 1993, are the super-empowered angry men. In one hand they have an explosive bomb and in the other hard drive. According to Stephen Cohen, such 'angry men' believe that they should first take over the possession of their (Arab) states and then with its power behind them, they must use it for attack against America. However, globalization has made it possible for them to made direct attack on America even as individuals. Globalization even provides them with the logical reason for doing so. The logic is that their state has no longer a structure of sovereign power in reality; the true and concerned power structure has now turned global and envelope the whole world. That structure is in the hands of American superpower, and supermarkets and multinational companies. They only dictate other governments about their policies. For their weak conditions, only America and the globalization process under its guidance are more responsible rather than they themselves. Therefore, chase out this superpower and supermarkets (mediums of newly developing world economic order) to destroy this true power structure; do not care about governments of Egypt or Pakistan.

The thing that worries Yusuf, bin Laden and such 'angry men' is that Americans and other western countries believe that America is not only much superior in terms of technology but its values are also much higher than others. To these men and the terrorists, on the other hand, "soulless consumerism and mindless worship of technology are the only American values; and one must keep it at as much distance as possible.

In the view of Bernard Lewis and Fareed Zakaria, the western values like human rights, equal position of men and women, democracy, secularism, etc., are disliked by the religion-centered terrorists. Examining the 'ecology' of terrorism, Vandana Shiva also emphasizes its non-cultural elements. At present times, elements like economic liberalization, privatization, etc., are trends that push globalization forward. These types of globalization trends make for feelings of economic insecurity and conditions go astray. It washes out the self-identity and diversity of the people concerned, and hacks at the political freedom enjoyed by them.

Taking the issue in its entirety, in the 21st century, we have entered a new age of global interdependence; and for turning back, there is no path, no wisdom, or not even any stronger or capable alternative leading backwards. Globalization of economy, cultural expansion and blending; intercontinental diaspora; explosion of information and communication technology; ever increasing and developing media and Information Super Highway; and developing biotechnology and its future effects and expanse—all these are now covering increasing populations of countries from the First and down to Third World. Unprecedented levels of interdependence and exchange would be reached among America, India, China, Germany, Scandinavia, Israel, Japan, etc., with the development in biotechnology and bioscience. Similarly, the changes in atmosphere and questions of environment have taken global proportions; and due to this the countries of West and East are gradually getting conscious and prepared for joint efforts to deal with them. In these conditions, the miracle of a quick and natural joining of hands by America and Russia, the former powers at loggerheads during the Cold War, also can and did happen due to such global experiences and fear of global terrorism. When the America-inspired allies joined hands for attacks on Afghanistan, acting against the Taliban and bin

Laden, China and Iran also lent an indirect support by their remaining silent. (Though, like economic globalization, terrorism and fundamentalism also have been partially globalized, it is a different issue.) Thus, an overall interdependence and consequential globalization is a characteristic and totally new development in the world history.

On the other hand, as Friedman points out, "Instead of criticizing in acid language American imperialism or Zionist colonialism while sitting in the drawing rooms at Beirut or Cairo, these narrow-minded societies' and their governments' foolish or destructive policies, we must try and understand well the forces and factors working behind it. They should not put them in clear-cut 'black and white' labels of 'we' and 'they'. Attempts must be made to avoid anger or contempt about the 'rage' felt for the western people but to try instead to digest its own historical and present role. It is recommended that in order to remove corrupt and anti-democratic state administrations and to improve the mistaken, and proved as dangerous, education systems, it is needed to understand and accept the realities of secular world." Thus, not so much cultural distance and conflict, the distance is greater in terms of political and ethical. The cultural smoke has spread over, it may seem, and therefore must be looked into carefully in this context.

This requires that episode 9/11 and its entire context must not be viewed with any 'colored or 'mono-cultured' eye. If we look at 'worldwide western culture', or global Islamic terrorism for that matter, with monoculture, then as Huntington says, we shall slip into the 'paradigm of clash of civilizations'. Or, as historian Francis Fukuyama says, we shall be liable to accept the thesis of 'The End of the World'. After the end of the Cold War, Fukuyama evaluates the end of communism and the final victory of free markets and liberal political thought as the 'End of the World'.

However, Huntington, Fukuyama and other such humanist scholars tend to oversimplify the issue of the vast multi-culture patterns spread in the whole world society. In the

Rio Earth Summit of 1992, Vandana Shiva, along with this author and others, had an opportunity to understand the world trends first hand. The successful environmental challenge of NGOs of the First as well as the Third World presented to America and President Bush (Sr.) at the Global Forum; the audio-video presentations of the original inhabitants, in America the Red Indians and others elsewhere against the developing economic and environmental systems; presentations made at Seattle, Washington DC, Jenoa, Gothenburg, Davos, Praha and at the end at New York-Porto Alleger (2002) regarding the paradigms and worldviews of other parallel cultures; and last but not the least, the fierce demonstrations of thousands of people—all these events go to show that even within the western world also the voices for an alternative worldview are getting louder and logical. Thus, we can see that the western culture is also not of one form in itself; nor is it faultless or absolutely naturally acceptable. Here, we definitely recall Gandhiji. When he was asked as to what he believed of western culture, he ignored it and replied in a short sentence, "It would be a good idea."

Such events mirror the counter-thoughts and criticism against globalization. By adopting corporate capitalism and seriously faulty models of 'progress', societies dependent on environment and their cultures have perished. The very bases of their traditional life for livelihood and lifestyles have been snatched away.

In reality, in the name of free economy and international economic dealings and exchange, the democratic foundations of politics and economy are wiped away. The reason is, for the concerned countries treat their domestic economy on the principle of centralization as needed by global principles. Thus, in the last decade or so, the World Bank, International Monetary Fund (IMF) and World Trade Organization (WTO) have hijacked their economic agenda; and the economy of the concerned country has turned into a hollow political shell.

There is now clear, convenient and open space for extremism, radicalism and fundamentalism to make an entry.

Besides, in the process of globalization, the multinational companies enter the countries of the Third World and displace the small industries and commercial ventures there. The people making living out of these enterprises lose their source of income. With coming of CocaCola, London Pilsbury Beer, and even about things like Uncle chips and Dove soap or automobiles, many countries have such experiences. Secondly, in the entertainment field also, the equipments and mediums like videos, DVDs, television shows like MTV and others make great impact on their young generation; and these symbols and insinuations of western, highly 'liberal' culture are felt as 'corrupting' the young generation. Thus, there is a large section of world population that is left poor by globalization, or in spite of it, disgruntled against this 'corruption', and it is fast turning against globalization. In such a fertile psychological ground economic insecurity, feeling of deprivation, cultural erosion or an imagined or true fear for its own sense of identity would easily develop. To 'go back' into their old and narrow cultural shell, Taliban or Islamic fanatics and even Vishva Hindu Parishad (VHP) in India, Catholics of Ireland or fundamentalist Islamic groups of Indonesia and Malaysia take advantage of this fear.

Thus, at numerous levels, globalization provides reasons for the development of fundamentalism:

- The conservatives, the poor, and the young class of societies and cultures, having turned into 'new colonies', feel alienated and create a cultural 'backlash', giving a push to fundamentalist thinking. "Those who have been deprived of economic security due to globalization turn to find emotional anchors in political type religious identities or narrow nationalism."
- In some countries, globalization leads to erosion of the power of decision in economic matters and some leaders lose their powers due to this factor and are offended.

Taking support from religious and cultural differences they spread a mixed feeling of rage and fear against the rich nations. Especially in the poor Muslim countries, they resort to Fascist fundamentalism even. As the gap between 'haves' and 'have-nots' increases with globalization, it leads to the ordinary people feeling a loss of material security. Taking advantage of this, the fundamentalists mix up religious element with it and misguide the followers of Islam against the West.

Thus, until the war against terrorism does not go into its roots and removes them, it cannot hope to discipline it. It is not enough to treat the outer traits of terrorism that have been expanding and turning more dangerous with time in the last decade, but it has become necessary to perform a 'surgery' of the system altogether. Such a treatment demands not just short-term but more effective long-term policies.

Vandana Shiva has studied this issue in the perspective of bio-diversity and environment of humanity, and she observes: Mere steps like a war would create violent reactions and spread the viruses of hate even more. The insects that feed on vegetation develop immunity by using insecticide on them, and as a result, even multiply. This is similar to the steps of military policy or sanctions that would make the terrorists even more innovative. To control the insects, it is better to make the vegetation more strong and develop immunity so that a balance is maintained; it is necessary to develop such a system of 'ecology'.

Here, we recall the observation of the famous scholar Olivier Roy. After 9/11, William Melly had edited a collection articles of experts from various countries under the title of *Afghanistan and the Taliban* with a long Introduction. In this work, Roy shows that Taliban is not made up of the 'Alims' (scholars) of Islam; it is made up of people who are out-of-employment, quickly trained in religious matters and called Talibans. In nurturing such 'instant Islam' a role has been played by their socio-economic conditions and fanatic bringing up. He says that established as Aamir Al Momin (commander of Islamic loyalists), who wears the shirt of a prophet, such a the fundamentalist leader like Mullah Omar would not be able to maintain such a force after his sound defeat (November 2001). Even then, we must go to the root of Talibanization. Otherwise, to take advantage of their disappointment and need for an anchor, organizations like al Qaeda with its net spread in 60 places and other local groups are just waiting to jump in and take over. Talibanization pushes humanity backwards. It would push it into a small and narrow world of 'communal existence'. On the other hand, if nothing else, at least globalization makes humanity prepare for keeping rhythm with 21st century, carries man outwards, higher and further, even with all his limitations. It is forgotten that the mixture of emotions and cultural opposition can become lethal. The emotional roots of the attacks on New York and Washington are in the feeling of injustice and western-style modernity.

Gray believes, "The opinion that the faith people with open market had in globalization has now evaporated...the age of globalization is over." Gray believes that the ideal of globalization is the creation of a new public culture as a solution to the eternal conflicts that occur in the world; but it is now a forgotten ideal. Global trade expects certain conditions such as not too many restrictions and peaceful relations of countries. But, the type of globalization that was imposed at various levels on countries and increased the conflicts of interests among them and sharpened the feelings of advantage or loss of it. Thus, having turned counter-effective, these are expressed in 9/11.

In her characteristic language, Arundhati Roy writes, "In the small lane behind my house, thin-bodied laborers are digging the ground to install optic-fiber cables; and thus working in the dark and cold winter night, they speed up our 'Digital Revolution'!" She indicates how in the last decade of liberalization and globalization the problems of the lower class and castes besides the deprived have multiplied.

Jay Dubash, once a member of BJP's 'Think Tank', also opposes globalization, and with illustrations. He says that bin Laden may be a Muslim and uses Islamic insinuating language expressions; and although it is one 'brand' of religious terrorism, the present great conflict is not Islam vs. West phenomenon. It is no cultural conflict. It is a fight of globalization, which is basically between the western countries and the rest of the world (West vs. Rest).

In 1999 at Seattle (WTO), in 2000 at Washington DC (World Bank and IMF), and in September 2000 at Praha where these financial institutions held their conferences, successful demonstrations were held against globalization by NGOs gathering from world over that included radicals, environmentalists and advocates of social justice. Run by 'Dow Jones' capitalist journals like *Wall Street Journal* called such demonstrators as 'idiots', while *Time* magazine had dubbed them as 'successful'. The reason for this was that Washington DC had lent its ears to the voice of the Third World, and the huge debt of a poor country like Tanzania, amounting to two billion dollars had to be written off by these financial institutions influenced by the rich nations. Accepting the arguments of the radical groups, *Time* magazine had shown that after granting an aid of $390 million, IMF had forced Czechoslovakia to agree to certain conditions like reducing expenditure on health, education and social welfare (just as in India pressure is brought on the government to reduce subsidies to farmers). The wealth that is shared by 41 percent of the population of the world, is equivalent to the wealth of mere 200 rich men of America and Europe. In the first eight years of economic liberalization, the debt of the poor countries had touched the figure of $1.66 trillion. This figure has roses in the next two years to $2.2 trillion. In Europe itself, there are 500 million poor people. In terms of social and economic welfare, the condition of Muslim countries has been indeed very poor.

Due to the pressure of IMF Haiti had to import rice from America in great quantities, and so its farmers have suffered huge losses. That same America stops imports of cloth, carpets etc. from India by putting forward social reasons (like child labor) and environmental reasons. On these issue, the West adopts a protective policy very cunningly. That is why, in India, employment in small enterprises is depleting fast. In Bolivia, the government and a multinational company have the monopoly for water trade, so the prices of water have doubled there. (Insistence of advocates of globalization to privatize infrastructural equipments like water, electricity, roads and bridges are also found in India.) In this context, one may wonder if this experiment of 'removal of world poverty by remote controlled digital equipment' is not indicative of a subtle and new type of colonialism. These are some great critical remarks against it. Finally, in the World Economic Forum in New York (February 2002), it has been accepted that the distance and gap between 'haves' and have-nots', among people and countries, has increased. When America's Treasury Secretary Paul O'Neil opposed the proposition to provide more aid to the poorer nations, the Managing Director of IMF, Horst Kohler reacted thus, "If we are serious that globalization should give advantage to all (countries), then the developed nations would have to keep their markets open for the poor nations rather than protect the interests of its influential farmer lobby...However, we (rich nations) do not want to give up our privileges available to us from international trade institutions in order to provide better opportunities to the poor nations."

In the Summit Conference of the rich elite nations that met at New York there were no such demonstrations of civil non-cooperation in commercial ventures of globalization that had taken place from Seattle to Genoa, but the basic issues of the demands were at last clearly acknowledged here. The French Finance Minister Laurant Frabius became the spokes-person of this new trend. He emphatically said, "The opposition and violent activities against the bigger powers of the world has increased. Poverty that gives rise to such events must be removed. In order to fight terrorism we shall also have to give a parallel fight to poverty. If we want to remove terrorism, mere military steps against it would not be sufficient. We shall have to fight another war by helping the poor nations for their development."

The suicides by farmers, only half-opened doors of 'open markets' for little developed countries, world order based on profit and consumerism (that gives rise to violence), etc., are a kind of indirect violence in itself and the other type of violence is connected with the suicide bombers, a type that is violence against oneself, while the former is a violence against others.

In this forum, Kofi Annan, the Secretary General of UNO, too exhorted the rich nations and corporate heads, "The leaders of trade and governments have to do a great deal to solve the problems of poverty and social justice; and only that would be their protective environment. Otherwise, that belief will continue that only globalization is responsible for what is happening today."

Of course, it would be unrealistic to hope to turn the tide back. As is noted in the beginning in these pages, powerful forces of technology, communication and economy have already begun to flow in all fields of life; and it is impossible to turn back such a vital phenomenon as globalization, though there is scope for improvement as based on above observations of course. Besides, there is a lot of truth and logic in the statements of those who oppose globalization, but they cannot offer any capable alternative of this immutable phenomenon either. Besides, globalization is not the only a factor that gave rise to terrorism, nor can the seeds or roots of terrorism can be searched out in globalization at all times. For example, in the Muslim world, there is a lethal cocktail of money and oil that would turn anyone's head; and when it touches rigid religiosity and fanatic backwardness, it nurtures terrorism that is dangerous for democracy, cultural co-existence and peaceful development.

Therefore, it would be wiser to change the face, basic elements and growth of globalization by making it more humane. On one hand, improvement in infrastructure, removal of bureaucratic delays, legal obstructions and of vested interests of state-centered economic enterprises and practices must take place in the countries of the Third World. On the other hand, the character and practices of globalization must be revised from time to time, with exchanges of ideas and demands at global forums and institutions with a determined and just hearing of the voices of each and every country for their interests. As Annan said at the forum in New York, "The idea that all prevailing problems must be blamed on globalization is indeed wrong. Instead of becoming a cause for poverty and other social diseases, globalization can perhaps become a beneficial medium.* But it is in your (the rich nations and corporate classes) hands to take concrete and result-oriented steps to lift up millions of downtrodden, exploited and deprived people of the world." In reality, one tower of WTC that has become 'Ground Zero' gives a message to increase communication among civilizations, while the other tower calls out for giving a new direction to globalization by adding in it ethical element of equality, new character and new global architecture as well.

---

* We have entered into the third phase of globalization (Globalization 3.0 as Thomas Friedman calls it). In his new book, *The World is Flat* (2005) Friedman argues that political, technological and economic change during the past decade have leveled the global playing field. This has deprived the developed countries like the US of the domination it enjoyed during the previous globalization phase. In the flattened world of 21st century, Asian countries like China and India are becoming equal global players, and jobs such as in info-tech field are moving from the US and the UK to India, China, Brazil, etc. If these countries can maintain the momentum of their economic development, the standard of living of millions of its population will go up. "Globalization 3.0 makes it for so many people to plug and play, and it is going to see every color of human rainbow take part."

V

Changing Scenario

11

Challenges of Reconstruction

Just as the Ku Klux clan is not Christianity, the terrorist attacks are not Islam...Today, many Arabs (and Muslims and some of the western liberal people also) are saying that 'Americans need to ask themselves why they are being hated so much in the world?' But this would mean giving indirect concession to the philosophy of the fanatic people and justify the terrorist action.

To explain thus the new widespread wave of anti-Americanism in the Muslim world would only result in encouraging violent acts like 9/11. Such logic would wipe out the thin line of difference between a few thousand people's religious thinking and the religiousness of millions of peace-loving Muslims.

However, the Muslims and the Arabs will now have to come to the forefront of a new type of war. This war is as if equivalent to a war for independence and for salvation of their souls. As those fortunate yet 'out-of-fashion' Muslim scholars say, 'this indeed is the real meaning of Jihad; but the terrorists and suicidal bombers have hijacked it.'

— A liberal Muslim leader

Afghanistan: Challenge of National Reconstruction

Afghanistan is so poor and little developed that it does not even get a place in the Human Development Report of the world.

Of its population of 27 million, 60 percent are women, and only 15 percent of them are educated. The average lifespan is 45 years. Of four children born, one dies before attaining age of five years. More than 6 million people live without basic life amenities such as food. In November 2001, 3.5 million of its people were estimated to be living as refugees in Pakistan and Iran. Before the bombings that began in October these were the biggest refugee groups in the world. According to the UNO Report 2000 potable water and electricity are rare here. "A quarter of the population would die due to war, poverty and hunger." During the decade of 1979-1989, 1.5 million Afghans were killed in the anti-Soviet war, and most severe drought of the last 30 years had occurred. At that time, nearly 66 percent of the goats and sheep had perished.

There have been ethnic conflicts between the two sections, viz., the Pushtus and the Tajiks that make up 39 percent and 25 percent of the population respectively. Their experience in warring is altogether far more than in peaceful life or civic employment conditions! Thus, to defeat the Taliban is to merely win half the war.

Besides, the general perception of the world about Afghanistan is that due to its local ethnic conflicts, its political culture is indistinct, divided and narrow and so it is not possible to bring about the necessary political stability. To a great extent this is true. This is a country where the efforts of reconstruction are bound to fail. Since last three decades it has witnessed political instability and it cannot be said with any certainty when any civil war might begin there. After the Second World War the Marshall Plan was drawn up for reconstruction of Europe, but to apply any such plan here today would definitely cost billions of dollars! This is the opinion of the observers as well as some influential leaders of both political parties of Washington DC.

However, Fareed Zakaria believes that if we lose interest like this in the task of reconstruction of Afghanistan, "not only would it be a grave strategic mistake, but it would also mean closing our eyes on the mist important lesson we have learnt in the last decade."

Let us play a game of connecting words. When we speak the names of countries like Uganda, Rwanda, East Timor, Bosnia, Kosovo, and Nicaragua, what do we recall first? We would recall that these are areas torn by civil and ethnic wars (Christian vs. Muslim); such areas that are in grip of wars and so devastated that they could be pulled up to normalcy, they are 'failed state', and so on. However, as Marc Brown, the Head of UN Development Program says, all these countries have begun, if slowly, to put their house in order once again. Once occupying the front pages in dailies and magazines, in all these countries peaceful and considerably stable societies are being developed, and we can feel the first waves of reliable economic activities also.

UNO and international community were unsuccessful in curing these countries of such chronic and incurable disease of civil wars and then in establishing and maintaining peace, and implementing projects of national reconstruction. But, in the last five years or so, they have learned their hard lessons. That is why, small and big powers, besides the UNO and other international development agencies, have also come forward in the matter of Afghanistan to work in better cooperation. In February 2002, the representatives of various countries at Tokyo accepted the task of creating a fund of unprecedented amount for this purpose. In this good work, America and Russia, Japan with England-France-Germany and India with China—all those countries warring opponents and rivals once upon a time, have come together today to uplift a neglected poor country and make into a stable nation!

In this *yagna* or holy work, UNO is the leader, and the contributors are countries of west as well as east. Also, international NGOs experienced in the fields of relief, welfare and development strategies have thrown in their weight for the project. It would seem that Pakistan, Russia, Iran and other countries have, at least for the time being, given up the policy of acquiring spheres of influence here, though in the long run we find the vested interest of America and in oil extraction and conduction interests would develop here firmly. For this, undoubtedly, it would set up its military base here. At that time, Russia and Iran would also begin to take greater interest here. Thus, then, can we hope that their present cooperation would not be sacrificed for their national interests at a later date?

Today, we already see a new young generation in the place of the old civil war-oriented generation of a decade ago. It is being emphasized that for this new generation such an education system be developed as to keep it away from Taliban type of religious upbringing. The youth looking for making their country modern find hope in the interim government of Hamid Karzai. If the uncontrollable 'warlord' Rashid Dostum reminds us of the past of this nation, the liberal and soft-spoken President Karzai, who is westernized in his speech and manners, is the hope and repose for its future. Even today, in Somalia and Congo, the primary question of security is not solved, and so, maintaining peace and efforts at reconstruction have remained impossible there. Whereas in Kosovo, Uganda, Bosnia etc. political stability and basic security are restored, and so they have advanced on the path of peace and reconstruction. The other lesson is that UNO by itself cannot provide such a security anywhere. After promising it, the main responsibility devolves on the important powers themselves. Fortunately, for Afghanistan (and in another way for Pakistan), most of the major powers are prepared to make joint efforts to restore peace and undertake the most difficult task of reconstruction.

Even today, we find groups of *jehadi* mentality with Taliban elements and war-like 'kabilah' or groups are still hiding in caves, and they want to hold on to their own local fiefdoms in Afghanistan. To get back the strategic position it lost here, Pakistan may be determined to take advantage of any possible loss of popularity of the rule of the Karzai government in case it comes under a shadow; we cannot deny the logic of the possibility. (The public promise Musharraf made on 7th February to Karzai at Islamabad to be helpful in the reconstruction projects of Afghanistan reminds us of his Lahore Agreement with Vajpayee that preceded Kargil conflict!)

Therefore, only a strong and multi-national military presence can give an assurance of security and stability here. America is not enthusiastic for leading such a force, as can be easily understood by the experiences it has had in other places. But it is good omen to find that its closest ally, Britain, has come forward for it.

Also, as the huge funds reach the people and begin to satisfy their necessities of food, education, employment etc. in creating and maintaining faith in the post-Taliban modern and liberal order, their vested and democratic interests also may begin to develop. In order to control 'warlords' also, such projects of financial and building of infrastructures like roads, health centers, settlements etc. must be done with participation of their own people in expenditure and management; only then can they meet the conditions of behaving in a way to maintain peace and stability in their country. All this also must be done under strict international system or management's observation. Thus, a new type of Marshall Plan is needed here. Unlike in West Europe, not just economic reconstruction and welfare approach, but also with a built-in cultural educational component. But, at the same time, the ironic need is to keep on our own side even the 'warlords' connected with the narrow-minded personal interests here.

It would take years to pull up Afghanistan to normalcy and able to make progress. The contribution in this would definitely be highest from America. It would also have the most at stake as well in keeping stability and reliable peace here. The reason is that it would need to obtain rights to use the nearly virgin oil and gas areas of the Middle East and then construct pipeline network in the Arabian Sea; and for such a network, the land of Afghanistan would be used as their conduits. The government can hope to collect appropriate fees for the land, its usage and proper protection from oil companies if such pipelines are laid from Afghanistan. As it is, Afghanistan does not have any big income sources like agriculture, trade and commerce or any other fields. In such a situation, the international pipeline projects can provide it an important support to uplift its own economic situation.

America also now wants to reduce its dependence on the oil fields of the Middle East like in Saudi Arabia. This is because it wants to have greater space to deal with them politically. The Afghan leaders also would be interested in such a source of huge and constant income for providing stability. Earlier, the great Soviet oil company 'Gezprom' had prepared an ambitious oil project called 'Centgas' in Turkmenistan. Another project was of the huge American company 'Unocal'. Both these projects aimed to develop the oil-rich fields (Turkmenistan, Kyrgyzstan etc.), to arrange the carriage of that oil and gas by pipelines running from Pakistan and Afghanistan all the way into the Arabian Sea. From here gigantic ships would carry the goods to America. (An alternative network was to begin at Daulatabad of Turkmenistan, run to Herat and Kandahar of Afghanistan, then on to area near Multan of Pakistan down to New Delhi.) This is an unwritten agenda of America for the Middle East and Afghanistan. This means that its presence here would be long term, and basically it would benefit Afghanistan. Similarly, the young children would be brought up under liberal education, and the 60 percent of women whose human resources have been wasted so far could be put to great use for the country by their education, and they develop a liberal social system—these are things that would be looked into by the Karzai government. Already by appointing two ladies on important positions in his government, Karzai has begun to take significant steps in the direction of de-Talibanization. As *Scotland on Sunday Online* reports (September 19, 2004): Pinned up by an unknown hand under cover of darkness hours earlier, their local name—'night letters'. The message read had a quaint, almost romantic, ring.

"A holy war has been declared against the infidel," announced the first. Christian invaders, led by the US, wanted to conquer Afghanistan's Muslims, said the second letter. Any Afghan working with them would be 'punished' warned the third. At the bottom of each was a common signature: "The Taliban".

The project of reconstruction and creating stability in Afghanistan taken up by the international community is an unprecedented one, biggest so far. Its neighboring countries, as well as America, Britain and India, are economically interdependent on the issue and that makes the chances of political conflicts are minimum. In view of the expectations of possible benefits the relations of Russia, Muslim countries of Central Asia, Afghanistan and America etc. would become closer. Besides, in order to continue stability of this strategic country and to confirm its progressive development, they would all make concerted efforts.

America and its allies have reasons to feel confident to continue its Afghan policy on this line. The first ever national election here on October 9, 2004 has demonstrated that how even a 'biggest refugee poll' can be held in a comparatively free and fair manner. In spite of the threats of the Taliban against participating in this poll, about 10.5 million (including 41.3 percent of them being women), Afghans registered to vote. The turned out at polling booths was termed as massive. Many women, who three years back appeared in stadium, were killed flocked to vote. Independent foreign observers noted that "threats of violence by remnants of the Taliban regime largely did not eventuate". *The Australian* (October 21, 2004) quoted a 25-year-old Abudu Haq, "Today, we can vote. We can change the future of our country and our life. After decades of war, I know that now things will change".

Pakistan: Hope for Reconstruction and Questions

Musharraf is the first such ruler of Pakistan who is not born there but in India and so is a 'Mujahir'. He can also speak Turkish language in style. Once he had mentioned in praising words that Ata Turk, who was responsible for making Turkey into a real modern and secular state in the 1920s, is his 'role model'. Now, in the statement of 12 January, he admitted that his 'real role model' is the 'Father of the Nation' of Pakistan, Muhammad Ali Jinnah. For, Jinnah also wanted Pakistan to make modern and secular (yet) Muslim state.

Kamal Ata Turk, eight decades earlier, had much better and firm faith in the western modern and secular thought processes than Musharraf has. Ata Turk had himself done far-reaching reforms in Islamic law and social system besides granting of civil liberties. In that context, although Turkey was geographically a part of East/Central Asian Muslim countries, it is very near to the West even today, and possibilities have come up that it would be accepted in the NATO membership too. As Ankara's veteran diplomat Sukreet Alectar says, 'Now, Turkey would be a member of the European organization, and then the dream of Ata Turk would reach its climax. That dream means to come very near to that (western) culture."

Like Ata Turk, Musharraf also is in a position to do a lot for carving out a secular society in a Pakistan that is so far inspired or run by military. However, he also realized his limitations in this direction in 2001. He attempted to change the prevailing laws that take strict steps against those who speak or write to criticize Islam for anything. But, the fundamentalists made great protest against this, and thus he had to give up his plan to provide space for liberal Muslims. He admitted, "Yes, I have retreated in this matter (of changing the strict implementation of Shariyat). The reason is, I want first to bring in economic stability, and I did not want to open all the fronts (of reform) together." He then also added, "There are many such delicate and sensitive matters."

Thus, while Musharraf assures us that Pakistan would turn into a modern and dynamic nation, there are some limitations he would have to face. Ata Turk had wanted Turkey to become modern-secular from within and with principle. Musharraf, working under pressure of circumstances, wants to do this as a part of a result-oriented policy, and therefore we may even accept his claim to be another Jinnah. That is why, Jinnah, who created Pakistan on the basis of religion, had sent overnight the group of showmen claiming that there is Muslim majority in Kashmir; and due to the circumstances of the time, the Azad Kashmir (PoK or Pakistan occupied Kashmir) did remain under Pakistan. Following this precedent, Musharraf had first concluded the Lahore Agreement and then from time to time, totally unethically in terms of international relations and standards, and then adopted the Kargil strategy. It is hoped that the Indian defense and intelligence administrators would be forever alert to this 'strategy of KKKI', i.e., Kashmir, Kolkata, Khalistan and ISI. They must remember the cunning and complex policy of Musharraf to provide help to some disgruntled elements like certain Sikhs still advocating Khalistan and other dissatisfied extremist and *jehadi* elements, helping them with infiltrating lethal weapons and trafficking in intoxicating drugs etc.—to work against India.

However, Musharraf undoubtedly possesses the ability and expertise to make Pakistan take concrete steps in the direction of change. In spite of his dictatorial type of rule, there are certain outer symptoms of democracy in his regime of Pakistan. The comparative freedom of the press; some widespread discussions on the important policy of Taliban, *jehad*, fundamentalism, support to America, etc., also take place; and not all actions of the state can be hidden.

Of his own 13 staunch supporting generals Musharraf dismissed five, along with some officers, who were supporters of Taliban. He also transferred the top leaders of a strong institution, 'a state within a state' type of organization, i.e., the ISI. He has also begun to implement a new policy to change the

Madrassa and such other infrastructures from its military image, and for this he has begun to take away weapons from them; and to change the narrow Islam-oriented education system by making it broad-based with improved curriculum in order to bring up liberal citizens.

The General has also captured more than 2,000 extremists and armed terrorists. After a little reluctant phase, he has also banned nearly a dozen organizations like Lashkar-e-Toiba (LeT) and Jaish-e-Muhammad (JeM). He has also taken care to stop terrorist activities within Pakistan. Not many anti-America demonstrations have taken place during January-February, or any anti-Musharraf demonstration after 12 January. However, that does not mean that most of the people of Pakistan have accepted the influence or the growing military presence of America. In an International Gallop Poll in this context, taken in February, as in all the Muslim countries, here also a critical attitude prevails against America. In the last elections radical Muslims have turned influential. Only time can say how Musharraf can manage the people's anti-American sentiment.

Observers question intentions of Musharraf. How many are arrested besides the terrorists? How many of those are serious offenders? How many have been released? Dawood Ibrahim and his 30 cohorts that India has demanded for extradition has fallen on deaf ears even after 17 months of persistence!

Secondly, some observers believe that in Pakistan the educated and middle class citizens support middle path or liberal type of Islam. However, the call made by the statements of Musharraf for liberal Islam and modernity has not received any spontaneous welcome. Even in media and intellectual circles it has not been widely accepted and given a favorable atmosphere.

Besides, as Musharraf administration played the game of blaming India for Kolkata and Daniel Pearl incidents, and even declared Advani as a terrorist, it only goes to show that

Musharraf has not changed basically. However, Bush and Powell had put pressure on him to take steps for improvement of 'system' in Pakistan, and his having done so, he received public accolades from them. It is an open secret that he had been also explained about the strict steps the US planned to take if he did not do so. Thus, only under the real pressure and monitoring of America and international opinion, he has made all these changes. On the other hand, a large number of the Talibans and Pakistani *jehadis* have spread into Kashmir as well as Pakistan itself. American administration has strong suspicions about still continuing strong ties and channels between ISI, military, religious fundamentalists, al Qaeda and other terrorists in new ways, as experts like K. Subramanian and others believe. Therefore, America would maintain its presence in Pakistan in some manner or other. The capable intelligence network of India also would provide the FBI with information and help in this regard. There is no reason to doubt that if the camps of al Qaeda and other terrorists were discovered there, it would hesitate in destroying them in a joint effort with the Pakistan government.

On the other hand, it also cannot be denied that a policy (even if undeclared) may be formed whereby in order to help fulfill the promises of January 12, international financial institutions would provide aid or grant in installments to Musharraf in proportion to the benchmark steps he would take for his liberalizing steps. As Musharraf may have obtained domestic support for his rule, but to get popular acceptance in the elections he has declared he would need huge amount of finance for development, and so he would accept such international monitoring or backseat driving. Thus, in order make it possible for Pakistan to develop sufficient determination and capacity to raise a liberal society and a free political system, Musharraf and the local influentials call all must employ careful and innovative policies.

Even in the context of such challenging tasks of national reconstruction before Pakistan, India cannot expect any respite about Kashmir or its internal peace.

The Indian policy makers would have to be very clear about one thing: it would do no good to naively view Musharraf as Ata Turk of Pakistan. If President Bush believes this, let him. At most he can become Anvar Sa'adat of his nation, and let the world hope that he does so. At the moment, however, he seems a mixture of the characters and roles less of Sa'adat and more of Arafat.

Fareed Zakaria (*Newsweek*, February 4, 2002) believes, "From a short-term viewpoint there is a greater scope for maintaining peace here. For the first time, Pakistan has got a ruler who is truly promising and bold." And, unlike any other parties, the Hindu nationalists in New Delhi would be better able to convince the come nation on this point. In this region, the American diplomacy also has been balanced, friendly and a good deal effective; and yet...no permanent or long lasting peace would be found here. For, Pakistan would not be ready for any compromise about Kashmir.

Besides, Musharraf is mercurial; he cannot be found resilient on issues of Kashmir or nuclear restraint, etc.—not even by the US. His past background cautions even its patrons in Washington to cultivate any trust in his word. Right from Kargil down to 9/11 and his own tight position thereafter, he has always played a deceitful game with India; and if he has relented a little, it is merely to resume it. He says, "For any strategy, its deciding factors are its timing, opportunity and strength." Then, he adds, "No democratic government would have been able to take such quick decisions and steps as I have done." So, in his own eyes, Musharraf would reconstruct his nation by establishing democracy as he defines it—that suits him. At the time of announcing elections he has used a certain phrase—Pakistan needs 'a fine-tuned democracy'. We would definitely remember at this juncture the fate of 'basic' democracy, 'panchayat' democracy, 'guided' democracy, etc., until now! In mid-September 2004, he let the cat out by stating that he would remain the chief of Pakistan's army.

Since December 13, Musharraf has had to face on Pakistan's eastern border a big neighbor that is taking a hard attitude, and in the west he has to deal with the post-Taliban government that he dislikes. Also, he is supposed to keep a close eye on the *jehadi* elements in his own domain that he had himself nurtured until now. And these extremists may be waiting for an opportunity to penetrate even such important areas as intelligence and army.

The General has yet to deal with a large variety of mines hidden under porous ground he stands on. His problems also include leading his religion-oriented country towards modernity. He has yet to find the content of thought and policy for this great effort. "He is a well qualified as a CEO of a word class PR (public relations) company; but in reality he is a ruler of a country wearing the mask of one integrated nation with snarling sectarian groups underneath it; a country with a shaky economy and a country trying to find its basis of being a 'Nation' in Kashmir." The last becomes both his strength and his weakness. On a tall stone in the main square of Islamabad the inscription with an arrow pointing towards Kashmir reads, "Srinagar 315 km." It is not a road sign, but a symbol of the foundation and objective of Pakistan!

As to the first issue also it may be underlined that in the long run, PR skill is not an alternative of concrete administrative work. His compatriot Aiyaz Amir wrote in *The Dawn* that is very apt here: "Religious fanaticism and terrorism are not new, but as they are now connected with high-tech, they have turned into issues of great worry. After September 11 and the fall of the Taliban we should have understood that the age of Jihad being fought from outside should end. Now, the matter that we should have understood ourselves, we have to accept under pressure of the circumstances. After September 11 President Musharraf adopted anti-Taliban policy and gave the slogan: 'Pakistan First'. It meant that now we have to put our house in order and keep away from any adventure in a foreign country." Then, he adds, significantly, "As in Afghanistan, it is necessary for us to withdraw our interest in Kashmir part under our occupation. This is an invaluable lesson of wisdom." In September 2004, he, however, again reverted to the refrain of no adjustment on LoC; no peace without solution of Kashmir. One needs to appreciate his deftness in managing the formidable cross pressures that he is trying to grapple with. The persistent domestic *jehad* in this Islamic Republic and thousands of jobless youngsters are ready to join the hand of Mujahiddins along with hardliner elements in his army and ISI on one side. But, the growing post-9/11 international pressures and the US are prodding that Pakistan is running out of options in Kashmir. Musharraf has therefore, adopted a conciliatory approach with Manmohan Singh (mid-April, 2005). Now, Musharraf is left with no option but to engage India in a unstained negotiation, where Kashmiri aspirations are imaginatively accommodated. For this, he has shifted his support from the hardliner Syed Geelani to Mirwaiz Omar Farooq, the liberal face of the separatist Hurriyat movement. Till now, that symbol of Islamabad on the stone remains emotionally more potent and powerful.

Palestine and Israel: Establishment of 'One Country, Two States'

For terrorists, besides India and America, Palestine and Israel region has remained the third major battlefield. Even prior to New York and New Delhi, terrorism has been rampant in the region of Jerusalem. But, after 9/11, as the circumstances have changed a great deal, it needs to be analyzed in a new context.

In 1948, the Palestinians were displaced to create the state of Israel in their land, and when those 3 million Palestinians had to live under the military rule of the West Bank region, it would no surprise if they developed a rebellious mindset. But firm hold and actual possession by Israel would not justify resort to such response as suicidal human bombs; and similarly the violence going on since the last decade under *Intefada* (uprising) and other ways by the Palestinians also cannot justify the occupation by Israel. That the series of violent acts began in November after the fall of 2001 when Israel killed a top leader of Hamas (Palestinian terrorist organization).

In ·fact, when the assurance of getting their own independent state became uncertain, the Palestinians would definitely not accept the pressure and strictness of Israel's rule. And, the other Arab countries like Saudi Arabia, Syria and Iran also would help them in their protest activities without doubt. The strong and violent steps of Israel would not break the armed opposition and political will of the Palestinians. For example, in the year of 2001, Palestine has lost 1,000 souls, yet it has not lost its determination about their objective.

In the videotape telecast on Al Jazeera channel, bin Laden repeated the accusation that America is using Israel to suppress the Palestinians. The Middle East expert Professor Edward Said, who was sympathetic to Palestine and is himself an American Palestinian, said, "Of course, in considering it as 'crusade' of the Christians and the Jews against Islam, bin Laden merely shows his own madness." Laden plans thus to join this region in his own fight. Most of the Arabs believe him. Said himself showed how, by support of latest weapons and diplomacy, America has allowed the Jew state to continue the massacre of the Palestinians.

Said considers such a possession of the land of Palestine as 'criminal', "...and it seems that America has forgotten this issue". Israel breaks up the basic infrastructure of Palestine (roads, settlements, etc.) and even schools. (Just as the Hamas members destroy Israel school buses and schools by bombing.) Thus, actually from both sides innocent children are being killed. On the other hand, just as America and Israel have not properly understood the demand of Arafat for the freedom and justice for the people of Palestine, even Arafat had not been able to present his policy and work wisely to them. In spite of getting millions of dollars for the Palestinian freedom movement, as Said points out, "whatever they got, has only nurtured large police force and corrupt officials only". He made a very important observation: "We must see that our opposition earns respect and that the other people understand the basic tenets of its thought. It should not happen that the others fear or hate this opposition. But even when dealing with such a just issue, by our suicidal ignorance and waging a war exhibiting total lack of discretion, we are actually losing the goodwill of many." The result of the steps taken in February 2002 by Israel was that the Israeli missiles and bombs were fired at the very headquarters of Palestine Liberation Organization (PLO) and even near the living quarters of Arafat himself. (He was forcibly confined to his house by Israel for more than three years till his death in the fall of 2003!) In October 2001, Arafat had two options: to support the Bush-inspired war against global terrorism, or allow greater freedom to Palestine's dangerous terrorist organization, Hamas, to carry on its work. Arafat banned the anti-America propaganda in the media, but on the whole he chose the second option and accordingly risked political suicide.

Zuckerman, the editor-in-chief of *US News and World Report* believes, "Thus, whatever is happening now in the Middle East is no longer spontaneous or a private kind of terror; but it is a systematic and regularly applied terror. It is not merely a work of Islamic jehad or Hamas, or the Tenzim or Force-17 any more; but a formal and regular committee of such people aiming to achieve their common objective is doing all this. The objective to bring so much pressure on Israel through terrorist massacre (like suicide bombers, etc.) that it would be forced to accept Palestinian demands (such as an independent Palestinian State, voting rights for 3 million Palestinians living in the West Bank region under Israel administration, etc.)." Indeed, neither Israel nor America has the weakness of character to give in to wars of nerves like this. (Strategic advisors caution India also that it should keep this in mind, in spite of the bloody and long drawnout terrorist activities in the cross-border terrorism it has been experiencing. For, Pakistan does not have a high opinion of India's capacity for determination and strength for maintaining a 'Hindu-secular' state.)

The one force to help, approve and organize all these attacks was Arafat, according to the middle path magazines and columnists of *Mercury News* (Silicon Valley), *Washington Post* etc. For example, the first one to ever hijack a plane was Arafat. He is known as the first person to have planted a bomb in a plane as well. The group that blew up a school bus carrying young Jew children was also Arafat's group. The successful conspiracy to kill (Jew) players at the Olympic Games was also his creation. "This is a leader who wants to bring pressure on the targeted nation by killing innocent citizens; hijack its plane, keeping the passengers under threat, and then make the government agree to their demands in exchange for them; and in all these incidents, using terror as his effective weapon, he is the first of its kind." However, he claimed and declared that he merely wanted to gain sympathy of the world by his attacks on other and even on the Israelis. (Does this not remind us of similar statements of Musharraf here?)

Palestinians must have their own state. This is an absolutely just demand, for which liberal citizens all over the world—from India, from Muslim countries and neutral states of Communist groups—also have given their respect, support and sympathy to Arafat for it. On the other hand, by now, Arafat was devalued among the Arab people, and America and Israel besides other nations had begun to consider him irrelevant in creating a somewhat contradictory arrangement of Arab countries formal acceptance of Israel and simultaneous creation of a new Palestine state, for co-existence of justified states that can enjoy international security. It is hoped that soon a new realist leader like Arafat or another leadership is found. As people had great love for him, Arab states that were allies of America had been providing huge financial help; but now it is currently believed that to continue receiving it, terrorist activities have become his vested interest.

Jordan and Lebanon did not allow Arafat any shelter, so he finally settled in Gaza. At that time he had two options to choose from: state or terrorism. Unfortunately, he chose the latter. Nearly two-and-a-half decades ago, freeing himself from the main currents and with the arbitration of America at Camp David, the Egyptian President Anwar Sa'adat made an agreement with Israel, and peace was restored between the two bitter rivals. Both the nations are enjoying the fruits of this peace. But, in the year 2000, at the time of another such 'Camp David', the Prime Minister of Israel, Barak, proposed for important concessions including formal acceptance of Israel and creating a state of Palestine that would include Gaza. President Clinton gave his consent to this proposal. If Arafat had accepted this proposal, the national flag of an internationally recognized, sovereign state of Palestine would have been flying merrily, and the occupation of Israel would have been a thing of the past. But, at the last minute, Arafat refused. A similar occurrence had taken place at Oslo too.

A major reason behind this is that Arafat himself had so much mixed up and confused his own Zionism and anti-Jew propaganda with the real Palestinian 'cause' and 'Arabism', and this had given his followers such hardened anti-Israel attitude, that if he now ever gives even a little concession to Israel in any pact, his own people would say that he betrayed them, and that means he would be inviting trouble for himself. So highly charged is the atmosphere there.

On the other hand, since November 2001, Israel has given a sharp and hard-slapping response against the massacres of its citizens by terrorist groups like Islamic *jehad* and Hamas in that region. So, under international pressure, as the President of PLO, Arafat had arrested very few from the list of 108 given by Israel who were really Palestinian terrorists. Most of the names were actually in the salary list of PLO! "In all this, the smoke and mirrors are many." (Here also India would recall tactics of Musharraf.) Arafat seemed to prefer criticizing terrorism in English language; for he always gives his real message only in Arabic, as his followers know very well.

That is why, there was a visible change in the attitude of America from its pre-9/11 stage for initiating compromises and pressurizing Israel to grant concessions. Now, President Bush had abandoned Arafat from any future negotiations for peace, considering him a chameleon, changing colors time and again and encouraging terrorism indirectly (or, one who had been virtually imprisoned by his own creation of violence and hate). When Arafat talked of a just and permanent peace, he meant a 'peace without a Jew state'. When he was handed over the West Bank region of Jordan, it was expected that he would make 'a down payment of peace'. But that did not happen; instead, he made his new unborn state into a flowerbed of terrorism.

In this context, even when we may not like it, the view of aggressive Prime Minister Golda Meyer is very relevant: "Only when the Arabs begin to love their children more than they hate us, we shall have peace." India and Pakistan also need to understand this philosophy, but 'the moment of truth' has not yet arrived.

The confidence that one-time experienced terrorist like Yasser Arafat would give a positive lead to the peace negotiations with PLO against terrorism held by many countries of the world was lost. America's more conservative magazines considered Arafat "a more divisive force than even bin Laden". Arafat had betrayed three decisive attempts at peace: one, he broke the confidence eight years ago when Israel had nearly concluded the agreement for peace with President Clinton's arbitration; second, he had continuously neglected his duty of working for a just peace for Palestinians; and third, he broke up the high hopes in the Middle East, built after great efforts, at Camp David in 2000. Besides, since November 2002, he had encouraged or ignored even suicidal steps of Hamas and *jehadist* Islamic organizations against Israel; and then as a 'reflex action', Israel had responded with sharp slapping steps of its own, doubly violent.

Till his death, he once again began to pursue terrorism for the objective of obtaining international acceptance to Palestine as a sovereign state.

Arafat had been in favor of Hamas-inspired or other suicidal bombings; while Israel Prime Minister Ariel Sharon was exuding flexibility and result-oriented approach for promoting peace efforts, and wanted everyone to take his proposals serious; but now it is lost. (Of course, in this context, one cannot forget a very insulting remark of Sharon, at a time when an opportunity existed for peace, that "If the Israeli mossad had ended the life of Arafat, everyone would have been saved from the terrorism from the climax it has reached today".)

Secondly, the main question may not be of ending the life of Arafat, as Sharon declares, intoxicated as he is with his power. For, if satisfactory arrangements were not made for the Palestinians after proper understanding of their *Intefada* and psycho-cultural roots of violent terrorism, other 'Arafats' or powerful leaders like Arafat, could also rise again and again! Even America has to contemplate that by merely bringing the political life, or even life, of Arafat to an end would not solve the daunting problem. The main question is that can President Bush, in view of the conciliatory attitude of Sharon and Abbas empower them to arrange as to how, when and with what reasonable conditions the motherland of Palestine in the West Bank be handed over to them with assurances of long-term peace and stability.

In this context, it is very important to watch how the peace process is forwarded by Prime Minister Abbas and President Sharon.

The most significant part is the philosophy of Golda Meyer applies not only to the Palestinians but also to the Israelis! And, a similar lesson must also be learnt by India and Pakistan as well.

12

An Untraditional War: Multi-Level Response

> If a compromise cannot be arrived at between religion-centered nation-state and the philosophy of religious yet secular liberal democracy, the world would have to turn a victim of a new kind of Cold War; and it would not be less obstructive to establishment and promotion of peace than the earlier Cold War.
>
> — **Mark Jurgenmeyer**

After 9/11 the concept and management of war have undergone great radical and qualitative changes. The usual questions and features of the past small or big wars, "what, when, how and against who, etc." do not apply anymore.

Osama bin Laden had observed in one of his videotapes very meaningfully, "They (Americans) want to live; we want to die." These few words convey a great deal. War is not going to be fought collectively, on large scale or in a battlefield; but there are going to be attacks, by those who are prepared to sacrifice themselves as martyrs for *jehad*; and these 'Mujahidins' would be acting under the instructions of their leaders, carrying out the attacks on selected place or building, keeping in mind a specific situation or program, using suitable and effective weapons and inflicting predetermined violence on their victims, aiming at creating a widespread psychological effect on all.

Secondly, this war is not to be fought with any specific army or a specific rival either. It is like dealing with someone who has no face, only a mask. Also, anyone such person also can attack suddenly anywhere in the world; he would just be changing his make-up, name, passport and national identity as per his need, cheating his way through customs and intelligence agencies at airports or other points of transport, attacking in a plane or in a mall or in VIP conferences or the government buildings, or anywhere he chooses.

Like Israel, now even India, America, Indonesia and other nations have also begun to understand that the greatest danger for one's security and defense is from outside and from outsiders. America used to find its enemies out of the American soil: it fought Soviet Russia, China, Vietnam, Sudan, Bosnia, Iraq and Taliban (or, it had found them to exist out of US!). However, now, the centers of its strategic and foreign policy 'think tanks' have begun to consider the challenges that are found from within the US itself, due to the internal contradictions resulting from globalized capitalism and cultural Americanization trends. President Bush has no doubt sanctioned the highly expensive system of defense so as to disrupt any missiles from outside America that would threaten its safety. (India has also shown a sympathetic to this system in principle.) But, how would this system provide promise of even domestic protection to its own citizens, when the terrorist hijackers could use American planes as missiles and attack even the Pentagon? As the experts of internal civic security like Gary North and Arthur Robinson observe in their study *Fighting Chance*, America that has spent billions of dollars for MAD (Mutually Assured Destruction) system, has not been able to set up any national civil security system against the biological and atomic fears.

Thus, with a superpower like America, having a great strength to attack the outside enemy anywhere in the world, having this experience as a 'super-cop', has made not only America but also the other nations, to re-think on the entire concept of security and defense all over again.

A faceless enemy does not observe the norms, techniques or practices of any traditional war; he makes his own rules ('rules of war' rather than 'rules of game') for it, and would open the war front as he plans and then attack. Therefore, to confront him, besides the great variety of the traditional, totally fresh weapons and equipments, practices and strategies would have to be developed.

The terrorists do not wear any 'uniforms' but 'muftis'; they do not wear 'khakhis' but civilian clothes. The author of *Doctors of Disaster Preparedness*, Dr. Constad Chester, who is also closely connected with the big laboratory for civil defense, also believes, "There cannot be any defense against those (like the suicide bombers) who want to die." (The fatal attacks on the Prime Ministers of India and Israel besides on the prestigious national buildings of America also support this.) By attacking the selected vital buildings in the West, "we cannot deny the possibility that they aim to paralyze the economy by discount". He says that a small terrorist group can manufacture Anthrax chemicals at home, but it is enough to kill 90 percent of New York population. Only 24 hours are needed for the spread of this chemical, out of which they can use some hours to escape from the condemned city! Merely $2,50,000 would be required to make the needed amount of the chemical; and from their population of 50 crores it would not be difficult to find enough rich persons who would hate America (or India, or Israel) to finance that money.

The world has no experience of biological and chemical warfare, but during the long-lasting Cold War between the two superpowers, the scenario was quite clearly portrayed with highly destructive nuclear weapons, 'Merv' and 'Marv', missiles of ABM series, etc., as part of the concept of military paradigms. However, the clear understanding of the power of this modern 'Brahma' and his 'nuclear theology', both America and Russia had realized the power of destruction not only against each other but also the entire world and put the clock back to the Stone Ages, had created a kind of 'balance of fear'. This had made the principle of 'nuclear deterrence' more real so that each superpower would hesitate before initiating such a war. But, the irony is that while not only America and Russia possess nuclear power, for it is also with China and India and perhaps others too; and yet none can stop this type of suicidal bombing tactics of terrorism. Which radar of powerful weapon based on military technology could be warned of a suicidal determination fuelled by the power of the mantra of *jehad*? Which 'anti-missile' could be directed? That is why, finally, instead of the prevalent concept of war, its counter-principle would have to be taken up.

Culled from the experiences from the episodes WTC to Tara Bora, mainly two kinds of clear thinking seem to be coming up: one, for short-term—war preparedness based on military technology against any possible terrorist attack and get a victory out of it; and two, long-term—non-traditional preparedness, by going to the roots in the psyche of terrorist consciousness and develop attitude of peace.

The mountainous and rocky land of Afghanistan (and later the desert land of Iraq in 2003) became the laboratory for testing the latest, most modern and powerful military technology of America. The difficult terrain and fighter population of Afghanistan that had shamed the armies of Britain and Soviet Russia, and so were considered invincible, were overcome by America, and this had been possible due to the opposition the weapons of the Taliban had to face in the latest military technology. The American bombers selected and destroyed the underground secret camps and bunkers that were impenetrable, with the help of satellite cameras with night vision! And, all this was done in the dark only. The small infantry troops on the ground were also protected against possible Taliban bombings and missiles by a protective cover in the skies. This was a strong response of America to the idea of war it experienced on the morning of 9/11 that even a small country or small yet trained suicidal group could challenge America and attack its impenetrable Pentagon! Thus, on both sides, now, the capacity of military strength is not to be measured in terms of number or spreading of the soldiers, but how quickly can it be mobilized and be moved on the target.

The American sensory equipments could not detect the hijackers and attackers only by looking at them. The anti-aircraft and anti-missile weapons costing billions of dollars could not stop them. But then, on the field of Afghanistan, the Taliban also faced an invisible enemy. However, the American satellite cameras were able to see clearly their Taliban opponent hiding under the rocky grounds in seconds.

Now, it has become possible to view the events taking place in a battlefield situated very far from one very clearly and easily. So, equipped and prepared with such high-tech materials, nations like America, without coming within the possible reach of little developed countries' strength in this regard and without incurring damage on its own soil, can deploy a great deal of destruction on the land of the enemy. The great battles fought at Kurukshetra, Panipat, Austerlitz, Waterloo, Stalingrad, Sing ben Fu, 38th Parallel, Ischhogil, Yom, and Kimpur etc., and classical land maneuvers from the age of bow and arrow down to rockets and bombs, cavalry and guns, tanks and jet planes, along with the generals and war heroes that exhibited great valor and ability—all are now shelved in the glorious chapters of military history.

In this new war against terror, the specially trained units detected their targets from a long distance, covered them in laser beams and connected them with electronic brains and then having located them exactly, bombed and destroyed them. Under the 'global positioning systems', catching the signals via satellites, these units constantly put under surveillance the Taliban's armed groups of different sizes, camps, bunkers and hidden ammunition warehouses, and even 'cavemen' of bin Laden. The spy planes of America could locate even moving targets from hundreds of miles away, and in places where special task forces could not approach physically, the unmanned airplanes dashed on to destroy. These unmanned airplanes also constantly videotaped the enemy armed units on the ground, sending the laser pictures and detailed maps of the areas covered right into the far-off American military camps.

With such subtle and complex technical equipments provided American cruise missiles and air force an extraordinary destroying power and effectiveness, and this is proved by the experiment in this new battlefield as well as Iraq.

Besides, the land forces of the Northern Alliance also so rapidly covered the ground battle for victory over targeted cities and areas that Talibans were paralyzed and shamed into inactivity and retreat. By this, however, the human loss in Afghanistan was even less than that suffered by the Americans in the damage due to the fourth terrorist airplane that crashed into New York and Pennsylvania. However, independent sources give figure of Afghanistan's human loss as higher.

Indeed, this is the story of a very small and poor country without any technical power or strength. But where the latest military equipments and preparations exist, with most modern submarines and naval force, fighter jets and tanks and other sophisticated arms and ammunition, and if one has to fight it in a war—then all the big powers—even the emerging power like India—would need the well-equipped and large land force. But, after the war with Afghanistan, America and India etc. would have changed priorities. Even the latest science and intelligence cannot fathom or know or estimate beforehand about the future terrorist style and fearful threats. The inadequacy of intelligence in America and India in matters of 9/11 and 12/13 respectively would mean that now a greater attention would be paid to not only high-tech but also to human intelligence capability and its development as in earlier times. By combining the mediums of modern skills of technology and human intelligence, security steps in wake of any suicidal terrorist attack could be taken with help of anticipating and tracing its probabilities and pro-offensive raids against them. A system for it needs to be developed. Indeed, in view of the resources, finance and policies, it is expecting too much. Yet, it is also necessary that the terrorists be stopped at the borders from entering India rather than facing them at any point in Kashmir, New Delhi, Ahmedabad or Mumbai. Within India also certain anti-nationalist and *jehadi* elements reside; and secret Pakistani or terrorist centers of activities must be identified and removed. This indeed would be a continuous exercise to catch and punish them.

Not only that, as Dr. Jasjit Singh, Air Commodore and a member of Defense Think Tank, suggests, "India should adopt an aggressive strategy whereby Pakistan itself is turned into a victim of its own cruel and cunning policy and strategies, wherever the centers of terrorism or its patronage are found; and for this a minimum of military presence also must be kept all the time." The promise of General Musharraf by his statement to take steps against terrorist and *jehadi* elements has proved so unrealistic that after a month of a liberal and non-aggressive defense analyst like Dr. Jasjit Singh also has had to voice such an opinion. Thus, in order to support the rebellious working against the influential Sunni Muslim section, or separatist elements (Sindh, Shia, Baluchi, etc.), and thus gradually create a situation of undeclared new type of war or another confrontation, there is now a need to set up an aggressive organization similar to Pakistan's Inter-Services Intelligence (ISI) (Indian Strategic Intelligence) also.

Zuckerman says, "We (Americans) should not ignore the 'wake-up call' of 9/11. Much more than whatever has been indicated by the 'Blue Ribbon Panels', commissions, studies, reports, editorial suggestions and books, this experience of war against terror has taught us to revise altogether afresh the qualitative readiness of our armed forces for a new king of war."

The new war would be fought with technology and high-tech equipments in the intelligence fields. Jack Swinson, the public matters officer, of the Air Force laboratory, where the latest weapons (electronic weapons, missiles, smart bombs, sensor and satellite equipments, etc.) are manufactured and tested, says that the equipments used by Americans in Afghanistan are no doubt insufficient and incomplete; but they are a new crop of weapons that can very specifically aim at the target, yet greatly reduces the possibility of damage to civil life. In the earlier wars, to aim at a particular target, the bombing and air wars needed a great amount of bombs and they resulted in massacre of a large civil population. "But now, even the war between bigger powers would only be a war of machines vs. machines only." America has the resources to spend trillions of dollars and also has an infrastructure and human resources to invent and develop such useful weapons. Therefore, the power patronizing the terrorists may be big, but America would have an obvious lead even here.

Yet, on the other hand, there is no longer the situation where one can dependent on any other one or more power, for we cannot be sure if even America would be able to foresee or anticipate correctly the point from where the threats may arise, in spite of all its achievements in communication and information technology (IT).

Here, we may recall the viewpoint expressed by the Defense Secretary, Donald Rumsfeld. In an interview (*Parade* magazine, November 18, 2001), he says, "This war is so very different from the wars we have fought in the past. The terrorists have not arranged any remarkable their army, navy or airforce that can oppose us, but instead our foes depend on other kind of things like fear that may not seem or be equal to it. Among such things terrorism and its fearsome psycho-cultural effects is one; and the other, such chemical, biological and nuclear weapons that make the community tremble with fear. There are such modern micro-weapons that can break enemy missiles and cyber attacks that break up cruise missiles and Internet. The terrorists could use for their attacks any of these techniques, at any time and at any place. It is not physically possible to protect ourselves at every time, at every place or against any technique that can be thought of." Rumsfeld adds, "Therefore, to meet the threat of the terrorists, there is only one way, and that is to snatch away the war from their hands and take it against them and finish them."

"Such a war could not be of just physical-military style. We have to fight for our values; we have to fight the rigid, Middle Age mentality, *jehadi* approach and narrow cultural paradigm. There is need to propagate and educate the Muslim society and other communities of the world about how the high elements of our culture and humanist philosophy (religious tolerance, secular thought and democratic system of governance, multi-culturism and pluralism, etc.) could lead to global and human security and peace. At the same time, we must also respect and remember to encourage the tendencies of people concerned to preserve their individual identity and traditions at their regional levels, indeed."

Rumsfeld also draws our attention to another qualitative change that has come in this field: "The neglect (was also) shown before Pearl Harbor or attack on Korea—but now we are living in another context altogether. The time was different then. Now, weapons of mass destructions have spread widely among a number of groups in the world."

"That is why, we cannot afford a little neglect shown earlier. For, the dangers of war have increased manifold now....It is our responsibility that we can never be inattentive. We cannot afford any misunderstanding or improper decision. We do not have the freedom to make such a mistake. For now, our one such mistake can threaten lives of not just hundreds, or thousands, but millions of people."

Like Israel, now America and India must see that there is no repetition of 9/11 or 12/13 respectively. For this they would have to fight a new kind of war before terrorists strike again. John Hopkins, one time Dean of School of Advance International Studies, and Paul Wolfowitz, a policy maker at Pentagon (till 2004), suggest to take care on three fronts:

1. To obstruct any armed attacks on our IT network centers by terrorists or suicidal bombers and be ready for attack them instead.
2. To develop IT and use it as necessary for this purpose.
3. To protect the infrastructure that supports our ground and space defenses and arrange for keeping them absolutely unobstructed and free of any interference for our use round the clock.

Indeed, the arrangement for this would require billions of dollars. The realists however argue that even if we have to spend astronomical amount for the latest spying and detecting equipments in America and Asia, we would then be able to save the great variety of resources and wealth besides the invaluable cultural assets that are far more valuable than anything else.

No doubt, thousands of patrolling airplanes and equipments would be needed for safeguarding these wealth and assets in America and elsewhere. But that is the only way to safeguard against terrorist attacks the lives of the people and the places of invaluable cultural heritage of the world. Besides, since now the most precise and 'smart' weapons and forces are to be maintained, their sizes would be reduced considerable. In the Second World War, only one out of 400 bombs fired could reach or go nearest to the target, and may or may not actually destroy it as intended. Now, as has been noted in Afghanistan, nine out of 10 bombs have been able to destroy the intended targets. Thus, as the weapons turn more precise and effective, and can operate even without pilots, the number of such human pilots would also reduce. Similarly, the number of the accessories and equipments to help them would also be reduced accordingly. American experts consider even the space as yet a virgin field. From the space the targets of the enemy can be located and easily and clearly seen by the light of laser beams, and so easily destroyed too. Thus, the ballistic missiles, cruise missiles, fighter planes, etc., could be circling the earth in skies and space to detect and destroy such centers! Rumsfeld and Wolfowitz (who visited India as the Joint Chief of Staff in

February), along with General Myers, are busy in planning such defense policy for America. George Will, the noted columnist of *Washington Post* considers this a suggestive step. One really wonders how such intense exercises of 'war-like' defense preparations are a result of the sharp emotions and the misdirected fierce passions of fanaticism and terrorism that make it imperative to give priority to such activities.

Where shall we look for a worldview that can provide a healthy balance between such war-like response and the nurturing of terrorist mentality that thrives on negative aspects of globalization and its adverse economic effects? Here, we find a statement issued by Nobel laureates, humanist gentlemen, in response to 9/11 that seems quite relevant: "We must look after the terrorist and gun mentality with farsightedness. War is not a conflict between religions and cultures. Only the attempts to remove poverty, backward conditions and weapons that can destroy large populations could prove to be the farsighted and result-oriented method of controlling the evil of terrorism."

Here, we must recall the statement of the inventor of atom bomb, Oppenheimer himself: "We are making the God of Destruction." At the time of the first use of atom bomb, these were his words of truth of 'Kalosmi Mahakalasya'. (Indeed, then America stopped 'high level security' provided to this great scientist!)

In this context, the father of the hydrogen bomb, Edward Taylor also made an observation that needs to be considered. He said, "(In 1945) We should not have thrown the bomb on Hiroshima but in the Gulf of Tokyo; or fire it at a height of 20 to 30 thousand feet above Tokyo, so that one crore Japanese could have observed it in the skies. Then, they would have been highly shocked about the possibility of the great destruction if it fell on them! At that time, even (the Japanese ruler) Hirohito would have seen it, and having understood the dangerous consequences, would have surrendered" (*Esquire*, January, 2002). Let us also look at this viewpoint: the power of atomic bomb is not going to remain with only a few bigger states; in nations like Iraq, Pakistan, North Korea also, it is likely to be in the hands of persons like future Muhammad Attas, bin Ladens, Omars, Zubaihads. "The next (terrorist) attack would not be a scene of clouds of smoke going from lower Manhattan (World Trade Center) to Brooklyn, but of a smoke-cloud, going up in the shape of a Mushroom!" Only the maker of the scene of bombing would change; and now the experts draw out attention to something that is even more possible: "The terrorists may not use the 'weapons of mass destruction', yet they can definitely use 'weapons of mass effect'! If they (terrorists) are successful in firing powerful car bombs, plane bombs...or highly explosives or six truck bombs, (the American) vast distribution network for electricity would be destroyed and economy of half the country would just be dead" (*Time*, October 2001).

In the present times, the form of terrorism has undergone a change. At first they used to plan such attacks where a large number of people could witness the terrorist act, and still would not die. Now, while undertaking such acts, they give their own lives as they destroy their targets. Besides, they now use the combination of high-tech equipments of the West and intelligence network of their own for getting the desired effect. Most of the episodes occur in a targeted country, but this has meant that the countries like India and Israel have had to suffer bloodied borders due to terrorist activities. On top of this, due to expert combination of western high-tech and adventurous and suicidal volunteers has made terrorism also go international.

This is a new kind of terrorism—great terrorism. The inspiration behind it is mostly political. However, more than that, it is the dreams of religious-nationalist identities, and changing the world order in keeping with their worldview only, etc. are behind it. Its weapons are weapons of mass destruction—biological, chemical and nuclear—besides the man to volunteers for suicidal use of these weapons also is the part of their destructive technology!

We shall definitely have to understand terrorism at the levels of its rise, development and conducting methods. We shall have to go to the roots of terrorist mentality. The pages flowing these provide details and analysis of issues like the rage of the Muslims, cultural conflicts, the globalization and the 'closed' non-democratic systems of governance—and indicate the causes of its development are subtle and complex and being joined provide great synergy to it. No doubt, the pragmatic response after the episodes of 9/11 and 12/13 is very necessary; but along with military-political response, we must also think on this as well.

The element of violence that has crept in the consciousness of man and nations is playing its role in all these forces.

It was more than five decades ago, UNESCO had learned this: "War begins in the minds of men; and so for the rows of protection against it also must be built only in the minds of men." Terrorism is a new kind of war of this century. To find ways to stop it also must be searched in the mind of men. "We have to address not only to the systems of terrorism, but also to the system of terrorism." The security and peace of our world or in any country lies in this philosophy—only a true and realistic 'ecology' of terrorism would lead the world on the road to peace.

13

Scenario of Change

The qualitative change has appeared in international relations after 9/11. Indo-Afghan relations provide its audio-visual profile in its pattern.

Before September 11, 2001, Pakistan was a dominant patron power in Afghanistan under the Taliban. It was as if India did not exist at all as far as that country was concerned. In November 2000, the government of Northern Alliance replaced Taliban. The new government, formed under Hamid Karzai, sent a special invitation to India for attending its oath-taking ceremony. When the Indian Foreign Minister Jaswant Singh alighted at the Kandahar airport, three high-ranking officials of the new government had come to receive him there. Meanwhile, when the Pakistan Foreign Minister, Abdus Sattar, arrived, no such official of the new government came to receive him. Only one officer from UNO was in attendance! In 1999, the terrorist leader named Masud Azhar had highjacked an Indian passenger aircraft and forced it to land at the Kandahar airport. Jaswant Singh himself then had to rush there for conducting negotiations with the terrorists in order to get the passengers released. Now, in the helicopter of the very same hijacker, Jaswant Singh was escorted to Kabul as a special guest by the new government!

The G-6 conference that met in Paris that very day for post-Taliban governance of Afghanistan as its main agenda, now included the name of India among its members, absent until then. In the new arrangement, the voice of India was heard rather than that of Pakistan that had given its support to 'moderate Taliban'. Keeping India away from such arrangement in September, Musharraf had brought pressure on Bush as if Pakistan was its member.

At this time, within one week of assuming power, Abdulla Abdullah, the new foreign minister and two other ministers visited New Delhi (and not Islamabad) from Kabul. This became a dramatic event that represented the shift in the history of international politics.

You can name any paradigm: Globalization vs. Talibanization, Jihad vs. Crusade, Islam vs. the Rest, West vs. Rest, or any other; during the conflict the nation-state that played the major role had to lose the most. The clear frontiers and protected boundaries, tariff walls and the nations with regional water-areas (*jala-vistar*) are being disregarded. The notion of global natural resources, religious loyalties that cross-national borders, Islamic states that go beyond national states, and such extra-national forces and currents are overpowering national boundaries now. Devils now throw bombs and missiles on civilized, law-abiding governments in the name of the Lord. In Lal Chowk of Srinagar one can ignite fires. The outside forces can attack the lawmaking houses in Srinagar and New Delhi. Secondly, without getting into the stance of war, a state can support and patronize such activities and forces. The instances in Pakistan of murder of Daniel Pearl, the killing of five persons, including American citizens, in a Protestant Church and attack on Shia Masjid—all indicate that it would not be surprising if in future al Qaeda and bin Laden may appear in new guises from within Pakistan.

— Abstracted from articles appeared in
The Indian Express (2002)

America

Ever since 9/11 America has changed. It is changing so fast that anyone coming here for the first time after 11th September cannot even think what it was like before, as he views America of today with its great preoccupation with highjack experts, security officers, spies and citizens harassed and terrorized by threats of biological weapons. This is indeed the same America that used to be traditionally occupied with consumerism and security earlier. Just as the baby-boomers generation after the end of the Second World War had given shape to a new, dynamic, prosperous and consumerist America, the post-9/11 generation of youth may also give shape to a new America. The polls indicate that more than half the young people now prefer to take training not in high-tech, Wall Street, industrial enterprises or management fields, but rather in the federal political institutions. The fields of study that had lost interest from younger people since a long time, such as army careers, aeronautics and flying, administrative and security services, medicine, most probably as help in combating problems of health after conflicts of biological or chemical weapons, foreign policy and other broad political and public careers have begun to interest the youth today again. Observers estimate that the power of youth may now put their abilities to achieve something intelligent in future in these fields.

Similarly, the American foreign policy is now being based on a new international perspective and new beliefs. Since 9/11 the American foreign policy has found new aspects. Thomas Augusta even believes that "rarely it has been seen that within one day the fundamental components of American foreign policy have changed so drastically".

Due to the attacks on New York and Washington, it seems now that after the Cold War the international situation was only an ad hoc arrangement for a decade. Now, an urgent change took place, with an international mission. "Let us get a global support of those who are against terrorism and ready to fight it." If President Bush took this to its logical end, it may also mean, "You (nations) are either with us or are with terrorists."

The decision to go alone in this taken by Bush administration was not approved by its close allies like Britain and Germany. The newspapers used to print cartoons of 'A Lone Cowboy' for him! Of course, even now, when we see the flowing international situation, it is difficult to say how 'global' and 'alliance'-like will these the hastily made international alliances fare in future. But, the America that wanted to break up the missile treaties, to adopt a strong stance with China, disregard the prohibitions of atomic tests, and adopt an non-cooperative attitude for the issue of global warming, now has to take the initiative for new friends and allies for concerted action, is itself an indication of demands of change in time.

Instead of one-sided foreign policy that focused on America only, now it is likely that it is developing a new one with multiple and multinational aspects. The fear of terrorism is felt in many nations. India, Israel and now America have experienced the bitter taste of terrorism on their own soil and this is troubling the future generations. This situation has given America (and also India to some extent) once in a lifetime an opportunity to shake up and waken up its foreign policy. The American Foreign Secretary Collin Powell has said, "We shall make the best of (such) an opportunity. Now, we have become so multi-dimensional that I have to be awake 24 hours a day to be in contact with the well spread (in time zone) nations of the world." Still, while America may have left the mentality of a huge self-sustained island nation, it has not left the real politic of non-feeling and even cruel mentality. This is evident in its so-called alliance with Pakistan and Saudi Arabia—the nations that have directly or indirectly continued their support and justification of the same for the Islamic fundamentalists.

Even then, ever since the very first month of 9/11, the magic of a 'new chemistry' and intimacy with America is felt even by those nations that had been distant until then.

After the disintegration of the Soviet Union and the melting of the Cold war, America became the superpower of the world. During the decade of 1990, the unprecedented material progress and prosperity made America's self-image and self-love reach new great heights. Historian Heinz Johnson observes, "We created new audiences. The focus of our talks was scams of OJ and Monica Lewinsky-Clinton. In many audio-visual events and politics we turned self-destructive: from Watergate to 'Monica gate'. In the world of even cultural entertainment also the society was busy in enjoying somewhat meaningless yet grand creations." But, after the event 9/11, the media, including *The New York Times*, suggested that those sections of reports of events as current affairs and the events of outside world that had been closed since some time be reopened.

America had believed that now the technology-created new economy would always be on a rising graph. But, the burst of the bubble of dotcoms in 2000 crushed this belief. Due to their prosperity and stable high economic position, the Americans believed that it is not important to note who runs the government and who is the President of the USA; there is no need to worry about the public services; they have the power to keep at bay any attack on its own borders, and so on. However, this last was the greatest bubble, and it burst on 9/11.

Now, the Americans have begun to take greater interest in understanding what is government, public service sector and politics. In addition, they have also begun to take greater interest in foreign policy. Its government is now very active in foreign policy, in keeping an open mind about the response of the other nations about the situations in the international field.

The people of America have come together as never before since the Second World War. This is no traditional and well-known type of war. Now, any state could be hostile, or any group or force that may not be in a form of a state. America will have to be on the look out for any roots of rage or contempt that such state or force has against it. Professor

Johnson observes, "We may like it or we may not, but the broad and outside currents do affect us. Not only that, these currents will play a role in changing our lives too."

Vikram Chandra, the News Editor of NBC says, "In the last three years a quiet revolution is taking place in the foreign policy of India. For 21st century, the Indian government security experts and most of the media persons have accepted that it was necessary that the relations of India with America become very close in 21st century—and may develop into even strategic partnerships. But, since 9/11, America has accepted Pakistan as its important ally in the fight against terrorism. After this and especially after the attack on the Indian Parliament by suicidal Islamic forces, the relations between the two was strained." India considers America as a partner in its opposition to terrorism. But it was not ready to accept this before.

When thousands of trained Islamic terrorists commit heinous crimes by their covert entry into Indian territory and when America knows it well, how could anyone accept the selective approach of the US to fight terrorism by ignoring Pakistan's role? Even Benazir Bhutto, the former Prime Minister of Pakistan, has spoken of this activity in different manners in her speeches and to various media.

Paul Kelly's comments (*The Weekend Australian*, May 21, 2005) is relevant here: Of late, the dynamics of global change and the factor of a fast ascending China is transforming the US-India relations. The US state department underlined its purpose "to help India become a major world power in the 21st century." If the US has provided F-16 to Pakistan, it is offering a top-of-the-line version of F-16, hi-tech defence and space cooperation in terms of satellites and launch vehicles, patriot and arrow missiles and access to nuclear (civilian) technology. Such a "new, strategic partnership" between the US and India with its far-reaching implication for China, Asia and international order is "rare in the past 100 years that a US president has sent a signal of this dimension."

India

9/11 was a challenge and an opportunity as far as India was concerned. It was an audio-visual presentation for the world about the fearsome span of terrorism. It was a real and actual experience for America. India had several times made its presentations of real experiences of terrorist activities within its borders in Kashmir that were inspired and patronized by powers across the borders and the grave difficulties it was facing due to these activities. Since years such presentations were being made to the US in the past. But now, they do not have to be briefed about the problem of India any more. And now, if the awakened do not want to get up, it is a different tale altogether!!

Besides, both America and India have very different cultures from that of Islamic fundamentalism or of bin Laden. From the day of 9/11 itself the memory of the thesis of an inevitable clash of two civilizations as presented by Huntington came to mind. Both India and America are sub-continental in geological dimensions and countries of multi-cultural societies. In terms of modernism, secular thinking, pluralism, democratic practices and other such important standards both have common background/role. In comparison with the mono-cultural Muslim world, India is definitely nearer to America. Religion plays an unusually influential role in the Muslim society. When such cultural factors are better understood by America after 9/11 in reference to India and when both the societies would work in partnership in their war against terrorism, to that extent the problem faced by India will lighten. However, America has belittled this thinking and instead opted for support from Pakistan for geo-strategic steps in Afghanistan and as a nation patronizing Taliban; and so the questions of India, specially its own, have turned even more tricky and wily.

Taliban has not been totally uprooted from Afghanistan, but rendered powerless; and after this also bin Laden and other similar elements have reportedly escaped into Pakistan. This has made it necessary for US to create political stability in Afghanistan and only then the projected oil interests and pipeline in Central Asia through the territories of Afghanistan-Pakistan can also be protected. America thus also needs to have airports and military bases and other facilities in this area for related activities. To protect its long-term interests, therefore, America will look after the interests of Pakistan. So, India also must turn practical and understand the policies of Pakistan as well as America in forming its own foreign policies.

UNO

Sometime ago, the importance attached to the role of UNO as the organization that maintained world peace and could mend the bloody international conflicts had touched a new low. This world institution was greatly devalued at this point of time. The 'detente' period saw that for tackling the tensions between America and Russia since 1962 the two nations neglected the UNO and made their own arrangements. However, this time, the Bush administration has declared that this world organization would play a leading role in the process of reshaping the post-Taliban Afghanistan. It also wants its services to some extent in the matter of Iraq.

The New Chemistry

The 'new chemistry' has also brought about some positive changes in the relations of nations in their foreign policy matters.

- Before 9/11 the relations of America and Russia were frozen. But President Putin, taking a great risk and responsibility, instead of showing happiness or indifference at the time of America's unprecedented crisis, at once raised his hand in friendship and cooperation. When in Texas both the Presidents parted from their meeting, both embraced each other with an open mind, determined against Islamic fundamentalism; and after talks, there was even a 'personal chemistry' between the two world leaders that was highlighted by the media too. Russia took steps against Taliban and gave the facility to America for conducting military maneuvers on its own land. Thus, Russia was 'reconnected' to America as well as the other nations of the western world. Russia hopes to get as a result a large investment from the US in its industries besides technological aid. This has already begun in the Christmas of 2001. As a result of all this, America was also able to establish relations that were absolutely and immediately needed with states of Uzbekistan and Tajikistan situated at the south of Russia (and it had been impossible for centuries for America to visit or contact these states before this altogether). In December that year, Putin had not accepted the one-sided step of the US of nuclear test, yet the new relations with it have not turned bitter yet. The US-Russia relations, however, soured after Beslan school siege and massacre by Chechen rebels (September 2004) when media and a section of US establishment sought to link the insurgents' terrorism with Russia's hard-handed policy towards Chechen's struggle for independence.

- Even China has accepted, with certain limits, the war in Asia under the guidance of America. A few months ago President Bush had declared China to be a 'strategic rival'. Due to the status of Taiwan and intelligence planes, the relations of China and US are fairly tense. Then, how did China take this stand? One, China is getting frustrated by the separatist movement in its western border province of Zinkiang that is being conducted under the leadership if Tajik and Turkmen Muslims inspired by Muslim fundamentalists like Taliban. Second, the increasing friendship of Russia with America also alarmed China that it will be left behind. However, China is aiming to remain the only power in Asia, and so adopting the policy of not allowing any other power to rise. So, even after the terrorist attack on the Indian Parliament on December 13, China has given 47 most modern fighter planes to Pakistan and has not failed to declare that it would provide considerable monetary assistance to its Ministry of Kashmir Affairs. This step is also suggestive.

- Nearly similar to the establishment of relations with Uzbekistan and Tajikistan, another unprecedented event has also taken place regarding the dramatic relations with Pakistan too. During Cold War and as a partner in its strategy of bringing the Taliban in power in Afghanistan, the US was quite dissatisfied with Pakistan in the last decade. Pakistan had become a problem in itself also due to the atomic bomb test, misadventure of Kargil and the military coup (1999) by Musharraf that ended the democratic government, and such other causes. In addition, patronage and encouragement extended by Musharraf to the Kashmir-focused extremists within India also had become a headache for the US. Pakistan continued to lend support to Taliban and this also angered the US. However, Collin Powell gave an open threat to Pakistan that if in its campaign for arresting bin Laden and in the strategy for removing Taliban Pakistan does not extend any cooperation, then America will have no alternative but to bomb out all the terrorist camps within Pakistan. To relieve its bankrupt government from great embarrassment, Musharraf asked for a large monetary assistance and uplifting of sanctions against it for this change and thus indicated a great political wisdom. Being in the inevitable pressure of the godfather of Taliban, its godmother agreed to leave nurturing of their child and provided an excellent example of merciless political games powers can play. In any case, "Pakistan, it seemed, had discovered itself anew". Only time can tell as to who was playing with whom in this game, and who would be gaining from whom. Today, at least, we find the two as partners for each other. Powell considers Pakistan as 'a valuable ally' in the war against terrorism.

  And, the old and permanent friendly relations of nations

have acquired new heights. The British Prime Minister Tony Blair has turned into an active partner for Washington DC. Acting as if he was another Powell, he has been active in the campaigns against terrorism in the countries representative of America, such as the Middle East, India, and Pakistan. In post-Taliban Kabul, his army and political presence is of primary significance. France has also remained a great supporter of British stance. Not only this. Even where peace ideology is strongly prevalent after the experiences of the Second World War, such as Germany and Japan, we find that they sent their token military units to indicate support.

- In countries like Indonesia, the Philippines, Malaysia, Africa and Latin America too the policy against terrorism has given place of priority. Mexican President Vincent Fox had been proposing that the security and checking arrangements on the southern borders of the US and Mexico must be lightened, and before 9/11 it was acceptable to Bush. But after 9/11 closing it is a precautionary step against intrusion of terrorists into the US, and so the great dream of an open border remains just that.

  In the new context the cooperation among those nations has increased that are potential victims of Islamic fundamentalism. Having very dissimilar government structures, national interests and even paradigms, in nations like America, Russia, India, China and of Western Europe, we find cooperation, in view of their experiences and vision of terrorism, on an unprecedented canvass.

  The major question of the year 2000 is how far and how long would the America-inspired war against terrorism spread out from Afghanistan? According to the scholars of this field, the states that nourish terrorism, such as Yemen, Sudan, Iraq, Libya, Syria, Iran, Somalia, etc., may become the new probable targets. This suggests that such 'rogue' nations must be brought to book is the current point of pressure raised by the war hawks. Among these suggestions the of war against Iraq is the loudest and most controversial. If Iraq is attacked, the Arab allies would be upset, anti-America/Britain demonstrations could be expected from the Islamic world and the problem between Israel and Palestine would be aggravated. Besides, in such global anti-terrorism war, would the role of Pakistan and the terrorism in Kashmir be included? Or, would the grave problem of terrorism in Palestine and Kashmir be tackled at a different plane? An estimate of CIA shows that the studies in these fields indicate that in 60 percent of such nations terrorist organizations like al Qaeda flourish. As these are scattered and the terrorist events that continue to occur time and again if locally, they will continue to harass local governments for a long time to come. However, if and when time comes, by getting monetary power and technology, such organizations may get into a network too. What then? President Bush has said that this war will go on indefinitely. In this context, we can glimpse the scenario of future.

- As the American journalist of NBC News Bureau at Pakistan, Farah Ispahani says, "At first the army and the Islamic *jehadis* used to work together for 'liberating Kashmir', but after giving up support to the Taliban, Musharraf has chosen another method." Then, he adds cautiously, "Perhaps he has had a change of heart. But has the Pakistan Army had a change of heart too?" No indeed.

Jasjit Singh believes that the most possible scenario is that the units of al Qaeda in Afghanistan/Pakistan will slip into 'Azad' Kashmir through its mountainous borders of northwest, and then going further it might cross the LoC to continue its activities of *jehad*. If we recall the work of ISI, then, we can see that under other names but with same purposes the *jehadi* terrorist activities will continue. Truly speaking, without reforming ISI and the army, terrorism cannot be eliminated from this area at all.

No person in power in Pakistan has ever used such a harsh language against the extremist religious activities, misuse of religious issues, communal violence and terrorism in his own state; or has anyone begun to take strict steps against such elements as Musharraf has.

Yet the fundamentalist forces have not been able to create too much trouble for the governing circles nor incite serious disruptive disturbances. However, the international Gallop Poll (February 2002) indicates that a large majority of the Pakistani people consider America as impudent and invasive. This dislike extends to the policy of Musharraf towards America too.

Activity like Taliban has now turned unprofitable for Pakistan politically, and one can easily say that Musharraf has put a timely break on Pakistan's Talibanization.

From the point of view of India thus, Musharraf has clearly declared in his policy statement that radical and armed *jehad* is not acceptable for Pakistan. The policy of taking strict steps to curb terrorism within Pakistan and also outside is an important and progressive turning point. Musharraf has differentiated for the first time between religious radicalism and *jehad*, and also between terrorism and *jehad*. But, simultaneously, his clear statement is that the *jehad* being conducted in Kashmir at present or in future will have his support. So, this statement is a challenge for India on this important issue. Of course, if the *jehadi* terrorist activities will be stopped in Pakistan, it is likely that the terrorism across the borders also will weaken.

As it is, the history of Pakistani governments is a history of braking the terms agreed by the UNO resolution or of bilateral treaties with India. That is why, if Musharraf can declare very clearly and before the international public that the tool of terrorism as a state policy will not be used at all, then only he can hope to begin a new atmosphere of trust needed for a reliable friendship with India.

If Pakistan stops attempts to find military solution to the Kashmir question, it should also mean that it would also not resort at the lower level measures like proxy war where armed conflicts of an undeclared war have already taken lives of thousands of people and it will honestly let go of any enmity towards India and policies based on that emotion. As Jasjit Singh comments, "As he speaks of unburdening of the past, Musharraf contradicts his own claim. He recommends that the Resolutions of the UNO be observed. Yet, he has not complied with the condition of removing Pakistan's armed forces from the PoK that lies to the north of LoC either then or when he wants to go for public opinion in his country." After the Security Council's resolution of September 2002 Pakistan has not been able to play the ball that has been thrown in its court. Singh says, "It is likely that while insisting on the implementation of UNO Resolutions, Musharraf has not understood the implications of the same. He has used strong language for 'state-inspired' terrorism of India and the 'Indian Occupational Forces' in Kashmir. But this attitude is like reading history from a wrong angle altogether. This can hardly support the stand he takes about peaceful and meaningful negotiations on the matter" (*Indian Express*, January 15, 2002).

In this context, the statement of Richard Boucher, the spokesman of the State Department at Washington, made in response to the speech of Musharraf, acquires a new significance. It says, "The focus of America is to get the promises made by Musharraf fulfilled; to see that he (Musharraf) takes suitable steps against terrorists working from within and on behalf of Pakistan; and not on any other issues with regard to its future (such as modernizing Pakistan)." In mid-January Collin Powell was to make an important trip to South Asia. On the eve of this visit, he said that the (terrorist) attacks on India are a matter of grave danger and insult.

After intensive discussions with the heads of both the states by Powell himself his statement is very significant: "the statement (of January 12) by Musharraf is indeed praiseworthy, but its actual evaluation will depend on how it is implemented in reality; and whether this happens or not, it is for India to say it." This statement clarifies the stand of America in this matter, indicating political support for India.

In spite of this support declared by Powell for India, Musharraf has hedged and howled about 20 of terrorists like Dawood Ibrahim who are of Indian origin and are wanted in many criminal and terrorist activities in India, and has not yet deported any of them to India despite detailed information submitted (FBI-supported) and request made. Musharraf has not even given any response also to the 'Red Corner Note' given by Interpol to hand over at least 15 of these criminals.

As early as June 2001, Hawash, an al Qaeda member from Sudan, had stated during his interrogation at Tihar Jail that "the next target of al Qaeda is going to be India". The Northern Alliance Commander Hazrat Ali, who had forced al Qaeda to run from Tora Bora, said in the Christmas of 2001, "After Afghanistan the militants of al Qaeda have escaped to Kashmir." On the basis of the arrests made by Indian security agencies in the later part of the year 2001 we can say that "now the worst possible this has happened; and this is that the first ranking international terrorist organization has now turned its guns towards India". After an in-depth research, Sayantan Chakraborty has shown in *India Today*, under his article entitled appropriately as 'Enemy Within' that "nearly 125 al Qaeda terrorists are now hiding within Indian territory".

During one month after the terrorist attack on Indian Parliament on 13th December, the security agencies at Kashmir and New Delhi have arrested militants and terrorists and these have revealed the constant relations of Pakistan and al Qaeda. Thus, Tavleen Singh (*Newspaper Today*, Internet, December 27, 2001) says, "We can easily see the footprints of string pulling of terrorist forces. Now, Pakistan has to face the danger of 'non-friendly' states on its east-west borders. Therefore, the Pakistan army is guarding its eastern as well as western borders. For the refugees from Afghanistan Kashmir has turned into a safe hideout." The armies may be present on both the borders, but the underground army is present only on the eastern one. Besides, we cannot assume that such a 'hideout' will not turn into the factory of *jehadis* from unemployed militants.

Looking at all this, from advisors from K. Subramanyam to Jasjit Singh had appealed to India, from early January itself, not to withdraw its army stationed at the borders even when not advising extremist steps of conducting a direct war, and this has been proved good logic. Subramanyam had said, "The Indian mobilization is a part of the war against terrorism." Singh wrote in the *Indian Express* (January 10, 2002) that "when the armed forces are withdrawn from the borders, even then we should bring soldiers of some Divisions, say two or four, to Jammu and Kashmir, so that the Assembly elections of this state in summer are conducted properly."

Of course, All-Party Hurriyat Conference, looking for seceding from Indian state altogether, also wanted to contest these elections based on these standards and organization. If they did participate in the elections and performed well, the equations in the Kashmir valley would have changed drastically. And, in this scenario, India would have had to change its total policy towards states qualitatively. However, in 2003, India had given out indications for such a change, too, at least for Kashmir.

Attention of the whole world had been on these elections. Pakistan created an atmosphere of fear and insecurity among the people of Kashmir so that this election may not turn into fair and just as well as peaceful one. But, the voters came out in large numbers to vote, voted against the BJP forces and in favour of its local Peoples' Democratic Party and the Congress. The international observers also declared that the elections were conducted in fair and just manner. After nearly two-and-a-half decades Kashmir enjoyed such elections and the attitude of India won praise from all quarters. Sayyed Muhammad Mufti heads the mixed government, adopted a liberal policy towards the militants, and this has also received, on the whole, blessings of Indian government.

However, armed militants, encouraged by Pakistan, still continue to enter this troubled state. The violent activities of terrorists continue to be small or large in scale. In April 2003 Indian Prime Minister Vajpayee has taken a bold and unusual initiative during his visit to Kashmir and declared the intention of beginning negotiation—a most amazing initiative in Indian diplomatic history. Pakistan has welcomed this move warmly. However, for both the sides, the issue of Kashmir and the acceptance of LoC are still as complex as ever. Under the changed scenario, what would be the role of US? Will both the neighbors be able to adopt a farsighted policy?

The US also suffered setback on other fronts in Europe where in the beginning of the war on terrorism, it had reaped the cooperation of its Atlantic allies. Its war on Iraq in March 2003 created a visible—rather bitter—rift with trans-Atlantic allies like France and Germany. Its unilateral approach and theory of pre-emptive war had few takers among its one-time global partners. As Victor Bulmer-Thomas, Director of Chatham House, an independent think tank in London observed, on the eve of the UN meeting in September 2004, Bush's UN agenda—multinational protection force for UN officials in Baghdad, faster training for Iraqi troops to replace much hated foreign troops and forgiveness for Iraqi debt—is stalled. The European Union's External Relations Commissioner, Christopher Patton said in a withering critique in Brussels, "Is the world today safer than before the overthrow of the appalling Saddam?" Patten asked in the European Parliament last week, "Is global terrorism in retreat? Are we closer to building bridges between Islam and the west? Is the world's only superpower more widely respected? Have the citizens in our democracies been treated in a way that will encourage them to give governments the benefit of the doubt next time they are told that force needs to be used pre-emptively to deal with an imminent threat? I simply pose the questions. The answers are well known."

14

Towards a New World Order

The future of global terrorism lies in the West. The Arab nations have been able to contain, normally, terrorism in their countries and divert the terrorist organizations towards Middle East, such as Bosnia, Albania, Chechnya, and Kosovo, etc., where the Christians and Muslims fought each other.

The more important point, however, is that in the infrastructure of terrorism has taken deep roots among the Muslims of western societies.

This infrastructure has been readied with subtle-expertise and that too in legal manner. All types of institutions and legal charity funds etc. cleverly manipulated strings to reach monetary funds to the terrorists. These people made the use of the liberalism and freedoms of the west to continue their own activities. Until now, the western nations were not sufficiently informed about such anarchical activities; but now that more than 800 persons have been caught in America and Europe who were engaged in such activities, one can realize how huge that network actually must be!

And, the hijackers of 9/11 were not poor by any means. They could have earned much by working as pilots. But they walked a

> path for their 'Mission' that could never be understood by the Western mindset.
>
> — **Dr. Reuben Paz** (Director, International Policy Institute for Counter-Terrorism, Israel)

After 9/11 the foundation for the new world order has been laid. Significantly, all the big powers are now welcoming inevitable changes in bilateral and international relations in the field of politics. The reason for this is not far to seek. Terrorism is a widespread phenomenon, and there are no precautions that can work in time against it. That is why, the global battle against it can be fought only by the means of interdependence.

Let us take the example of India. In the first week of February 2002, that is, within one week, talks began in India on one hand with Russia and with America on the other for bilateral military agreements. These were not merely for defensive purposes, but the fact that political relations flowed simultaneously on such matters was significant. These had been uncharacteristic of such international contacts during the Second World War or Cold War, and there is no pattern of currents and counter-currents now; for we find here that these trends somehow touch each other at some points or even together make a greater trend.

The Deputy Prime Minister of Russia signed a new Security Protocol in New Delhi that will aim to develop futuristic defense system. Now, India will be supplied new Russian nuclear submarines and long-range bombers and weapons of higher technological level, and also impart knowledge about atomic energy to India.

Forgetting the tension after Pokhran II atomic tests made by India, America has signed agreements with India about army-to-army high-level exchange of military expertise and cooperation. This will extend to latest and most sophisticated and complex technological cooperation too. The American Army Chief General Myers visited New Delhi in February. He declared his country's willingness to make agreements about naval and air power development. He also added that America has agreed to provide India with electronic and satellite equipments to detect intrusion of terrorists in borders of Kashmir and other such methods being used by them to terrorize the state. Post-9/11, when the American fleet needs any assistance in the Arabian Sea, Indian Navy provides it, whereas during the reign of Indira Gandhi as Prime Minister, when American fleet made a naval post at Diego Garcia and began its movement, India protested to America about a possible naval threat to India.

Thirdly, two other new policy attitudes have taken shape during this period. One, President Bush in his 'State of the Union' speech declared that America would from now on work with India, China and Russia "in a very different way from the past" in the matter of terrorism. It was impossible to think of such policy lines during Cold War days. In those days, America vs. Russia, an understanding in context of Russia between America and China (since 1971); overall cold relations between India and America; close relations between India and Russia; lack of trust between India and China—such equations had been seen. Then, it was Russia that suggested that tri-country friendly relations develop among Russia, America and India. (This reminds us of the earlier Russian 'Primikov formula'). China and Russia are highly sensitive to the idea or indications of America becoming more influential in the Middle East, for they consider it as their field of influence. In this context, again, the alliance known as Shanghai Connection has been clearly marked. Its members are China, Russia, and some originally states of erstwhile USSR, viz., Uzbekistan, Turkmenistan, Kyrgyzstan, etc. Their international agenda includes actions to limit the interventions of America in economic matters such as oil, and its influence on this field besides containing the separatist and terrorist activities of their nations too. Such 'oval alliance' from Beijing to Moscow has not been seen before this. As 'axis of evils', America aims to next deal with Iran, Iraq and North Korea as possible targets.

On the other hand, such an organization is not a political or military alliance against America. For, there are bilateral friendly relations of India, China and Russia with America in any case.

A remarkable point in this context is that China has behaved with good sense with regard to the question of terrorism. In 1971, during India-Pakistan war, China had adopted a threatening posture against India (accusing India of having driven away hundreds of goats and sheep of China that roamed Tibetan lands, and issuing an ultimatum about this imaginary 'crime' of India, demanding that these be returned or else...). But, in 2002, when 5,00,000 Indian soldiers were guarding Indo-Pakistan borders, the Chinese Premier Rong Zi made an official visit to New Delhi and concluded a treaty of cooperation and friendship. Moving closer, India and China have signed an agreement on substantive matters like border dispute and trade during Prime Minister Wen's New Delhi visit in April 2005.

On the other hand, China has also continued gestures to confirm and support the notion that it has a special friendship with Pakistan as well. In the winter of 2002 Musharraf visited Beijing twice in two weeks. China gave 46 latest bomber fighter aircrafts. Also, there is a treaty for increasing military cooperation between the two nations. All these points also have to be noted in this context.

China has extended help to America in its recent so-called war against terrorism. In the western parts of China, in the province of Sinkiang, the areas bordering the Muslim countries such as Turkmenistan, Kirgizstan etc., Islamic fundamentalism was on rise. The separatist movements and rebellions against the central government of China have been suppressed by Beijing with a strong hand. Even then, the fear of this fundamentalism made China support on the whole the new US Afghan policy and ignored the indication of displeasure on this issue by Pakistan. On the other hand, its economic, military and strategic help to Pakistan indirectly intensifies the problems for India, and has its own interest in it. In the triangle of Pakistan-China-India, the first two sides may seem to be different, yet are together. Although it must also be noted that China has avoided giving open encouragement to Pakistan against India. Also, China has supported the international opinion that India and Pakistan must undertake negotiations. President Bush visited Beijing in the last week of February and even at that time the Chinese President had indicated preference for negotiations by the neighbors—a suggestion that was music to ears of Musharraf. About the role of China the senior fellow of Council of Foreign Relations, in an interview to CNN, Elizabeth Economy says, "I do not think China wants to wage a war against India on this matter, for I believe that it cannot afford one. In fact, China persuades Pakistan to keep itself under control." Robert Hathaway, an analyst, believes that "China is behaving in a very balanced manner (in this issue)". However, in a recent book, named *Seeds of Fire*, the author gives examples of China's double talk and cunningness by citing examples and warns India and America to be wary of China. He also recommends that they should not judge China from its short-term behavior and think that it has forgotten its long-term objectives against these powers. Both the democracies must remain constantly vigilant and alert on this issue and still may welcome the positive role of China on this issue for its cooperative world order and it may achieve the purpose of a new international political scenario.

By giving up the old traditional enmity and politics of old principles of 'one against other' or 'an enemy of enemy is a friend' and by joining at once with America on the issue of war against terrorism, China and Russia have encouraged the addition of new positive trends and a 'paradigm shift' in international relations. But, there are also some complex elements as well. For example, when the Under Secretary of America made a statement as to whether micro-electronics equipments be given to China or not, he also stated that they are checking out the possibility of 'a probable strategic danger' from China to

America in the next decade. At the same time, a stage has been set for a policy, upgrading military relations with India. Years ago, America had backed out of the understanding with India for supplying Light Combat Aircraft (LCA)—a very important fighter aircraft project. But, today, they have extended their hand in friendship once again. Collin Powell, disregarding the pressures to make Pakistan recall its border forces by de-escalation, declared that "only India can decide whether it is satisfied by the call of Musharraf (of January 12)". Demobilization can be undertaken or even thought about only after the border and Kashmir are no longer made forced entry points of militants and terrorists. Besides, America also found the movement of Indian Navy in the Arabian Sea as a good move. The kidnapping and then the murder of a journalist like Daniel Pearl was not well investigated and Musharraf could not come up with any satisfying answers about whether any ISI or fundamentalist elements of Pakistani army had committed these crimes. He may be playing a double game here. This point was discussed in American mainstream media openly and even some officers of the Bush administration also have aired their suspicion. Thus, the context has now come into existence when the triangular relations of India, America and Pakistan must come under closer scrutiny. In addition, bin Laden or his associates may have escaped to Pakistan from Afghanistan and taken refuge in fundamentalist camps, according to some of the doubts raised in Washington in the second week of February. Thus, the search for bin Laden and the hiding of terrorists in Kashmir, who can again resume activities, has made the war against terrorism enter yet another stage. That is why, America has to see to it that Pakistan really, honestly and effectively plays the role it claims for itself. India also will have to be very alert and watchful of the developments of this second stage of the war for they touch its own borders too.

Russia

The greatest and picturesque changes in the 'paradigm shift' of international relations after 9/11 can be seen in the example of the relations between America and Russia. When the smoke from WTC towers was flowing towards Brooklyn, at that time, the Russian President Vladimir Putin immediately contacted the American President George Bush on hotline. This hotline had begun during Kennedy-Krushchev period to let the other power know if any atomic missile was launched by mistake. But this was the first time when it was used for a friendly purpose. Putin at once condemned the terrorist attack and expressed Russian people's sympathy for the victims. He also promised President Bush to lend Russian support to any steps the American government may decide to take in the matter. If America were troubled like this in earlier times, Russia would have been secretly joyful!

Putin, who had earlier headed the dangerous intelligence agency of Russia, KGB, had however, extended this friendly gesture. For many Russians this America-inspired agreement against terrorism was indicative of great inclination towards liberalism in political matters; but due to it, Russia was to gain a great deal on the whole.

In spite of running to the western camp, Russia has not been given a primary seat in the bus of NATO (not made a full member). Even then trends are seen that could not have been imagined earlier. American army units were placed in the backyard of Russia. The American warplanes brought military equipments for the Northern Alliance forces via Uzbekistan and Tajikistan. After some sharp displeasure Putin is believed to have given out signs for acceptance of friendship of Georgia and America. It is the same Russia whose great influential political presence in Afghanistan (1979-89) was eliminated by America through massive help to Taliban forces to uproot successfully with Pakistan as its front. Now, they had joined hands in the objective of the removal of Taliban that was patronizing terrorism under the inspiration of bin Laden from Afghanistan.

Putin met Bush in the latter's Texas ranch and their 'personal chemistry' was said to have 'matched' too. That the President Bush found in Putin a great friend was a statement that was more suggestive than the common declaration made by the two powers after a summit meeting even.

For decades the contempt, dislike and indifference of the American people had felt for Russia were now replaced by the praise for Putin and Russia in the media. The fruits are for the Russians to taste. Unlike his predecessor Yeltsin, Putin did not thrust his begging bowl for money, and yet as the journalist, an expert of Russian studies, rightly observes in 'Mercury News' that "he will stop a bullet even for us".

That one day, by merely one phone call, Putin achieved what the bear-hug of Yeltsin had not achieved, and received more than ever from America. "We want to become their friends", the secret information sources of White House said, and that is what actually happened.

Today, the Taliban who was considered by Russia as the most dangerous force against it after the separatist tendencies of Chechnya, has now lost its power foothold in Afghanistan. The American dollar mostly paid the expenses for this in the attack on Afghanistan, jointly undertaken with its allies, and the blood that flowed was Afghan. Also, the fear in Russia that Islamic extremism will enter its southern borders any time has subsided with the defeat of Taliban. Besides this, the separatist camps of Russia operated by Chechen terrorists also must have been destroyed in the warring actions taken.

Now, the owners of oil companies, who have good relations with the powerful persons in Russia, may hope to turn into global/international level entrepreneurs in this field. For sometime now the western countries including America are already feeling a sense of relief that they are no longer helplessly dependent on the Middle East. In the latter half of 2001 the OPEC the oil producing nations thought of reducing the production of oil, then Russia, had remained away from it. As a result, the production of oil had continued as before and so the prices had not increased. By such gesture of friendship Putin had won the goodwill of the superpowers and great oil companies that could have suffered from the effects of oil shortage. This indicates the significance attached to the geopolitics and geo-economics of the Middle East. America is interested in the oil production of Turkmenistan and Uzbekistan and Russia also join in; and for the constant supply of oil by pipelines the stability in the political sphere and security for them in the area of Afghanistan, Pakistan will draw great interest for them. Thus, the geopolitics along with geo-economics has acquired a new significance. It would seem that from Pakistan to Russia a new political economics would take shape as American security circuit.

From the viewpoint of Putin, the greatest advantage would be that America would give him greater space to deal with its own border areas. Earlier, when Chechnya was agitating against Russia for secession, America supported it as a movement for right of self-decision by a people and both criticized the policy of bombing that Russia resorted to for curbing that movement. Now, after 9/11, such criticism is not being heard. (Indeed, this also indicates the absence of ethics in its own stand, and once again exposes its true character of being absolutely self-centered!). In December 2001, Russia sealed the semi-independent styled television centers, and at that time the American media had forgotten to sing the song of protest for freedom of speech, expression and so on.

To silence the opposition elements and increase social obedience Putin took strict measures; he even made out the order to train the students of 11th standard for compulsory military training and thereby once again aiming for militarization of Russian society; but the topmost nation of the free world has preferred to keep silent on the topic. The 'Duma' of the period of Gorbachov-Yeltsin also seems to have turned into an obedient body. "On the whole, the steps of Putin indicate that he is keen to take actions and turn Russia into a modern and economically lively state. Of course, it will not be a copy of the western model altogether."

These Russians now will increase trade and commerce with the West and their leaders and rich men will not spend their vacations in the beautiful Pyongyang (North Korea) but in the comfortable resorts of the West. Whatever was aimed for by his predecessors and were not able to achieve, Putin may be perhaps able to do soon. He has created a bridge for Russia with western wealth and technology. And, this he has done without losing much of the freedom and prestige of Russia. 'Advantage of 9/11' indeed!

Japan

The hijackers who destroyed WTC towers and attacked Pentagon also brought to an end the 50 years old policy of peace by Japan. The shock of 9/11 has brought a total qualitative change in the Japanese policy.

In the Second World War the murderous marches that it had undertaken in the mad excitement of illusive pride of strength it felt within it, Japan had now totally abandoned as a reaction to it of any policy of war or military forces. But, as Daniel Snyder notes, "Now, we can feel as if there is a revolutionary change in the thinking of Japan...In the last half century when America was involved in three big and some dozen of smaller wars, its political ally Japan had not sent a single soldier to fight in these war zones."

But, after 9/11, with unusual speed, the Japanese government, for the first time since the Second World War, passed a law by which Japan could send its army in a war zone outside its borders with the approval. By October, six of Japanese warships were taking rounds in the Arabian Sea. Touching the Indian coasts, these supplied the American ships with oil, relief goods to Pakistan, and carries American soldiers from Guam to Diego Garcia base. A decade ago, at the time of Gulf war against Iraq, Japan did not send even one soldier to assist America that had provided it with a military security for the last five decades (but it did provide funds to the tune of billions of yens). Quietly bearing with the criticism of other allied nations for this, it would seem that Japan is now turning into a 'normal' country. It has begun to believe in military preparedness. There have been observations that due to this change, the balance of power in Asia may change too and the relations between Tokyo and America may turn stronger.

Japan was afraid not only of the terrorists that had attacked its powerful protector nation, it also feared that they themselves might become a victim of such an attack, as they witnessed the event on the night of 11th September at 10.48 hours (the two nations have a time difference of 14 hours).

Their officer in foreign department, Norio Hakhori admitted, “Earlier when these things happened, we felt them so far away from Japan, but now times have changed. Japan has come to realize that the earth has become so global, so small that such a danger seems to have arrived right in our neighborhood!” Talks of making constitutional changes in this context have already begun there. A Terrorist Act has already been passed by its Diet (Parliament). Japan does not want to turn into a military nation again, but steps in the direction of better military preparedness have begun there. America also wishes to promote such a trend. Against North Korea and suspicious about the increasing strength of China, America would be interested to see its colleague in Pacific region turn into a military power. A Diet member Suto states a reality when he says, “We have not crossed the Rubicon river (in a decisive manner), but we have had to jump over it. And now, there is no going back for us.”

Important nations like America, China, Russia, India, England and Japan are carving out, after 9/11, a new cooperative multi-sided shape and structure in their relationships. At this time, there are two parallel cooperative relationships that are taking shape within this structure. These are, on one hand, the Pakistan-China relations, and on the other hand, the India-Israel relations.

India-Israel Friendship

When Pakistan’s President Musharraf visited Beijing twice in the second week of December and the early weeks of 2002, during that period, from Israel a high-level body of representatives visited New Delhi. In 1992, the relations were established between India and Israel. After a decade, this relationship had touched new heights of friendship in a number of fields. There were a number of visits exchanged by important high officials and military officers of both the governments. These visits were not only successful but also fruitful for both Tel Aviv and New Delhi. Especially, in the defense matters, the relations of the two governments have prospered. After Russia, Israel has become the second allied nation to supply military equipments to India, and this speaks a lot on this issue.

The leaders of both these nations have to deal with similar type of (terrorist) dangers, it has been declared. Arriving in January for a visit to New Delhi the Israeli Defense Minister Shimon Peres has promised to extend all types of help to India fight its war against terrorism. At the end of his visit, Peres said, "Israel and India have sought mutual support for exchanging secret information and security matters, for both have a common enemy, i.e., terrorism."

Israel has concluded a treaty with India to supply the latter with three Falcon systems that can catch the enemy planes and missiles to give timely warnings, and the price is one billion dollars. Earlier, Israel had an agreement with China for the sale of the Falcon system but since America did not approve of the deal this agreement was not signed and sealed. China had turned angry at Israel for going back on its word, and had asked for compensation from Israel.

After 9/11 Israel has become active to find new markets for its weapons in America and India. Giving this information Tehelka.com says that on the whole the quality of Israel weapons are considered best in the world. America's great need for airport security equipments also is to be supplied by Israel. Pakistan criticized as 'strategic' the growing relationship of India and Israel. At the international conference regarding missiles that met at Paris in February, the Pakistan representatives aired the concern that Israel is going to sell India anti-ballistic systems like Falcon and Aero. To protest against such a possibility they argued that it would threaten the stability in South Asia. Tehelka.com quotes the Hebrew daily *Mariv*: In this conference a senior official of Pakistan had told a high official of Israel, "Do not get entangled in our (South Asia) region. Otherwise, we'll have to do something similar in your region." In defense, India has adopted a milestone policy that is easy to see. There has been a deal with India's private jeep company, i.e., Mahindra's, to equip the motor vehicle with technology of Israel that can sense and detect humans, animals, weapons and other vehicles by the temperature of their blood and laser beams and convey information of the same for its place or movement in air or land at day or night in all seasons. The deal is between the two governments and to be used for military purposes. Thus, a new pragmatic approach of joining hands with private enterprise in the sector of defense is suggestively new step from India.

Concern over Unilateralist America

On the other hand, in managing the world's small or big events or trends, America must not turn unilateral has become a sensitive issue for certain big nations. For example, in the International Security Conference at Munich, the defense ministers and foreign ministers of Germany, Russia and China clearly expressed their concern about the war against terrorism that was being fought under the leadership/guidance of the US (against Iraq, Iran, etc.) and which is expanding it based on its own policy. Similarly, known as Shanghai Group, the nations like Russia, China, and members of erstwhile USSR like Turkmenistan and Kyrgyzstan, etc., have made up a joint strategy against America's increasing presence in the Middle East. Similarly, Russia and even the colleague of America itself, i.e., European Union have criticized the policy of Bush administration to attack Saddam Hussein in Iraq after Afghanistan, declaring them to be 'axis of evils' and take the steps against them by itself. Turkey, the most modern and West-oriented

Islamic nation, has also expressed concern and caution against such a possible policy of America. Again, in the Munich Conference, the then Deputy Defense Secretary Wolfowitz had said that if in future America does not seek a mandate from UNO to take steps against any nation that harbors terrorists, it can march on alone. At that time too Germany, Russia and China insisted on first getting a mandate from UNO. This attitude became solid during the war against Iraq.

Thus, China keeps Pakistan under its wing in the context of India, but after 9/11 Pakistan handed over to America two air bases and other help for land strategies. This has displeased China and it thought to put into cold storage the Gwader Project that has military significance for Pakistan. However, China continues to complete buildup of Gwader at the earliest. In fact, the Beijing leaders have begun to suspect that with the help of atomic technology they have provided to Pakistan might render negative results instead. America also would like to see, and do everything to see the Chinese influence lessen in Pakistan and make the latter a moderate and soft nation. Yet forces like bin Laden and al Qaeda seem to continue their underground activities in Pakistan, as can be seen in the events related to Aftab Ansari and Ahmed Omar Sayyid Sheikh and also in the murder of Daniel Pearl. That is another reason why America would like its presence strengthened within Pakistan. All the important nations have become now more alert to receive the waves off the antenna of South Asia.

Thus, within a very short period, such vast changes have occurred in the international scenario. Some of these may look like currents and anti-currents that seem to contradict each other. However, most of these are complementary or cooperative working for each other. For example, nobody looks at the relations of India with another nation in terms of a bipolar politics. For the first time India is continuing the proven friendship with Russia. America too is giving high priority to relations with it in not only economic but also in political and military fields. When America aids Pakistan in economic and military matters, India does not raise the protest to the level of earlier times. If India has to emerge as a world player rather than a player only in context of regional context of South Asia, it has to learn keenly the new political and diplomatic imperatives and trends. One symbolic and yet a very significant example is this: Israel has provided India (ignoring the protest of Pakistan to America) with the Falcon AWACS system, developed by American technology, and that from the Russian platform.

Now, as in the age of 1945-1991, Russia had no opponent to compete with in the technological field or to face an equal power, America is the only great atomic and missile power in the world. The contemporary geo-political context also makes America the one and only superpower, thus giving it the capacity to turn into a unilateral decision-maker. However, it does indulge in this type of unilateral behavior, it would only undermine if not defeat the very system of democracy that it prides itself as the greatest champion in the world. Therefore, to combat the threat of terrorism, America must take help from its friends in the European Union and in addition also from other nations like Russia, India, China and Japan. The revolutionary and new healthy trends that are seen in the international security paradigm give out only this message.

Viewed in overall perspective at global level, three significant developments seem to be shaping the new world order:

1. 11/9: The fall of the Berlin Wall, in November 1989, brought freedom and entrepreneurship to East Germany and eventually to scores of other countries; "the advent of Microsoft's Windows 3.0 software six months later unleashed the PC revolution and digitization of content. Together, the events empowered the people (including, ironically, the terrorists networks globally) around the world."
2. "From the primordial swamps of globalization have emerged two genetic variants—one is al Qaeda and the other is companies like Infosys (India) or Jet Blue (USA). Our focus, therefore, has to be how we can encourage

more of good mutations and keep out of the bad." (Infosys CEO Nandan Nilekani). Adds, Friedman, "I could not agree more. Indeed, that effort may be the most important thing to learn to do in order to keep the planet in one piece."

3. "People who are connected to the world and exposed to different cultures and perspectives are far more likely to develop the imaginative of 11/9 (fall of Berlin Wall). People (like Islamist fundamentalists) who are feeling disconnected, for whom personal freedom and fulfillment are a Utopian fantasy, are more likely to develop the imagination of 9/11." (Thomas Friedman, *The World is Flat*, 2005)

VI

Theatres of Conflict

15

South Asia: Time Bomb in All Directions

9/11 has dramatically changed the world. After this, we looked the best nation in the world. Hijacking airplanes, making them crash into towering buildings, killing thousands of innocent citizens to take revenge of imagined injustices—this new young generation was not raised by India; nor has it prepared any youth that believe terrorism a respectable activity in the name of Allah, as Pakistan has done. In the next October also no frenzied crowds shouting angry slogans and showing pictures of bin Laden marched in India's towns and cities. In such a huge country, except for one incident, communal harmony was also intact. And, in fact, there was no communal incident in the last decade (since Ayodhya). But we were then merely in a land of fantasy.

The 'Godhra Massacre' and the violence that followed changed the scene. We were not given any idea about the culprits for the next whole month. Everyone is still in the dark as to why did the Godhra incident occur and who were behind it. However, the Chief Minister is not worried on this point anyway.

Indian media may pride itself for upholding the 'secular' tradition they also have not been able to go deeply in this incident of Godhra and to get the threads together. Then, isn't it a little strange for the 'investigative journalism' to come out

> with picking up details and contexts of murders of Muslims only? But in such matters journalists providing one-sided reports and the 'investigative groups' have really speaking a twisted sense of 'secularism'. Has it ever been clearly reported how the Babri Masjid Action Committee and similar organizations were as much responsible as the fundamentalist Hindus for breaking the Babri Masjid? We do not pay attention to fact that Islamic fundamentalism has nurtured fundamentalism of the Hindus as well! For us, neither is acceptable. We must become totally clear in this matter. Our rulers are indulging in activities that feed each other and share their prejudices and fanatic activities even! After understanding this context the citizens would have to adopt the right sense of equality for all religions.
>
> — **Tavleen Singh** (*India Today*)

In the present context, centers of conflicts of terrorism and violence of religio-ethnic variety that cause greatest concern are situated between the Mediterranean and the Bay of Bengal. If, in the wake such conflicts, the two vast and little developed regions of Asia, from Israel to Bangladesh and Sri Lanka, remain deprived of development, there will be a threat to world peace. These two regions are the Middle East (West Asia) and South Asia. The attention of the world has long been drawn by the extended war-like situation of Palestine-Israel and Iraq that has often enough created a crisis. Also, in South Asia, the communal conflicts, Maoist strategies, ethnocentric armed movements etc. are like a silent volcano, and cannot be ignored anymore. The 'fault-line' in their socio-religious and philosophical grounds is widening and the distances are increasing among Pakistan, India, Nepal, Bangladesh, and Sri Lanka. The balance among them is getting upset, and the likelihood of a man-made earthquake or widespread political instability is perceived. It needs to be studied well in time.

Muslims have to be considered as the largest community that lives in a very narrow and unsteady ethno-religious environment in the whole world. Three of the first four nations of the world with the largest Muslim population (India, Bangladesh and Pakistan) are located in South Asia. Of these, Pakistan and Bangladesh have a considerable orthodox as well as extremist Islamic population. The regime under the present lady President of Bangladesh is noted for harassing the Hindu minority. She forces them off to India by harassing them. Adopting a harsh policy at home since January 2002, Musharraf has been camouflaging behind words and some cosmetic changes, and nurturing armed Islamic forces and secessionist groups in Kashmir. For the first time in the history of South Asia, as reports go, since Christmas of 2001, as many as ten thousand soldiers equipped with war weapons were guarding the Indo-Pak borders. That is why, President Clinton and some noted strategic analysts of the world called it as 'the most explosive' or the 'most dangerous' zone in the world. Musharraf's meet with Manmohan Singh in new Delhi (mid-April, 2005) seems to have considerably diluted this explosive eventuality. The General himself has change the tone and tenor of his aggressive postures when he stated: "The post-9/11 transformation in the worldview has underlined that violence or terror cannot be the basis of dispute between nations." In their joint statement on April 18, both leaders have emphasized that terrorism cannot be allowed to hamper the peace process sincerely promoted by these neighbors in South Asia.

Nepal

But, in this region, the most heard and seen point of conflict was the small Himalayan kingdom of Nepal in a worrisome manner.

Nepal has sounded alarms for many events that threatened the security environment of India and South Asia: one, in 1999 under the ISI, the Pakistan intelligence agency, a passenger plane of Indian Airlines was hijacked and flown to Kandahar, and it was done from the base of Kathmandu; and second, since 2001, the Maoists have been able to set up very powerful centers of action in the mountainous region of the Terai in

Nepal. Since 1960, during the rule of King Mahendra, they had begun to demand removal of privileges of the rulers and granting of rights to the poor class of peasants. They also have considerable influence over some sections of the Magar and Gurung communities. It is significant that Maoist influence is spreading widely among the backward and poorer regions. After 1996, their influence has reached the peak point. Their workers seem to number anywhere between 5,000 and 10,000. They have either driven away the police and administrative officers of the Nepal government or made them ineffective in the western Nepal. They are collecting taxes and dispensing justice and other such functions to run parallel government there. Of the total 75 districts of Nepal, 20 are virtually run by them. This gives them an image of their armed power.

After 1996, till 2002, Maoist guerrillas have killed 1,600 persons and 700 policemen. And, they also blew up two towers of the airports of Nepal. These facts demonstrate of their prowess. Since mid-2002, the Nepalese government has adopted a tough attitude towards them. After November 2001, within five months, the Nepal government also got rid of 700 Maoist rebels. Indian help in arms is made available to it from time to time for this purpose. Thus, the revolutionary politics and civil wars continue to advànce. The Nepali Maoists have secretly forged their links with India's militant People's War Group (the most active armed rebels of Andhra Pradesh) and the Maoist Coordination Committee (Bihar) too, that help them strategise to carve out a zone of insurgency between Telagana to Nepal.

Maoists are in no mood to negotiate with the king, or the human right activists and even the various governments of Nepal. These trends in the neighborhood of Nepal may become threatening to India in the context of the intrigues of Pakistan and the forced intrusive policy of ISI agency. When it was revealed that the Health Minister of Nepal, a Muslim, had facilitated the hijacking of Indian Airlines plane to Kandahar, he had to resign. As it is, the Indian intelligence agencies have reported that the anti-India activities of ISI have begun to spread into Nepal and the nearby rural areas of Uttaranchal, as also in Bangladesh.

Secondly, the Maoist rebels of Nepal have found their strength, courage and what's more, the arms to make direct attacks on Nepalese soldiers, police, officials as well as citizens. The political influence of China in Kathmandu is on rise and the pro-Chinese forces are becoming increasingly powerful in Nepal. In March 2002, the Nepalese Prime Minister Sher Bahadur Deuba had come on an official visit to New Delhi and submitted a list of Maoists hiding within India. He informed the officials of South Block (Foreign Ministry and advisors to the Indian Prime Minister) that Bihar (where the poor farmers have become easy recruiting constituency of extremist Maoists) and the neighboring areas of Nepal with West Bengal have turned into 'launching pad' for the Nepalese Maoists (to operate in India).

After the hijacking of the passenger plane of Indian Airlines (by Masud Azhar) India had informed Nepal that the policy of open borders between the two nations that did not require any 'visa' to cross over from one country to another, is being misused by the ISI-inspired terrorists to enter India through Nepal. The former Indian ambassador to Nepal, Deb Mukherjee had told *India Abroad* (New York), "The Maoists are seeking clandestine refuge in India, and the concern about it in Nepal is not without a basis." Both the countries are now busy in building up a network for exchange of special police force and information. During the visit of Deuba, it was decided that the extradition procedure to deport to the place of his origin any criminal or traitor of either country be made more effective and purposeful. India has not agreed to the suggestion that it take up arms to fight the Maoists on the Nepalese land. However, keeping in mind that such extremists are a helpful conduit for China, India has accepted to provide better arms and training to the Nepalese army personnel.

On the other hand, in mid-April, the Koirala government had announced that until and unless the Maoists would return the weapons and hardware they robbed from government arm depots, no negotiations can take place with them. As the Maoists have not conceded to its condition, the government also declared its decision to drive them away from Nepal altogether. In the meantime, cooperation is on the rise between the two neighboring nations with Hindu majority regarding the security of the borders against operations by ISI and Maoist organizations, for its monitoring and management as well as care against any intrusions.

It is significant that Nepal is a Hindu kingdom, and the majority of Indians are Hindus. Pakistan, the traditional 'enemy' of India on one hand and China through strategically arming Pakistan on the other also want to increase their influence in Nepal. From this point of view also, India would naturally prefer that Nepal remains by its side for its national security. Four decades back, *The Times of India* editor-in-chief Girilal Jain, an expert of foreign relations, had written a book entitled *India Meets China in Nepal*. The title is relevant even today. Now, Pakistan also meets India in Nepal and in India's northeast and Assam through its ISI. Nepal is a buffer in the three-way street of Pakistan style terrorism, Chinese style communism and Indian style democratic system.

Sri Lanka

The civil war that has been on in the mountain area in Jaffna region of Sri Lanka is not the only problem for Sri Lanka. The civil war situation in Sri Lanka and its effects are also major concern for India. In the northeastern Jaffna region of Sri Lanka the secessionist organization of LTTE or Tamil Tigers has divided and terrorized this small island country since a long time now. India's Prime Minister Rajiv Gandhi had sent a peacekeeping force to help the Sri Lankan government. Thereafter, the LTTE, even before the Palestinians had tried it, used successfully the weapon of a suicide bombing for killing the young ex-Prime Minister of India in May 1991.

Earlier, India has often asked Sri Lankan government to handover Prabhakaran, the extremist leader of LTTE, hiding away from law. But this small country had avoided complying with this request even when opportunities had been present, and in fact, turned it down most of the time. This request had been made in the first place because some political parties were aiding Prabhakaran for his group who belonged originally to Tamil Nadu. These parties helped or sympathized with this ethnic and violent group and Indian government disapproved of it. However, the present Chief Minister of Tamil Nadu, Ms. Jayalalitha has been with the Indian government (from Narasimha Rao to Vajpayee) for taking steps to strongly suppress the ethnic violence.

On the other hand, in April, Prabhakaran has indicated his willingness to press reporters to end the divisive conflict of ethnic violence by negotiating with the government. He has put up his demands such as an autonomous province for northeast region where the Tamils are in great majority and freeing of LTTE prisoners or treating them with sympathy, etc. It is a hopeful sign that the Prime Minister who did not want to see his face has now shown willingness to meet him. Prabhakaran has also sent signal of peace to New Delhi. These are signs for end of a problem that created a lot of anxiety for both India and Sri Lanka. India had burnt its hands by offering help in keeping peace in its island neighbor; so after the assassination of Rajiv Gandhi India has remained wary of extending military aid or presence in Nepal in either Sri Lanka or Nepal.

Bangladesh

India is more worried regarding the role of Bangladesh in aiding the terrorists instead. Its widespread poverty drives thousands of its citizens illegally cross the border into India and live there. A large number of them have been caught doing illegal businesses and are even working in traffic of weapons and

Talibanization of Bangladesh

Fundamentalists Demonstrate Against India

drugs, etc. They join the networks of powerful mafia gangs and carry on anti-social and anti-nation activities. Earlier, some of the Islamic organizations used to deny the involvement of Bangladesh citizens in such activities, but even intelligence agencies like India's IB also have documented their involvement. In addition, ever since the present Islamic political party has assumed power, thousands if its Hindu minority people are being driven off its soil to enter into India. The size of the Hindu minority in Kashmir, Pakistan and Bangladesh has diminished visibly in recent times and this must be noted as a sign of current trends.

The seven states in northeast India, popularly called as 'seven sisters', which created after the split of erstwhile state of Assam, include besides Assam, Nagaland, Manipur, Mizoram, Tripura, Meghalaya, and Arunachal Pradesh. The original inhabitants or tribes in these states also desire to carve out political identity for themselves based on their own sub-cultures. For this, a number of rebellious movements are undertaken, often armed. Nagaland, Mizoram and Manipur have often faced situations of internal strife and separatist struggles until now—thanks to the support to the insurgents of this area given by Pakistan's ISI.

For sometime, Indian intelligence agencies have been alerting successive governments of the dangers posed by the strategic demographic shift in favor of Muslims in India's border districts. It is estimated, for example, that as many as 5,000 Muslim youth from Assam and the northeastern states have received arms training in camps set up by the ISI in Bangladesh. In addition, the wave of Islamic radicalism in Bangladesh that has virtually destroyed the legacy of the liberation struggle is beginning to be felt across the border. Yet, both India's union and the state governments choose to be willfully blind to the dangers inherent in the rise of another Muslim separatist movement embracing eastern India (Sapan Dasgupta, "An Ostrich in India", *Rediff.com Online*, September 14, 2004).

China is handing out weapons and training in them to Naga and Mizo rebels through routes from Burma/Myanmar or from its border areas. Also, the ISI is cynically carrying on its nefarious activities against India through Bangladesh, it has often been reported. Thus, India is facing the challenges on its fragile, porous and uneasy borders in all directions due to a variety of intrusions, armed interventions, terrorist activities, separatist movements, and armed rebellious groups. The country has to tackle not just the outside threats but the very real dangers from within too. The leading strategic journal, *Jane's Intelligence and Insight* reports on the rising Islamic extremism in Bangladesh, with the militants there seeking a greater Islamic nation covering some adjacent areas in India. After her visit of South Asia in the late April, 2005 Condoleezza Rice stated that Washington is interested in working with India on "deteriorating stability level of its esteemed neighbour." The journal cast the spotlight on the "increasing muscle of radical Islamic parties" in Bangladesh.

Gujarat (India)

In such a delicate situation, events like Godhra (Gujarat) in the heartland of India itself can endanger the stability of the nation. Such events may lead to divisive forces turn powerful in political and social spheres, and this also may adversely affect the capacity of the nation to meet the challenges of outside terrorism. If the mindset of a section of India's largest minority turns anti-national or if the nation loses its national integrity, the contribution of the Hinduist Sangh Parivar in that situation will not be anything less than noteworthy. In such a context, ISI and the forces nourishing terrorism will easily find raw human resources across the border of Gujarat and Uttar Pradesh. In that situation, if the religious fundamentalists and militants outside and within India will join hands, it will pose the greatest danger to India. There will be totally adverse effects on its security, political stability and development projects. It may be still a far-off possibility, yet Gujarat has given out enough signals that from within the country too, terrorization process of *jehad* movements or civil wars can erupt. The poisonous seeds of violence have been sowed in the minds of the large minority, and this is evident from events of Gujarat, and protest demonstrations at West Bank in the first week of April 2002. At that time, one Muslim girl showed a placard in her hand displaying this message: 'Sharon–Modi of Israel' and another placard read: 'Modi–Sharon of Gujarat'.

The hatred and desire for revenge against Israel in the Arab/Muslim world are very strong. If it is thus even only symbolically linked with Gujarat, have the leaders of political parties and leaders of the two communities in India given any serious thought as to what would be long-term repercussions of it for the nation? These leaders have long been vying with each other for victory in elections, in exploiting community vote banks, and are characterizing not just bad administration but a lack of governance. It is the imperatives of 9/11, 12/13 and Gujarat events that the government of all political parties and all members of parliament and state assemblies give the highest priority to inclusive matters of national security and inclusive integrity above politics of cuddling on communal entities.

16

Indian Subcontinent: 'Nuclear Terrorism'

Al Qaeda is not just an organization. It is a symbol of the mindset of many in the Arab and Muslim world. Oriana Flassy, an Italian journalist, has had an introduction to this mentality. As (the Hindu extremist) Dr. Pravin Togadia believes, this mindset will not stop by waging a war against Pakistan or ending the terror in Kashmir. This is a long, long war. One can win a war on battlefield; the war to change mentality will continue for long.

Dr. Magnus Reinstarp of the St. Andrew University's 'The Study of Terrorist Center' says that this war against terrorism will cóntinue for long now. It is a sophisticated operation. Who has taught to fight a serialized war? The intelligence department of Musharraf!

If you will try to pacify Pakistan, it will keep on demanding more and more; it will not be pleased with merely with Kashmir...Showing its nuclear teeth and with that fear as a hanging sword on the head it will blackmail India and also continue its indirect war by terrorism. This makes it difficult to work with them. Attempting a dialogue with them is unthinkable, Flassy says. It would be suicidal even to try and fulfil the affectations and demands of Pakistan.

> Pakistan will not rest even it the whole of Kashmir is handed over to it. For Pakistan is now neck-deep into international terrorism. Nuclear blackmail is now its magic armour and psychological missile.
>
> — Extracted from Flassy's works

Since May 2002 the possibility of war between India and Pakistan was on the horizon. But there was no clear picture of what would be the political and military results and effects of such a war and its subsequent impacts. The Prime Minister of India declares on one day in Kupwara in Kashmir to the military 'jawans', "Be ready for a last war"; and on the very next day, points out to the sky and says that "The skies have cleared"; and yet made parting remark, "Let us hope that no lightening attacks from that direction" too. Such statements of Indian Prime Minister indicated the two-fold mentality of a pigeon and a hawk. Pakistan's President too gives out mixed signals by his simultaneous and contradictory actions of peace talk and missile tests. Should these then be considered lines drawn on sand? Or, are these the lines on hard stone that must be seen at any given time as a political reality? However, the question is not merely that will there be any war? The similarly important or perhaps even more important question is, in case of a war, are the two nations ready completely ready for it? Do they have proper political conditions and capacity for it? Are the rulers of both the nations sufficiently aware and equipped about the consequences of such a conflict?

In present-day war, one cannot use any military logic about its trends, turns, surprises, and results. Yet, wars do have their own logic. This 'logic' can be understood only with simulation exercise of the war struggles, events, strategies that change or need to be changed, only as the war progresses—and not before it commences! Before undertaking a war on land, air or seas or in traditional or nuclear conflicts the simulation through computer model of the techno-military scenario can be visualized beforehand—may be for one event or so. However, in reality of actual war, several factors and forces that defy imagination enter into it and totally distort the scenario the war scientists had visualized in such a simulated picture. That is why, not just Pakistan but even when looking better equipped India must be prepared for a totally unforeseen great shock.

One thing, however, seems to be clearing up. Such a full-fledged war, big war would undoubtedly cause a great earthquake of 8-point on the Richter scale for not only Kashmir but all of South Asia and create a great upset in political equations, where people will have to be ready to redraw the map of this region.

Although, we may not be able to find answers to some of these questions today itself, even then, we shall need to understand some of the basic issues clearly and totally, so that we may have an idea whether the two nations are ready for the 'after shocks' of such a great war-quake.

1. When Pakistan had created a war-like situation in April 1965, that conflict had taken place in the region of Kutch only for few days. The real war took place in September for 17 days. Pakistan used to import its ammunition in those days, and so its stock was empty soon. The 1971 war did not last even for full two weeks (from 3rd to 16th December), and the result was that Pakistan was separated from Bangladesh (its earlier the East Pakistan region).
2. Today, a full-scale war on all fronts would mean that the airplanes and bombs, ammunition, rifles and guns, missiles and the spare parts of the weapons would be used up in such a short time that, according to American experts, this war cannot last more than two or three weeks. However, India could count on other friendly countries like Russia and Israel (besides America) for its major military hardware and other weapons, whereas Pakistan would be relying on China and Saudi Arabia besides some other Arab countries. Yet, it is assessed that countries like Saudi Arabia may not be very enthusiastic to help Pakistan in

such a situation if America brought pressure on them. Therefore, both the nations would rely on speedy and surprise attack to grab the important coveted region from each other and destroy their military bases and infra-structure as much as they can.

3. Besides, the pressure of America as well as other nations of the world will begin to be felt at once by both the nations. For preventing the traditional war from turning into a nuclear war the nations like Japan, America and of Western Europe would bring a joint pressure (in economic, political and techno-military forms). Pakistan and India, then, would find it difficult to ignore and remain firm on their stand. As a result, the country that has obtained greater area/military bases from the other would be in a better position to make a deal for it. Pakistan wants that by such short war activity the question of Kashmir will be internationalized and India will have to abandon its present stand and accept it in that status.

The 'Kargil war' or conflict took place in July 1999, but it did not take the form of a full widespread war. An armed conflict or a limited war on borders is possible (and the suggestion that some Indian military officials may take such steps to quash terrorist bases has been widely accepted, and after this another suggestion has also been made that to free certain parts of Pak-controlled 'Azad Kashmir' such 'limited' war also can be waged) and such a war may last as long as a year even. A war like Kargil can create havoc on both the sides of the borders and yet would not involve the entire nations on this one. Especially, after 1986, when the two nations have acquired traditional yet powerful weapons and since 1998 are equipped with nuclear weapons (mid-ranged N-missiles) cities like Mumbai, Delhi, Ahmedabad, Bangalore, Chennai etc. and many large cities of Pakistan may turn victims of mutual air attacks and in the first atomic invasion as many as three hundred thousand people may die at once. Such estimates must be taken very seriously indeed. Within hours the decades of work for the development of industry, science, communication, health and education with their best institutions etc. or the civic infrastructures that have come up in the two countries would be totally destroyed. Has anyone the insight, mental courage and power to recognize and admit such a destruction of civilization built over centuries within some minutes?

4. Kumar Ketkar, the editor of *The Maharashtra Times* insightfully observed in one of his lectures in the US (May 2002) thus: "Even if a modest size of Indian population of India has contempt for or dislike of Pakistan and a class of Muslims, at this point in time, is our central government (except for their military organization) equipped or capable to meet such a challenge in the border states like Gujarat, Punjab and Rajasthan to protect their main institutions and citizens? Pakistan is indeed weaker in this context or only half-prepared than India; and that is why Musharraf insists America or Russia to intervene or through negotiations by their diplomats wants to put off the moment of confrontation as much as possible."
5. Public opinion, by and large, in India favours a war. Most of the political parties are with government. The parliament has the power to take decision on this crucial question. Whereas, in Pakistan, most political parties boycotted the 'Referendum' of Musharraf and it remains a question whether his administration has received the support of the people or not. However, if a war takes place, then people would definitely lend support, such is the mindset there—what if so far any conflict with India has been dangerous for the people of Pakistan.

   After the defeat of 1965 the position of the then President of Pakistan, General Ayub Khan had become weak. After 1971 war, General Yahya Khan had to relinquish power. After Kargil 'war' the lines of contact were severed from Nawaz Sharif. In summer 2002, rumours were on in influential circles of Pakistan: would Musharraf survive the war with India? If so, for how long? The Mullahs, the Maulavis, al Qaeda and even some of the high military officers seem to be waiting for such opportunity. These militant elements believe that Musharraf has betrayed Islam and surrendered the self-respect of Pakistan to America. Indeed, Musharraf seems to believe that he will get absolute public support any time in case of a war with India. He has already become very popular after the intermittent nuclear missile tests and by his anti-India statements. However, the instability of economy as an aftermath of a war may not get a long tenure for him and even this tenure will not be very long! (As it was, General Ayub Khan and General Zia had even the constitutional support for their position, but what happened?) In any case, no Pakistani ruler has been able to experience a sense of security for long, emphasizes Ketkar.

6. In 1971, Bangladesh broke away from Pakistan. Now, Sindh and Baluchistan, and even Punjab from within have begun to experience some detachment from Islamabad—waiting for the weakening of Pakistan.

No big war or long-term war has gone on the lines drawn by any powerful or capable leader at any time in history. Napoleon entered the capitals of all Europe (except England) as a victor rather than a royal guest, began to face his downfall from Russia onwards. Recall the sight of Red Square of Moscow and the buildings surrounding it where once, Napoleon had its finger-prints. Aiming to become the 'Fuehrer' of the world in 1941-42, Hitler was also forced to step back by a 'weak' Russia. In 1967, when President Nasser began the war to crush Israel, his efforts only led to complete routing of Arab nations; Egypt, Syria and Jordan lost a lot of their territories. Expecting to wipe out that small insect-like power of a farmer nation called Vietnam, America had to abandon bag and baggage, its possessions in Southeast Asia. In this context, the 1960s had brought America on the brink of a civil war. Trying to gorge up Afghanistan, the Soviet Russia had to move every inch away against the Taliban counter-attacks.

7. India also must remember the lessons of history. Not only Pakistan but India also must be prepared for unexpected shocks and wounds. The possible shocks may be somewhat like these:

- Has India a definitive scenario if the people of Kashmir declare themselves 'independent' with the outbreak of India's war with Pakistan? It must be accepted then that most of the people of Kashmir do not love India but in fact want to break away from it. They also seem to think of themselves not as a part of Pakistan either, but are much nearer to it than they are to India. In such a situation, Pakistan may use its short-term tactics, and support the movement for a separate and independent Kashmir.

  Earlier, India also extended support to movement for Bangladesh. How could Pakistan forget that! There is no reason to believe that now, after 1971, there will not be any redrawing of South Asian map, that Kashmir will not turn independent and once again after 1947, India will never be divided, that no such thing can happen; for any development may take place. This does not mean that it would be happening, but a war has its own dynamics and its own rules. And, like a hurricane, al nino or fire, it makes its own way that is not always unpredictable. Not only can the astrologers say anything in the matter, even the expert war strategists cannot foresee all twists accurately every time. If Kashmir turns independent (with the jointly supported military-economic guarantees by America, China and even UNO), then Musharraf may emerge more powerful from the war. Although a probable result of the war would be that Pakistan would be facing military ruin whereas India may become a more powerful regional entity.

- However, if Kashmir breaks away from India, this may encourage the separatist tendencies in the northeastern parts like Mizo, Naga and other similar elements; Bangladesh would also butt in; the forces for disintegration of Indian nation would receive encouragement and another Kashmir question may be created in the northeast by ISI-Bangladesh machination! Thus weakened, India would turn into a 'cocktail' of central political instability and separatist 'Kashmir' tendencies that may be then colored with extremists and fundamentalists too.
- Besides, if India has to lose Kashmir, wouldn't the attitude of the Hindus of India change towards Muslim community? If on the basis of insistence and arguments of majority of the Muslim community India has to suffer two partitions, then why should that community, a minority for India anyway, live here anymore? If this line of thought gains ground, then, the experiences of Gujarat may be duplicated in other parts of India as well. If Pakistan loses the war, then the responsibility of the Indian leaders will be heavier, i.e., to see that if millions of Indian Muslims turn rebellious and anti-Indian, can India keep its environment stable and secure? Even more worrisome than the Israel-Palestine region are the living pattern and mutual balance of religious groups in India and entire South Asia. In innumerable cities of India the majority/minority communities live side-by-side or concentrated in separate areas. If they do not have good relationship, then more blood can flow here than ever did on the West Bank. After Indonesia, India has the largest number of Muslims in its population, next come Pakistan and Bangladesh in the world. "In South Asia Muslim population can become powerful. There are indications that another Kashmir can be created in the east through Bangladesh." The Islam-centric worldwide terrorist network can easily be established here. The serial bomb blasts of Mumbai (1993-2003) and the railway incident

(1998), the criminal bases of the minority community (Juhapura in Ahmedabad, factory for weapons and ammunition in Bihar, large arms collections hidden in farms and godowns in UP, Gujarat and of Punjab, etc.) are examples of the local terrorist criminals. There are signs of violent forces active in Mizoram, Bihar, Andhra, etc., also indicating a network with them.

- If as a result of war Pakistan comes on the brink of defeat and disintegration, then, Musharraf will use the nuclear power at his beck and call! A few days before December 13, 2001, the attention of two Italian nuclear experts had gone to Pakistan's nuclear power and they met a responsible official of Pakistan on the matter. That official had said that if any of these four situations occurred, Pakistan would use its nuclear weapons: (1) if it has to suffer a crushing defeat in a traditional war; (2) if it is on the brink of disintegration; (3) if it loses a great part of important territory; or (4) if its economy is seriously endangered or if it is deprived of distribution of waters of the Indus or Chenab or other main rivers.

  In December 2001, the Indian government took steps to limit political relations or introduce Samjhauta Express and flight of Pakistani airplanes, etc. But, in spite of the great demand from the Indian public, the Indian government made no move to annul the international understanding of 1960 about the waters of the Sindhu, and given a fitting reply to Pakistan's three atomic missile tests in May by its own 'Kalchakra', and shown great self-control about it; but has Pakistan given these things any consideration? However, the former Italian ambassador, K.P. Fabian rightly asks, "We say that life has to be supported in Pakistan; but then by killing people in India terrorism increases, what of that?"

  At the places where all main roads meet in the cities of Pakistan posters of the area where Pakistan had conducted its atomic tests are put against the background of the likenesses of Changhai mountains and the decorations of that centre's is done with small and well manicured gardens. This has become the symbol of Pakistan's pride and power among its people. After only four years four missiles of Gaznavi, Ghori and Abdali were tested in the same month and their models were also placed in these public squares. In his address of May 28 that Musharraf delivered, we can see indications of his policy of terrorism and uncompromising attitude in Kashmir matter that are dangerous signals—and all this, in spite of international pressure including that of America against it! David Alwright, an expert of nuclear weapons, says at this very time in a report of Pentagon that if nuclear clouds rain on the subcontinent, unlike the earlier estimated casualties of 300,000, now 120,00,000 persons will lose their lives; and another 700,000 will be affected by the radiation. However, R.R. Subrahmanyan, the expert from the Institute of Defense Studies and Analysis in New Delhi, challenges even this estimate. In any case, the main point is that if we can prevent it, millions of people should be saved from such disastrous end at all.

On the other hand, an argument is forwarded that while Pakistan may threaten to use its nuclear weapons, it will never do so actually. First, the 'first use' by it will invite an immediate replying 'second strike' from India, and in that attack the entire nation of Pakistan can be wiped out! President Musharraf and high commanding army officers and ISI officials also themselves would perish. (But we do not know who would live from the leaders, whether in India or in Pakistan!) Second, Sandeep Vaslekar of the Institute of Peace Studies at Mumbai analyzes that Pakistan's army is dominated by Punjabis, as he explains with the help of statistics. These Punjabis would never give up a lucrative situation and take such self-destructive steps for the cause of Kashmir. That is why, only using the threat of nuclear weapons over the head of India and use it for the war of nerves is a line that Musharraf may not cross, it seems. Any ruler under such circumstances, ultimately, will behave with restraint, wisdom and intelligence according to the 'rational actor theory'. Similarly, in spite of a number of pressures at different levels, the Indian government will not break the 1960 agreement on Sindhu waters. B.G. Verghese, a development expert, who has made a deep study of north India's water resources, has given technical and pragmatic reasons and explained that waters of the rivers like Jhelam, Chenab or Sindhu cannot be diverted without building very huge dams, and that is neither practical nor in good interest of the nation. That is why, in spite of a great wave of public opinion demanded that the Indian government take up an aggressive stance and stop waters of the river Sindhu flowing into Pakistan, under the 'rational actor theory', it is not possible for the Indian government to do so. However, one must also not forget that the pre-First World War race for colonies between the UK and Germany and a bitter atmosphere in the UK against the reports of the warships built by Germany that brought tremendous pressure on the British Parliament and the role of encouraging enmity played in the newspapers of both the European powers, and in such a volatile atmosphere the news report of the assassination of the heir apparent of Austria at Sarajevo in 1914 brought the First World War on. One cannot rule out the possibility of the unrestrained *jehadi* terrorists putting a defiant President/General into such a situation; and this may not be too far either!

- It is an irony of history, though, that at a time when the American army is present in Pakistan to ferret out and crush the terrorists of al Qaeda and Taliban, and it is asking Pakistan to exercise self-control and is making all possible efforts for it too. The intelligence agencies of the US are also monitoring the nuclear installations in Pakistan. One India expert says, "The 'nuclear button' of

Pakistan is in the hands of America only." The American navy also has been making rounds of Pakistan-Afghanistan all the time. Thus, as far as possible, America will prevent Pakistan taking any extreme, desperate step. On the other hand, the presence of American armed forces and sophisticated war equipments on the soil of Pakistan also puts a limit on the options available to India; for if India opts for a full-fledged war, the attacks would harm the lives and interests of Americans present there. However, Jaswant Singh, India's Foreign Minister then had denied any possibility of keeping a restraint on India for taking any steps against Pakistan by mere presence of the American forces on its soil. Yet, this issue is quite weighty too.

- There are many other riddles too. Germany, America, UK, and some other nations are not with India in the Indian stand with regard to Kashmir. With India clearly unwilling for re-opening of the question, the international pressure on the two nations will find yet another opportunity for it in case of the next war. While fully aware that Pakistan is responsible for terrorist activities in Kashmir and the rest of India, America has not declared Pakistan as a 'terrorist state' so far; but, in fact, has provided new arms and billions of dollars either directly or through the World Bank to Pakistan. Contextually, sooner or later, in one form or the other, India will have to be ready for the internationalization of the Kashmir issue.
- On the other hand, a war against Pakistan might, perhaps, turn out unexpectedly for India too. Kashmir may become 'independent' and the issue between the two nations may dissolve altogether! Or, without the use of nuclear weapons, Pakistan becomes too weak to carry on. Musharraf would go out of power and more radical and fundamentalist party/forces take over. The badly beaten Pakistan would face separatist movements in Baluchistan and Sindh, besides Pakhtunistan/Waziristan on its northeast border. Thus, from the viewpoint of political

stability and integrity, and even in terms of its very existence, it seems that not just Pakistan but India—both have nothing to gain, but only lose on all sides.

There, however, is another issue as well. Suppose, Musharraf is not in power. There are reports that two generals, viz., General Yusuf and General Aziz are there to see that the Pakistan does not pass on into the hands of revolutionary fundamentalists in his absence.

- One important issue also cannot be forgotten in such a serious discussion. From the speeches of Musharraf we cannot assume that he would try or be able to suppress or stop the terrorist activities in the Kashmir valley or stop anti-Indian waves. But supposing that he tries it even with honesty, can he stop the terrorist organizations or individual terrorizing activity? Nearly 2,000 to 2,500 militants are already with al Qaeda and the Taliban who are trained by these organizations and are present in the PoK (Pakistan-occupied Kashmir) area. They are ready to escape into the valley or Jammu area through the launching pads prepared by Pakistan government along the LoC (Line of Control). In the snow-capped mountain area, full of dense forests and nearly 740 km long route of this LoC Pakistan had at least 123 camps or bases and of these at least 36 are active in 2002. Such or new camps will get support from the Pakistan army and ISI war hawks (and there are many such), whatever the policy of Musharraf. Thus, with a parallel autonomous infrastructure of its own, the cross-border terrorism and intrusions or violence cannot be stopped by Musharraf. On the contrary, India has explained to America with the help of statistical figures that after the promise made by Musharraf in his speech of January 12, the terrorist intrusions and activities have increased in the valley from April-May 2002 to summer 2004.

  This is where the question turns even more complex. India had explained to America and other nations that there were two conditions that would make India not take any military step against Pakistan. These were: one, Pakistan stopped altogether the intrusions and violent terrorist activities across the border and in the valley and elsewhere in India; and second, it took an attitude to allow fearless and peaceful State Assembly elections in Jammu & Kashmir coming up in September-October 2002. But, the statements of Musharraf delivered in May did not allow India to hold any such trust. However, India could hold the elections earning international legitimacy.

Thus, for India, the dilemma continues. Expressing disappointment before President Bush and other senior American diplomats, Vajpayee, Brijesh Mishra and Jaswant Singh stated that during the terrorist attack on Indian Parliament, the nations including America, had failed to meet the guarantee that "Pakistan would now abandon terrorist activities against India, and so India should keep self-control".

- Then, how long should India carry the burden of an undeclared war that enables its wily neighbor to continue to inflict thousands of wounds to bleed it? Even in such a low-level fighting 50,000 people have already lost their lives. Every month billions of rupees are spent by India for nothing achieved with concrete results. Since later half of December 2001 to April 2002 India had already spent Rs. 4,000 crore for the army posted on the borders. To maintain such a large army on such a large scale and for such a long drawn out time in the burning heat of Rajasthan or in the freezing cold of the Himalayas without any type of focus, time schedule, and no military-political focus too at that, the law of diminishing returns began to operate not just with regards to the coffers of Indian treasury, but also affecting the morale and health of the soldiers adversely. This fact also perplexed the leaders of the army and government.
- Some officers suggest a way out thus: one who attacks first, wins. They say that taking the initiative and sudden

invasion of Pakistan should be undertaken, destroying its major camps and occupying its sensitive areas. This would ensure defeat of Pakistan within the week. When pressure is on for a truce, during the negotiations, India will be at an advantage, and so a new LoC can be drawn then. (Even Pakistan may adopt this surprise first attack strategy, though!) Second, after June, the monsoon season was on and the army movement on land became difficult. Then came the election in J&K; and who knew what would be result of that? If uncertain verdict produced political uncertainty leading to chaos militants might destabilize this border state. In the context, certain senior army officers suggested 'limited war'.

Columnist Anita Pratap came up with her poser: "But what is a 'limited war'? Against whom would it be limited? Against the Kashmir terrorists or the Pakistan forces that nurture them? Again, could it remain 'limited' at all? If there were a war, how would it remain limited? And, if it is limited, how could it be called a war?"

There was yet another issue: Will such a war remain limited only to Jammu & Kashmir or will it turn into several theaters of war? (In 1965, Ayub Khan had made surprise attack and sent the tanks to Samba area of Jammu, but the small bodied Prime Minister of India, Lal Bahadur Shastri then showed exemplary courage and at once made air attacks on these tanks and within two days the war had spread to the borders of Rajasthan and Kutch with Pakistan.

- A war across LoC between any two nations is fought on all borders and beyond (with tanks, planes and missiles) and if in the traditional war Pakistan comes on the brink of defeat of any of the types described above, the possibility remains that it would resort to using nuclear weapons. The Ghaznavi-Ghori missiles are tested only with this threat in mind for India; and CIA has after three years suddenly, and suggestively, opened the secret that Musharraf was ready to use atom bomb against India without the knowledge of Nawaz Sharif as he was failing in his strategy in Kargil in 1998.

On the other hand, nations like America, the UK, Russia and others are wondering how to effectively bring pressure on Musharraf after his famous address. For, America, India and their media besides other countries also have put forward documented reports of cross-border intrusions, but Musharraf coolly denies it all. That too, after President Bush and Secretary Powell had personally intervened to tell him to curb the terrorist activities and *jehadi* interventions! That is why, the Deputy Prime Minister of Russia and the British Foreign Secretary Jack Straw had to comment on the observation of promises made by Musharraf. Also, he had denied that there was any movement of independence of Kashmir.

- Thus, India is going through an unprecedented dilemma in its foreign policy. Before this it has never experienced any such crisis in taking decision. Pakistan, on the other hand, is going on in its bloody terrorist activities without caring for consequences; and this must end. For its inhuman and rude behavior Pakistan must be answered with great force and unbearable shock of physical-military action, so that it would stop such activities in future. This is very necessary.

  Again, taking advantage of the events of bloody carnage in Gujarat, Musharraf harangued on the tortures of the Christian-Sikh-Muslim minority communities and 'dalits' in that state and India as such. This was an unbecoming gesture, made with the purpose of spreading divisive and discordant forces in Indian people. However, leaders of all the four 'minority' communities made smashing replies to Musharraf, thus displaying integrity of the people of India.

  In the incident of Kaluchakra, three of the culprits were from Pakistan, and there are foolproof evidences for this contention. Even the opposition parties are with the Indian government on this issue. The media and sharpened public opinion also show inclination for lending support to the idea of taking effective steps against Pakistan. On the other hand, Musharraf is capable of adopting a new trick of arming highly trained terrorists and similar non-state forces with even more powerful weapons just to enter India clandestinely.

The India's then Foreign Minister Jaswant Singh has very aptly pointed out that "today's context has two great dangers that are put to use together, and these are: (a) use of nuclear weapons, and (b) accompanying terrorism". In his unique style, Singh has put this phenomenon succinctly as 'nuclearization of terrorism'. Another critic calls it 'nuclear terror'. If India succumbs to it, then it would suit Pakistan very well to continue interventions in this manner and weaken India further. However, showing a great self-restraint so far, the vastly more powerful India may at least sometime try and teach it a lesson to back off by such drawing of the line! Pakistan has successfully packaged the entire episode as a problem related to Kashmir. Hard-headed strategic analysts say that India must think of such a strategy so that its efforts can get the label of "war not for Kashmir but war against terrorism". Only by this change of strategy would the Indian interests command support by international understanding and efforts, and this would include America too.

For, after all, the real reason/s behind such dangerous military steps and entire war efforts must be 'political aims', no less. Have Indian government and military leaders been able to clear with each other any such 'political aims' for efforts behind the war?

Thus, the 'fall-out' of 9/11 has come to this frightening point. The planes that dashed onto the WTC towers and the Pentagon were as good as normal missiles, but in the Indian subcontinent the scenario is changing into one in which not just missiles but, as if, even nuclear missiles could fly into action!

Had 9/11 not happened, the West Asia would not have faced the bloodbath it already has, and is going through, nor would have India and Pakistan been put in a situation full of imminent danger as they now face each other—tank against tank, fighter planes against anti-aircraft tanks, and nuclear missile against nuclear missile. Also, the things that have not taken place at the World Trade Center or in the West Bank, may take place in the Indian subcontinent, viz., 'nuclear terror'. Such a scene is no longer confined today in novels like *The Nuclear Winter* or in films like 'The Day After'. President Clinton had described Kashmir a few years earlier as the most flash point on the earth, though many in India did not agree with him then. Today, not only Kashmir but entire area of the border states of India and Pakistan, and even beyond, are facing the threat of nuclear war clouds—possibly though not probably. Kumar Ketkar says, "Today, not only the Indian subcontinent has turned an insecure region, but the entire world is experiencing the sense of insecurity."

The reason? In the long history of the world and of wars, terrorism of today, with the help of a threat of using nuclear weapons, is now capable of hijacking the peace, security and development of the whole world.

The fact is: the international fabric has been woven round 'nuclear terrorism'. India and America have to diffuse the nuclear blackmail by Pakistan as a first step of basic blow in the war against terrorism. Indeed, this seems nearly an impossible task at the moment. Yet, it would not be a surprise if this issue is being discussed in the high power circles in America for creating a serious strategy for it.

First, after 9/11, gradually, Pakistan has turned into an epicenter of terrorism. It has become the strategic headquarters of anti-terrorist efforts of America and allies against the Taliban in Afghanistan and al Qaeda. In its own eastern region it has patronized and nurtured terrorism in Kashmir against India and elsewhere too. Again, thousands of members of the Taliban and al Qaeda who left Afghanistan after defeat have sought and found refuge in Pakistan where they have spread widely including Wazirastan and mixed with the local *jehadis*. These are pressurizing and controlling the Islamic fundamentalists and militant terrorists against America. After the carnage in May at Kaluchak 2000, India has adopted a tough policy, and only now they are somewhat ready, feeling the international pressure, to reduce the intrusions in Kashmir across the border and the terrorist activities and training of locals in it, etc.

If they would do this, it would be welcomed by India; but this may create dangers for Musharraf, the experts believe. The reason is that if these terrorists, who have been captured from northwest borders or those members of al Qaeda/the Taliban who were driven off, are stopped from being active in Kashmir, they will make havoc within Pakistan itself, says *The Los Angeles Times* (June 17, 2002). Citing the Washington officials, it says that the army and the forces that believe in ISI policy of terrorism may try to end the rule of Musharraf. The very life of Musharraf may be in danger too. (In fact, the latter two attacks on his life in 2004 proved its assumption.) After the promises made by him on January 12, as many as four violent terrorist attacks have been made on American and French citizens by mid-June, and these are considered a show of the weakness of Musharraf and striking power of the terrorists. The estimate of 3,000 trespassers that have crossed over into Indian territory in Kashmir indicates that at least half the number is Pakistanis, Afghans and Arabs. If controlled, their anger also will turn against Musharraf. There are indications also that these would be receiving support of 'Islamised' army leaders even.

Thus, the new center of terrorism is Pakistan and the elements of al Qaeda that have spread within it. If these two facts are put together, the country that America is thumping on the back as its ally in public needs to be very closely monitored by it. When diplomatic persons like President Clinton call Kashmir as "the most dangerous place in the world" and this has been accepted in the spring of 2002, it's pregnant with reality. However, Rajiv Malhotra, a scholar, who has studied this problem in great depth, writes in his important article "America's Last Chance" (June 8, 2002) and warns, "Today, if there is any place that is of greatest danger, it is the region sandwiched between the western Afghanistan and the land to its east." In this 'Red Line' area, he includes the border areas of eastern Afghanistan, the western Pakistan made up of aboriginal tribes, and even the 'Azad Kashmir/PoK. And, he says, "because of this, entire Kashmir has expanded into a theater of the al Qaeda-Taliban terrorism".

Musharraf does not exercise his power in this area. In fact, the uncontrolled activities done here by the al Qaeda and bin Laden's associates, Mullahs and Maulavis, and ISI that lends support to all of them, such as murder of Daniel Pearl and threatening steps to shake up the American Consulate at Karachi—all has actually embarrassed even Musharraf.

America has, thus, two issues for worry: one, if after Musharraf the Pakistan's nuclear missiles and weapons come under the control of the terrorist or *jehadi* forces, it would pose a great threat to security of not only India but of the whole world; and second, if Kashmir or Pakistan are lost into the hands of Pakistan's militant and fundamentalist forces, its northern neighbors of Central Asia (Uzbekistan, Kazakhstan, etc.) and India in south, also may turn into the distribution centers of activities for *jehad*. In that case, the Islamic Crescent would shine, as the *jehad* dream is, over lands from Morocco to India, and then curve over to the other side at Indonesia too. In other words, more than half the world population would be covered with green color and the Crescent. Of course, a secular India is a great and central obstacle to realization of such a dream. In the geopolitics and geo-economics of America the Central Asian nations, with backward Muslim population and rich oil treasures, occupy a strategic significance. One American scholar even says that the future international wars will be fought not on the land of the Middle East but on this land of Central Asia that has remained neglected so far. The reason is that the oil and gas stocks in this region are eyed not only by America but also China and western nations. Here, the tug of war would be between big nations like America-Britain and China-Russia along with the Shanghai Group for their own interests.

In the new millennium then, the terrorist-quake at New York has created new global concerns from Jerusalem to Pakistan and India and is giving many aftershocks as well. So, if America takes a selective approach, considers the problems of its own and that of India as separate ones and treats these also separately, it is neither logical, nor prudent in the long run. Perhaps it is better to remember that while America is fighting al Qaeda and other terrorists on the land of Pakistan, they can carry the fight on the land of America too and damage the global presence of America. Both 'Shoe-bomber' Richard Reed, and Jose Padilla (alias Al Mujaheer) who attempted to throw 'Dirty' radiological bomb in America were sent by Pakistan. That must not be forgotten. Thus, America will have to try and understand the constant unbroken danger in its continuous and undivided war against terror with Pakistan at the epicenter of the terrorist shocks. It is comforting to see the reports that America intends to monitor constantly the actions and activities of Pakistan, and so it is not in a position to reduce its military presence in that country. If this is so even in order to control Musharraf and *jehadi* extremists, it is in the interest of India too.

Thirty-eight years ago, late Sisir Gupta, who was an expert on Kashmir and its relations of India and Pakistan, wrote a solid and reasoned book, *Kashmir: The Centre of New Alignment*. In this and in one of his articles published in a research journal he established that Pakistan is very keen and eager to be on par with India in all spheres. Again, it is troubled by an identity crisis whether it is an 'Islamic nation' or a 'modern nation'. It also experiences a dilemma as to its own image as an integral part of the Indian subcontinent or the western most face of the Islamic world of the Middle East. Also, it considers itself equal to India. This three-fold crisis does not allow it to come to a compromise about the Kashmir imbroglio. Even by becoming equal to India and getting the Islamic identity and the question of Kashmir question resolved, it would oppose India in other matters. On the other hand, after years of unsuccessful negotiations, understandings or treaties and end of armed conflicts, and after unsuccessful talks even with the separatist groups of Kashmir, India too needs to re-think about a new policy for 'political surgery' of this festering wound, as the demand of the time is pressing. If by the present 'proxy war' or attacks against terrorists in the matter of Kashmir India is placed in an unbearable situation by heinous blood baths, it will be constrained to engineer similar situation created in Pakistan (and if it is inevitable, it can resort to full military intervention on full scale too), and thereby create a situation that is acceptable to the local residents of Kashmir and restore peace and stability in that region within a year or two.

Selig Harrison fears logically that if the Muslims of Kashmir make a choice to have an independent Kashmir, or to join Pakistan, reaction against such a choice among the Hindus of India may turn out of limit or very frightening. The intensity of the Hindu ire would be indeed very high, as they would hardly accept partition of India twice on the basis of majority residence of a particular community. And, if the Muslims in Kashmir would behave in such a communal manner, again dividing India on the same basis, they would question the right of the 13 crore Muslim minority population in the rest of India; they would logically want them to leave for their Muslim countries of Pakistan and, now, the new 'Kashmir'! What can the aroused ire of violent communal feelings of the Hindus can do to the Muslims is already evident from the riots of 2002 in Gujarat. Such a scenario worries Harrison and other analysts. "India is ready to wage a war for Kashmir because it wants to save Kashmir for itself. This is not just an objective; but otherwise the situation of 'status quo' that prevails at present in the whole of India, may change, ushering in an unstable situation. However, India would definitely want to prevent this happening" (*The Standard*, Hong Kong, June 15,

2002). According to Gupta, in its search for parity with India and finding its identity besides unravelling its internal and congenital 'genetic' knots, Pakistan will continue to fight with India—if not Kashmir, then on some other issue all the time! However, if the question of Kashmir is finally over, it would be a great relief and open the way for restoring peace in the subcontinent.

In the context of considerable external pressures at present, General Musharraf may be able to reduce the intrusions into India from his borders for sometime, but when the pressures begin from within what would he do? Even three years after Musharraf's famous reformist addresses (January 12, 2002), the reality is not changed in substance. Dr. Jasjit Singh says, "Changing the madrassas to a more modern secular framework may take much more than another decade with concerted efforts which are not yet in evidence. These and other factors continue to sustain a deep emotional and ideological commitment to religion with a significant proportion resorting to radical extremism and terrorism in the name of religion. And the Pakistani army remains a leading partner in this process" (*Indian Express*, September 20, 2004). Harrison believes that when the present crisis subsides, during the administration of Musharraf or his successor, the intrusions into Kashmir would resume previous proportions again and the violent terrorist activities too would shape up as before. That is why, the LoC that was drawn at the initiative of America 56 years ago must be restored once again, be approved, with some modifications, by both the nations concerned. Provision of an international guarantee besides monitoring arrangements is the only possible step in the interest of both the nations. The question of Kashmir too can be dealt successfully with its help. If such an arrangement is given support by the moderate governments of the two countries, it is likely that the extremist forces are marginalized or somewhat softened up. America should provide India in time with the latest satellite and other intelligence equipments to detect any intrusions at its borders for convincing India that it is serious about this issue. If even then, the intrusions abetted by Pakistan do not end, then America should commit itself to India that it will also provide not only predator airplanes to halt such disruptive activities, but also provide highly placed satellites to check the borders by early detection. Besides this, India should take a flexible posture with Pakistan and the armed rebel groups within Kashmir and associate them in the framework of negotiated settlement so that the widespread demand of the Kashmiri people for autonomy can be satisfied. In April 2000, the 'Mori' agency had conducted a survey about the public opinion of Kashmir in which 61 percent of the respondents preferred to stay with India—an encouraging point for India. After free and fair elections in 1977 to the J&K assembly, but for some moderate Hurriyat leaders like Mir Waiz, the last elections in 2002 have been so much free and fair that the people really felt that these elections have echoed their voice accurately. It would be a great opportunity as well as a big challenge for India to consensual grant a workable autonomous status or 'azadi' to Kashmir and see that such a step receives locally (Kashmir) a wide public acceptance, free from the emotional and intimidating pressures from Pakistan-abetted extremists/militants. Even when America, the UK, Russia, UNO, etc. had observed 2002 elections in that state and positively appreciated its free and fair conduct that gave pro-India party a legitimate government, it still needs a firm legitimacy by consensually obtaining the approval of its mainstream population as partner in its final settlement agreed to by India and Pakistan. "For New Delhi and Islamabad, while meeting Kashmiri aspirations is the best way toward an agreement, balancing the quantum of independence with Indian and Pakistani vital interests will have to be done by them alone." If the tangled Kashmir question, which erodes the body politic of India for so many years, can be solved, Pakistan will lose its trump card of terrorism in the subcontinent and the Indian subcontinent will breathe a fresh air of peace, cooperative ambience and development.

17

Terrorism Flows into Gujarat

Some Jihadi groups, especially like the Deobandi group, have penetrated into the border areas of Gujarat. The Central Bureau of Intelligence and other intelligence agencies did have reports of the estimates of these Deobandis, but no steps were taken in the matter. Recently, one person arrested in Sopor of Kashmir admitted that he had taken training at a Madrassa conducted by the Deobandis. Even after such a revelation, no steps were taken.

It is suggestive that the persons involved in the Godhra incident were also connected to Jihadis who are closely connected to the Deobandis, it is believed (though not yet proved).

On the other hand, the uncontrolled Hindu crowds attacked selected individuals and settlements, as the reports suggested, the police just looked on indifferently.

Whatever the truth, these riots have weakened the case of India (that it was taking steps to curb terrorists) before Pakistan and the ruling elite. By using self-control, even when terrorists attacked its Parliament, India had somewhat succeeded in bringing international pressure on Pakistan regarding its policy of Jihad. But, the communal war in Ahmedabad may shatter the

> strategy of its bigger war (against terrorism), is the current point of worry.
>
> The terrorist attacks have threatened even the security of Narendra Modi, the Chief Minister, and he has had to live within the highest category of security provided by the state. The Sachivalaya Complex at Gandhinagar looks like a military fort!
>
> — Based on reports of H. Aiyar and Uday Mahurkar (*India Today*)

Developments in Gujarat need separate examination for several reasons. Religion-based violence, probably encouraged by the state, which occurred in 2002 in this developed, western part of India, continues to get critical reference in India and outside. Muslim community worldwide gets irritated when reminded of this communal carnage. In fact, the Muslim zealots use it as a handy ruse for promoting their Islamist agenda. Ever ready, Pakistan has used it to plant anti-Hindu and anti-India terrorist strategy built in its agenda to weaken its neighbor. Unbearable conditions in riot-affected refugee camps in Ahmedabad in 2002 had created a fertile ground for some Muslim youth to revenge on the Hindus by turning to terrorist activities, and ISI was quick enough to avail of this opportunity to plant terrorist dens in India. Unlike in other countries, the conditions, however, were unwittingly offered by the dominant Hindu groups—religious and political—of this region—the land of Gandhi's birth, work and influence.

The Gujarat of 2002, for a while, was pushed back into the medieval age. At the same time, it has turned into the land of spreading the wave of terrorism that began in this century.

This experience has developed five dimensions: (1) a new and unprecedented trend in Gujarat for religious symbols, definitions and activities; (2) after Godhra incident the creation of aggressive Hinduism and the Muslim minority turning into the target for ruthless attacks in the name of religion; (3) sharp communal polarization between Muslims and Hindus including Harijans-Adivasis; (4) one-sided role of the state which helped the communal section of the majority to indulge in communal carnage and thus escalate this process even in a 'secular' democratic structure; (5) some persons of influence and the intelligence agencies were in the know of the fact that one section of the minority was in hand in glove with communal forces and 'underground' anti-national activists. Thus, dry fodder was ready and available; the climate was hot, while the ember was provided by the massacre of 59 Hindus in the Godhra train incident, and the massacre of Muslims by the Hindu zealots. Islamic extremists from Pakistan took advantage of this situation; and (6) The international impact of the communal carnage in Gujarat is dramatically recorded when, following determined campaign against him by the secular left forces and minorities in the US and the UK by his critics, Modi, an elected head of a state government of a friendly country, was denied entry into USA by its visa authorities and when he was forced to abandon his visit of the UK in the last weak of March, 2005.

Gujarat became the theater and victim of the communal policy, communal mindset and the widespread violence and terrorist atmospherics. Gujarat, once nurtured by non-violence of Jainism, Swaminarayan sect and Gandhi, enjoying a long standing tradition of non-violence in all fields of life, commercially-tuned political culture orienting it to adopt middle course of action and pragmatic approach for centuries, crumbled at this occurrence. It is a great irony of history. The carnage in Gujarat has created a reaction in a section of Muslim minority that is endowed with only closed minds and stilled thoughts that the fundamentalism of Hindutva must be met with terrorist and violent revenge. The step-motherly treatment by the Modi government that the Muslim minority thinks it has received has made deep scars on its mentality. The first audio-visual example of this feeling was the incidence of two

Muslim youths who fired their bayonets in the beautiful Akshardham Temple at Gandhinagar and killed 31 innocent visitors.

Gujarat and Terrorism: Lengthening Shadows

ISI has been providing training, especially in Gujarat, for sabotaging activities to its informers and supporters. For example, the terrorist belonging to Hark-ul-e-Islami, and arrested in Surat in March 2002, had taken his training at Pakistan. He used to travel from and to Gujarat and Pakistan during 1994-98. Similarly, a former soldier arrested in July had been trained by ISI in Dubai.

After Godhra, it is natural that Pakistan and its allies who support Muslim resentment and incitement would use these sentiments and turn it into their own advantage. After Godhra incident, the Kashmir police arrested two youths from Kashmir who had been recruited by ISI agent, Abdul Gani. They were about to crossover into Pakistan at the border. They had been active in Bharuch, south Gujarat since last two years; and Abdul Gani was to train them into sabotaging activities by penetrating into Azad Kashmir region. In mid-2002, as many as five activists of Lashkar-e-Toiba (LeT) were arrested in Delhi, and they revealed that they were to prepare Muslim youth of Gujarat for terrorist activities. The main accused arrested at the time of an attack on the American Center at Kolkata, Aftab Ansari said that three of his colleagues were from Gujarat. In fact, he also confessed that he had sent 14 kg of RDX to Patan in 2001.

Two terrorists were killed during the attack on Akshardham Temple at Gandhinagar. They were not 'suicide bombers' nor had they come only to die (by closing down all avenues of escape). If that were the case, they would have bounced off with grenades tied to their bodies on the closed doors of the hall where all the visitors were gathered. In any case the information about their original intention or of plans, if any, about their activities in Gujarat will remain a secret since they died at the hands of the defending police. But, the experts of intelligence wing suspect that the sharp tongue of Modi is readying the terrorists as well, if indirectly.

Certain countries have recently experienced terrorism. But, if the terrorists have made anyone region within a nation their main point of action, it is Gujarat. Within 12 months of 9/11 from WTC terrorism crossed the distance all the way to Gandhinagar (the capital city of Gujarat). The terrorists have targeted not just the Pentagon—the symbol of American military power—but even Akshardham Temple—the symbol of peaceful religious center. The serious implications of this are worrying the people of Gujarat. However, the results and implications are not for just Gujarat but for entire India as well to experience. Thus, the trend set off on February 28, 2002 of 'action and re-action', violence and counter-violence has turned into a vicious circle that has polarized Gujarat. If not checked prudently, the process could endanger and weaken the security and stability of India itself.

The negligence of the ruling circles in helping, compensating and rehabilitating the victims of these riots added fuel to fire and many pamphlets made circulations against Hindutva leaders. Sheela Bhatt, a reputed journalist, was told in a refugee camp in Ahmedabad by some young Muslims that they were so disgusted that they would rather follow the suicidal human-bomb type of activities as in Palestine, against the leaders and advocates of Hindutva. During this period, it was widely reported that the area of Gujarat is selected or preferred in the map of terrorist activities. In early April, the Muslims took out a 'Protest March' in Mumbai against the carnage of minority community in Gujarat. One of the girls carried a placard that read: "Sharon–Modi of Gujarat"; and another: "Modi–Sharon of Israel". This probably indicated the link of Israel-Palestine-Gujarat-Modi with suicidal terrorism in Gujarat in the Muslim psyche.

During 2002-03 one could make a seismographic note of the lengthening shadow of terrorism on Gujarat, as illustrated by the following cases:

- ISI is cultivating the supporters among the minorities who are prone to collect and provide information for causing sabotage in Gujarat and Maharashtra. An operator of Haraq-ul-Islami who was caught in Surat in March 2002 had his training in Pakistan. The used to travel between Gujarat and Pakistan during 1994-98. In the same way, ISI had trained a former soldier in Dubai. He was caught by the Indian security guards in July 2002.
- It was natural that Pakistan an its cohorts in India took advantage of the anger and dislike for India among a small section of Indian Muslims in the wake of the post-Godhra carnage. The Jammu police had picked up two Kashmiri youth, who were hired by an ISI agent Abdul Gani. They had stayed in Bharuch (Gujarat) and were carrying on there their sabotage-related activities. Gani was arranging for their surreptitious entry into Azad Kashmir (PoK) in order to get trained in sabotage actions. However, they were nabbed just when they were almost to cross the border (LoC) in Kashmir.
- In the mid-2002, the Delhi police arrested five active operators of Lashkar-e-Toiba. Information elicited from them revealed that they proposed to train Gujarati Muslim youth for carrying out terrorist operations.
- As the main accused of the event of attack on the American Center in Kolkata, Aftab Ansari admitted, three of his colleagues belonged to Gujarat. In fact, he himself had sent a stock of 14 kilo RDX explosives to Patan in October 2001.

B. Raman underlines how Dawood Ibrahim has been operating from Gujarat and Maharashtra. The US has declared this don as a global terrorist for helping al Qaeda. Branding him thus, the US has order to seal all the properties of Dawood Ibrahim. It has also requested UNO that whatever, wherever he has his properties in the world, should be seized. It is not yet known whether Pakistan, where he has a cosy hiding, has taken evinced follow-up action in this matter or, how the US has pressurized or persuaded its ally in war terrorism in this matter. Anyway, Pakistan has not handed over this dangerous don to India, despite the latter's demand to this effect in 2002.

In its Executive Order, the US Department of Treasury had stated that Dawood Ibrahim, the kingpin of the criminal underworld in India was assisting al Qaeda in various ways. He is the main accused in the Mumbai bomb-blast case for providing fund to carry out the related terrorist operations. He is also funding the terrorist organization LeT in India.

The US Department of Treasury has clearly referred to Gujarat, stating that Dawood provides fund to LeT for spreading unrest in Gujarat (October 16, 2003).

However, after Akshardham, the happy indications are also discerned, indicating that there will not be any Godhra II in Gujarat. When the revenge and counter-revenge actions reached their peak in Gandhinagar, the common public of Gujarat and even the ruling circles used a language of self-restraint and reacted to the incidents calmly and coolly. In this way, the calculations of the patrons of terrorism to spread provocation and sharp reactions were defused and made ineffective by the basic and practical wisdom of the public, along with media and government, besides political parties.

The call for a 'bandh' given by Shankar Singh Vaghela of Congress as a public protest against Akshardham attack did not get much public response. When Vishwa Hindu Parishad (VHP) gave the call for 'bandh,' the Bhartiya Janata Party (BJP) remained officially away from it. On the day of 'bandh' the Chief Minister Modi, known for his sharp tongue, and his administration as well as the police saw to it that the situation does not slip into the February 28. The suspects for anti-social activities and violent behavior were arrested beforehand; no crowds were allowed to gather and the police dispersed any that were about to be formed. Even, the critics of Modi were also pleasantly surprised. Some of the secular activists even appreciated all the work. The 'rajdharma' (the duty of the ruler to maintain law and justice) that Vajpayee had advocated to Modi was put into practice!

Elected to Lok Sabha from Gandhinagar constituency, L.K. Advani, Home Minister took weeks before visiting the torn region of Gujarat. Prime Minister Vajpayee also visited Ahmedabad only after two months had passed after Godhra. But this time, Advani was in Akshardham the very next day of the attack and the Prime Minister also reached Ahmedabad after cutting short his visit to Lakshadweep. Right from the day first the central leaders had insisted to the Gujarat Chief Minister that law and order must be preserved at all costs. The media also acted with restraint after this incident and its possible aftermath as they covered it. The minority leaders of Gujarat as well as from the rest of India at once condemned this incident; even the Sangh Parivar behaved with restraint in the matter.

The general public had come to understand that by giving overreactions to Godhra I incident, both the communities, of majority and minority, would have to suffer a great deal. Thus, instead of a ruthless reaction, a mature reaction set in at all levels. No pretext was provided for ISI to instigate the Gujarat-based *jehadi* anti-national elements to light up communal fire and keep it burning in Gujarat.

The reaction of the ascetics or 'sadhu-sants' themselves was most soothing. When the Chief Minister went to meet Pramukh Swami, the head of the Swaminarayan sect; he requested that the Swami must make a statement that two terrorists who attacked Akshardham were connected with ISI and Pakistan. But, Swami did not accept this suggestion. On the contrary, he advised the Chief Minister to act in a restrained and discretionary manner. Thereafter, a meeting of 15,000 people was held at Akshardham to miourn the death of those who lost their lives in that attack. All the political leaders, including the Chief Minister, were present. In any meeting, if a

CM is on the platform, a speech from him is a mandatory protocol. This time, however, no one suggested that he could give even a short speech for the occasion! The ascetics of the sect themselves made short speeches and requested people to behave in a self-controlled and peaceful manner. Pramukh Swami said, "All religions are good. Everyone must have a space to observe his religion. What matters is that he must also have the equanimity to learn about others' religions too." The speeches of other religious leaders elsewhere, in Ayodhya, Mahudi, Vasna or other conferences, had the color of political inclinations or provocation for action to the followers. This element was conspicuously absent here. Not only this, peace and harmony were the two points emphasized the most. This author and Ramesh Menon, the journalist from *Rediff.com*, in their publication *Caste and Communal Time Bomb* showed with illustrative examples how during the 'Rathyatra' of 1885 and the 'Shobha Yatra' of 1986 the religious leaders had become a salient feature of politics in Gujarat. Now, however, a totally mature reaction was seen in an atmosphere that could be otherwise surcharged by provocative commotion. Decades ago the cooling breeze of a patient and non-provocative tradition that prevailed in Gujarat seemed to flow at least for the time being. The October issue of *Outlook* magazine conducted a survey and found that 70 percent of the respondents welcomed the tolerant strain of Hinduism. This conclusion is also confirmed by the fact that in spite of the murder of Haren Pandya, a popular political leader of Gujarat and a significant entity of BJP, which occurred in a high-profile area of Ahmedabad, no unrest followed and peace reigned.

The 'sadhu-sants' or swamis of this sect separated themselves from the high-pitch Ayodhya-brand meets and the Akshardham episode and also from politics of the state. That helped Hinduism to return to its natural tolerant and middle and moderate path. What would be the policy of the Chief Minister may become clear in future, but at least now New Delhi has understood that the episode of Akshardham is an indication that the shadows of terrorism has not only loomed over Gujarat, but for the entire nation where as many as 120 million Muslims reside and may usher in terrorist violence any time from within and create an intolerable situation for the country. The terrorists killed in Gandhinagar may have belonged to any place, it was evident that a section of the local Muslims and Pakistan had supported and trained them professionally to promote their own ends. It was a mere part of a network that operates from outside India.

On the other hand, the head of the National Security Guards (Black Commandos), Mushahri has assured that central government is determined to pick out and destroy such terrorists, and for this purpose, the latest equipments and training are being provided to them.

At a time when due to the Hindutva forces and their politics of violence and hate, the Muslim society was burning with similar emotions in reactive reciprocity, a voice of sanity came from Dr. Najid Hussain from America. The son-in-law of the political worker Ahsan Jafri, a victim of the riots, visited relief camps and calmed down the excited youth there to think coolly and with equanimity if they wanted to lead a peaceful life in India. "If we resort to extremism against extremism, ultimately only we shall have to become the victims of extremism", he explained. Social activists, along with sane citizens and the state government in restoring in the civil society of Gujarat peace and harmony are trying to make it free of extremist mentality even among the victims of the fundamentalism of both religions who have borne the brunt of the disturbances. They must chalk out long-term projects to provide civic education to live with acceptance of multicultural climate in order to bring this about. Only then would the people of Gujarat be free of the fear of insecurity that chases it today, and thereafter turn its attention, energies and resources for further development. Is India ready to avert the dark clouds of ISI, al Qaeda and the likes of bin Laden that are raining havoc Kathmandu to Kashmir; and those overcast in Delhi, Gujarat,

Mumbai and Bangalore as well. Mixed experiences of Gujarat and India in 2002 send out enough indications and messages for actions—pro-active and preventive.

One can make out a few traits of this context: one, the social psyche of Gujarat has been communalized and it has been strengthened by 'brutalization', so that persons of both the communities have begun to keep some small or even big arms with them for ready use in case of a sudden need. If any state that has come under the clouds of Islamic *jehad* after Kashmir, it is Gujarat. Of all the states, its chief ministers have to bear the highest cover of security.

Secondly, the democratic system of India will gradually put Modi and Sangh Parivar on the defensive by strengthening itself. Institutions like the Human Rights Watch, European Union, Election Commission, and most of the media—had put both the Prime Minister and the Deputy Prime Minister on the defensive about Gujarat on their foreign tours. Their confessions on the details, the alertness of the social workers and intellectuals, and reports of reputed and reliable NGOs like SEWA and Citizen's Initiative, etc., working at the state, national and international levels, forced to change the adamant attitude of the Modi government into a soft and open one. Democracy has a great potential to calm down and overcome radical and extremist forces in its processes, and this too will swing the pendulum to move towards center or equilibrium rather than the extreme positions. Democracy has 'in-built' forces that go in for 'checks and balances' against extremes. Would now this come to the aid of Gujarat in the present circumstances? The prevailing insecurity, uncertain peaceful conditions and the impending nightmare of terrorism have reduced the budget of Gujarat: its expenditure has gone up while income has reduced by 21 percent; in comparison with the previous year the development projects have been cut by as much as 40 percent, the investment from out of the state have reduced to a trickle. It is very necessary that this highly important part of the consequences is embedded in the psyche of the people as well as the politicians.

In the meantime, both the Hindus and the Muslim minority have been reviewing the events of 2002 and trying to learn lessons in their own ways for their own security and overall peaceful atmosphere. This means that now the conditions are changing into a 'balance of terror' to keep at bay the ever-present threat of riots and violence. The minority will try now to be as far away as possible from situation of 'Godhra' even in miniature, so that it can avoid the reactions of the majority community that followed in March-April. Even the majority community will read the writing on the wall after the episode of Akshardham and would be certainly afraid to allow terrorism entering, or putting its roots, into the state. Of course, the people of Gujarat themselves will have to remain alert on the whole, that no fundamentalist elements of either community take such steps again so as to shake up the peace of the state again.

May be religion and politics will not be separated, even then if those religious leaders on whom Modi and VHP banked withdraw their names from politics it can really put a break on religious politics effectively.

It would be interesting to see if this will have a 'ripple effect' or not. If Hindutva loses its priority on the political agenda, one great weapon in the hands of the Islamic terrorists would be blunted.

18

Iraq Monomania

In 2002, the U.S. was superbly well-placed, financially and diplomatically, to deal with terrorism. For longer-term efforts against Islamic extremism all that was required was to think broadly about threats to the country, and creatively about the responses.

The Bush administration chose another path. By the end of 2002, it placed all other considerations second to regime change in Iraq. It hampered the campaign in Afghanistan before fighting began and wound it down prematurely, along the way losing the chance to capture Osama bin Laden. It turned a blind eye to misdeeds in Saudi Arabia and Pakistan, and to WMD threats from North Korea and Iran far more serious than any posed by Saddam Hussein, all in the name of moving toward a showdown with Iraq. It overused and wore out its army in invading Iraq—without committing enough troops for a successful occupation. It saddled the United States with ongoing costs that dwarf its spending for domestic security. And by every available measure it only worsened the risk of future terrorism. In every sense 2002 was a lost year.

— **James Fallows** (*The Atlantic*, October, 2004)

Speaking at the forum of 'Peace Vigil' organized by Gandhi Foundation at Martin Luther King National Memorial in Atlanta on March 15, 2003, this author had quoted Martin Luther King, "We have guided missiles, but we have misguided men!" Due to such missile men a complex scenario of long-term trends and situations had arisen before the war with Iraq.

Everyone agreed about the results of the US-led war against Iraq in March 20, 2003, but the question was not that militarily much superior America would destroy President Saddam and his iron-clad administration. Also, the war, as America and few of its allies claimed, be short and with least loss of men and material; or would Saddam, by adopting guerrilla war tactics, lengthen the conflict, thereby bringing about destruction of American men and showing the pictures of Iraqi suffering create wider sympathy in Muslim society and the world and bend the public opinion against the steps taken by Bush?

Even before the war America has had to suffer huge losses. After the Second World War its alliances with European powers had collapsed. In the next six decades France had still remained at its side, and now France and America were at loggerheads in public, exchanging arguments and blames on each other. After the Cold War, America made friendship with Russia, and after 9/11 President Putin declared and provided support to America to fight its war against terrorism. Even Tony Blair, although on shaky ground for support from his own Labour party, was giving an ultimatum of 48 hours on 17th March midnight to President Bush! It was all right when he was finally able to get the support of the British Parliament later on.

More than 65 percent of the people of the other allies of Bush, Italy and Spain, countries with ordinary strength, opposed any war effort without consent from the UNO. However, Japan and Australia extended support. On the whole, however, in First World, Second (Russia) as well as Third World countries, (governments as well as the people of the entire world, at this stage) and even in Australia, so many huge opposition rallies were organized as have never been seen in history. On February 15, 2003, about four weeks before the invasion of Iraq, ten million people marched against the war from New Zealand to London. On March 15, 2003 Peace Vigil programs, from Sydney to Washington, DC, were observed by millions of people in 100 countries. Once again, organized opposition programs and prayers of peace, and participation were audio-visualized worldwide to caution against the war. Again, one million had peacefully marched in the streets in over 575 cities of 66 countries against the Iraqi war a year after the invasion. That people of Muslim nations like Indonesia, Malaysia, Pakistan, Egypt, etc., would take to street for this cause is easy to understand.

In spite of using all kinds of strategies and policies for it, America could get support of only four out of 15 member-states from UN Security Council for seconding proposal it suggested on 17th March! Not to lose face, America and Britain now decided not to present another at all. And, the 'veto' of France with support of Russia and consent of China was still hanging on their heads. Even Bush Sr. himself clearly, if indirectly, observed when he spoke at the Tuft University in a special speech that to accept the need to disarm Saddam would be like cutting off relations with those European allies who have been friends of America so far.

Thus, one and only 'superpower' America came to be isolated. Once an advocate of the principle of power, the political scientist Professor Hans Morgantho, having eulogized the war policy of America in Vietnam, wrote the famous essay "Limits to Super Power" after 1968, portrayed how even great powers cannot do everything as they think they can; there are limits to the freedom of action to them and making such observations for he had warned the then President Nixon. And, finally, America had had to back out of Vietnam with loss of face.

After 35 years of this, now America is behaving like a 'hyper power', it would seem; isolated from the world and separated from his traditional allies, President Bush, Jr. and America of FOX channel and CNN, and British government-influenced BBC are not prepared to accept such limitations. President Bush even ignored the warnings, given two months before, by certain 'think tanks' whose words are paid great attention even by the Departments of State and Defense in America. The journals like *Foreign Affairs* that are prestigious and supportive of established government most of the times, also sang a different tune for the first time from the President. But such timely warnings could not shake the White House in to awareness of reality.

Thus, although there were a number of indications of opposition and warnings, President Bush, who had won his elections on a disputed counting, took a very serious decision. In this we have had to witness the tragedy of democracy and of the world. The support or approval from Security Council of UNO, important nations of the world and public opinion were not forthcoming, and so the policy of Bush has lost its 'legitimacy' and widespread acceptance of people. Influential mainstream dailies such as *New York Times* and *Washington Post* and others round the world have published editorials and other articles with great insight (from Thomas Friedman to B. Raman) and scholars from Noam Chomsky to Kristoff have exposed, with forceful arguments, the mistaken policies of President Bush.

But President Bush banked on the certainty that Iraq would fall. While it is definite that America would be the winner any time, but the question here is if it would be getting the laurels of that victory! Bush assures that Iraq after Saddam will enjoy stability and growth; that he has a plan for reconstruction of an Iraq suffering the effects of a war. But, as his experienced father Bush Sr. has said, having quarrelled with the European allies, would their support be available in the process of rejuvenating Iraq after the war? If a time comes to do this without international aid and only by resources from America, would the people of America cooperate with the President? It is more difficult task to manage the peace and new 'reconstruction', rather than the war itself. Would the Iraqi people, having suffered under Saddam for so long, accept the direct presence and help from America from their hearts? What if America is found short in fulfilling their expectations or even fails altogether? Suppose, after having used its own resources and equipments, the Americans still have to face their opposition; what then? Whether the question of Iraq would be solved after the exit of Saddam? All these and such other 'American questions' would need to be solved.

The world's peace, security and welfare would depend on how these questions would be solved. To get the answers to these questions, following issues would need to be kept in mind:

- People welcomed the fall of Saddam Hussein as they felt liberated from his repressive dictatorship. During his rule, one million Iraqis had lost their lives. By using poisonous chemical weapons on the Kurds, Saddam had exposed his demonic ways. The TV footages on popular rejoice in Baghdad at the sight of the pulling down of Saddam's statue on April 9, 2003 graphically underlined this point. But they had not bargained for the long-term occupation of their country by the US-led coalition which they were soon to detest.

When we look at it in a larger perspective, even after having brought an end to the Iraqi question, as Fareed Zakaria, the editor of *Newsweek* points out, the problem of the 'American question' remains unsolved.

- Banking on its own superior strength, America has shaken up all the established foundations of the world organizations. The Western Union, European Union, and UNO—all structures faced fractures. The wide-scale international understandings and unanimity are washed off and stand eroded. (In the very first year of his first term,

President Bush had withdrawn America from the treaties made with Kyoto and other such five international treaties!)

- The present generation has met with terrible failure in its transparent attempts to stop war at any cost and to bring about diplomatic solution.

"President Bush has not travelled in foreign countries much; he is the least so travelled among the heads of American state in the last 40 years" (till 2003). Similarly, Saddam also had not quite gone out of his country; and actually never beyond the Arab countries! Productive occasions necessary to have a mature understanding of summit conferences, personal equations with the heads and important personalities of foreign countries, presidential dinners with visiting dignitaries at White House, and so on as channels for understanding the changing world and relationships have not occurred in the Bush administration. Thus, as luck would have it, both the bitter rivals are leaders with no or little understanding of world matters and without a farsighted worldview for tackling such questions of major significance to the world.

- America is standing at the turning point of history. After the Cold War, what should be the nature and architecture of the 'new' world order? How could America, as the most powerful and effective leader, provide leadership to shaping of such an order? On this issue President Bush has not been able to adopt any farsighted approach. America's ideal (from Carter to Clinton), in its foreign policy has been to deal with internationalism or the common problems of the world (terrorism, war-like situations, or ethnic conflicts within a nation, etc.) keeping all the nations on its side first and take a multilateral approach. Bush has dropped this approach. America, instead, has fought Iraq war without any urgent necessity or unavoidable pressure, and that also almost on its own responsibility. Its objective is right, but the means are seriously defective.

- That is why, for those countries that badly need peace and stability in this century, especially India and China, are embarrassed by the American policy. (However, these countries would be inclined to provide cooperation for reconstruction of Iraq, and that would be beneficial for all the parties concerned—Iraq, America, and India).

As stated earlier, the question of management of the reconstruction and peace after the war was a much greater challenge than the management of war itself. The hope that America would adopt a liberal approach and enlist cooperation from most of the countries of the world in this matter was belied. America could not turn this great moment of anxiety of history into one memorable and statesman-like undertaking.

Since its start, the Iraq war has created a complex scenario of far-reaching questions and enduring trends and complications. Bush ignored the sound of cautions at considerable costs—human, material and psychological—for USA and the world's fight against terrorism. Contemporary views of some perceptive analysts (even of just March-April 2003) documented in following section underline how Bush administration was to behave in an ostrich-like manner to remain impervious to the storm in the desert.

Far-Reaching Questions

The Iraq war has thrown up certain far-reaching questions.

- America has not been able to prove that that there was any urgent or real danger to its national security from Saddam's Iraq. Even before the war clouds were hovering in the sky, respected American scholars and former diplomats were cautioning against Bush's intransigent rush on this issue. In spite of this, Bush took pre-emptive and anticipatory measures against the perceived threat of Iraq; and thus sought to establish the principle of ignoring or hurting the sovereign rights of other nations, and it was done with success. Iraq of Saddam was surely not going to withstand America's military might for long. Even the support extended to it by suffering under the dictatorial system of Saddam fast washed off. America has absolutely failed to prove that Iraq is in possession of weapons of mass destruction and that Saddam and al Qaeda had any connections.

A Precedent for India/Israel?

Besides, with this success, within America, the basic one-nation theory (even if nearly 40 countries including Britain had lent support in some manner) has given greater importance to military steps rather than diplomatic ones for solving conflicts among nations. Other nations like Russia, Israel and India also may be emboldened to imitate it in future. William Caff says in *International Herald Tribune* that by following this new example, India, failing in diplomatic tactics against Pakistan, would use this as an excuse for military attack on the latter. At that time, would America have any moral base to stop India from doing so? (Six years ago, America had bombarded terrorist camps in Afghanistan, and at that time India wanted to carry similar raids on the camps of infiltrators in Azad Kashmir, but America had not given consent for it.)

- On the other hand, in time, Pakistan has continued to be quite useful to America to break the network of al Qaeda and the allies of bin Laden. President Bush has lifted the sanctions against it and even declared willingness to provide military aid and billions of dollars worth largesse. Under these circumstances, America would not allow Pakistan to be weakened by India more than a certain extent. Thus, if India takes any military steps imitating America, the relations of the two countries would deteriorate. Monopolistic superiority of America would be on the increase in this matter.

It could become difficult for most of the nation to be in bad books of America after its impressive military success in Iraq during March-April, 2003. One cannot ignore certain realities in this situation. The military budget of America is bigger than that of Britain or Germany together. Its economy too is bigger than the joint economies of Britain, Germany and Japan. In 2004, the defense budget of America was higher than the total 191 countries of the world. (With the beginning of Iraq war, for the security of the city of New York alone as much as 50 million dollars have been spent every week!). Thus, it is a country that possesses power that has never been seen in history until now; and if that country does not adopt liberal and farsighted approach, and loses sensitivity for the welfare and dignity of the world, it would be too serious a problem that concerns everybody.

'Lemon to Lemonade'

B. Raman, the profound scholar, warns that in the Muslim world, a feeling of rage and opposition to America would increase. In his speeches of 17th and 19th March, 2003, delivered with the people of Iraq in focus, President Bush declared his commitment and readiness for change, make it very necessary to win over the trust and goodwill of the Arab countries. The war imposed by Bush put in a quandary nearly 57 of his allies, with Muslim affiliation, from Egypt to Pakistan. Also, Saddam and his propaganda machines have played an important, if cynical, role of nurturing in Muslim youth a terrorist and anti-American attitude. Professor Hussein Haqqani of Carnegie Endowment, giving examples from history and *Hadeeth* (a collection of the words of Prophet Muhammad), says, "Whenever the Muslims have lost in military battles, they have turned to fundamentalist *jehad*." He warns, "Now, the wheel of 'Hate America' will begin to move on fast, from Morocco to Djakarta." Thomas Friedman's advice on this matter needs serious consideration. He says that now on the matter of Iraq not just rowdy 'Arab Street' (Arab people coming out in thousands on to streets to demonstrate opposition) and the people of all the nations of the world taking out large rallies against the war, and organizing non-violent 'Peace Vigil' has turned into a phenomenon of a

A Shia Believer Praying for the Fall of Saddam's Sunni Regime

Anti-America Rally of 2,00,000 Moroccans even in a Liberal, Modernizing Muslim Country (2003)

'World Street'. At such a time, America would need to demonstrate the responsive sincerity and sensitivity of turning 'lemon' into 'lemonade', that is to say, to change the soured minds of the Muslims (lemon) by judiciously adding the sweetness of goodwill and aid (lemonade) into better relationship.

Otherwise, instead of 'globalization', America would be alienating many countries of the world by its 'unilateral' foreign policy. It will escalate the process of globalization of anti-Americanism.

It is comparatively easy to manage a war; but then, later on, the President must adopt a policy to nursing sensitivity not just of the Arabs but also the one time close allies like France, Germany, Russia, etc., by its imaginative policy. Otherwise, the reconstruction of Iraq that could become 'models' for democracy and development was to remain a pipe-dream. Much more difficult than war is the management of peace. It is a great challenge too, and if America is able to meet it successfully, it would indicate a happy turning point in the history of mankind. The US and its allies celebrated the dramatic event of nabbing Saddam alive from his hideout in a hole on December 12, but they were soon to learn that even post-Saddam was to prove more troublesome and a costly occupation.

In this context, a review of developments one year after America's military victory in Iraq is in order. A year after America launched its 'shock and awe' campaign in Iraq, as *Mercury News* (March 14, 2004) stated, "The awe is a distant memory. But hardly a day goes by without shock—for Iraqis, for US soldiers and civilians, for Spaniards, Poles, Italians, Britons and other members of the America-led coalition". It adds, "The prospects of our sowing democracy in Iraq—never mind the rest of the Middle East—remains a chancy." On April 19, the date of invasion of Iraq, it wrote, "The Bush-Cheney team likes to talk about Iraq in simplistic terms: Saddam, one of the world's most brutal dictators is gone, and that's a good thing. But other rationales for the war—the 'imminent' Iraqi threat, the weapons of mass destruction, the ties between

Saddam and al Qaeda—have proved illusory. The goal of establishing a safe and stable Iraq is more important than ever."

Following killing of hundreds of passengers on bomb-blasted train in Madrid, the people of Spain feel that their cooperation with the US did not make them safer—it made them a target of the terrorists. So they pulled out. Poland, another staunch ally, was showing growing unease on this point. On March 18 that year, total deaths of coalition forces reached 670. Out of them, the US lost 570, the UK 59 and Spain 10. Iraqi military causalities was estimated between 15,000 and 45,000; Iraqi civilian casualties between 3,200 and 10,000; 181 killed at Shiite shrines in Karbala and Baghdad by March 2, 2004 (figures depend on the political orientations of the sources). In the one year during the occupation and the construction work that meanwhile had started, a middle class

Political Effect of Post-9/11 Terrorism

Saad family found their household income increased three-fold. But Alla Saad, an engineer in Agricultural Ministry stated, "There is no stability, there is no security, no clear future. Alongwith a feeling of humiliation pervades all along." Rued a daily in Bay Area, "The first anniversary of Iraq war cannot be a time for celebration. It ought to be a time of national reflection and a renewed search for real solutions to a war that is far from over."

That pattern and assessment were to continue when the coalition, hurriedly and without the mood of celebration of the event, transferred the power and governance in Iraq to an interim government on June 28, 2004 under the lurking fear of insurgents' attacks on the venue of transfer of power to Iraqis. For the preceding two months had been marked by the developments that exposed how the occupation had increasingly become untenable. In early May, for example, prison pictures of ghastly cases of the torture of Iraqi prisoners by American soldiers coming out of Abu Ghraib prison hit a neuralgic point. A picture of a uniformed American woman soldier with a cigarette in her mouth holding a naked Arab man on leash was prominently featured in several Iraqi and mainstream papers. It had disastrous implications for the Americans as stereotyped in the Muslim world. Charles Krauthammer tersely comments on its neuralgic point in *The Washington Post*: "One aspect of the Abu Ghurayb makes horrors even more incendiary. The pictures of American women soldiers mocking, humiliating and dominating naked and abused Arab men created shock waves worldwide. One could not have designed a more symbolic representation of the Islamic warning about where western freedom ultimately leads than Thursday's *Washington Post* photo of a uniformed American woman holding a naked Arab man on a leash" For the *jehadists*, it was a telling proof of what they caution against freedom in America and Europe that brings with it sexual license and corruption, decadence and depravity that symbolize modernity. Other pictures also graphically exposed the torture of the Iraqi soldiers in prison from

Abu Ghraib that Tarnished the US Image

summer 2003. A photo showed Iraqi inmate pinned under a stretcher. One was of a wired Iraqi who was told that he could be electroculated. In yet another, underpants were forced on an Iraqi inmate's head. One should not ignore here the facts of far more tortures and atrocities committed during Saddam's regime, and gruesome butchering of captured westerners by terrorists in Iraq thereafter. "But American offenders should surely be judged by our standards, not by others," writes Krauthammer.

Some interrogation tactics being used in Iraq are far more aggressive than sanctioned in the US Army Manual. Excellent reports, possible in a highly open democratic polity of USA, appeared in influential papers as *Newsweek*, *New Yorker* and even in American army's in-house journal, *Army Times*. Even *Army Times* (May 17, 2004) editorially stated: "The entire affair is a failure of leadership (military and civil) from start to finish... at least 14 have died in custody in Iraq and

American Forty: Why America is Hated?

Afghanistan." Even this army journal cautioned, "This is not the way a free people keeps its captives or wins the hearts and minds of a suspicious world." The Anglo-American acts are logically charged for the breach of international law on this count. Violent events in the Sunni city of Fallujah near Baghdad during April-May continued unabated despite heavy air-bombing by allied planes and choppers. Car bombs exploding near coalition headquarters, Khobar Petroleum Center near the Persian Gulf Coast, etc., during May killed the US soldiers and Iraqi police and others. The Khobar incident was significant for the signals it gave. The terrorists apparently sought non-Muslims and westerners in Khobar. They took 22 lives, many foreign. The terrorists were believed to range in age from their late teens to early 20s. They demanded, "Where's the American men? We're looking for non-Muslims" (*Mercury News*, June 1, 2004). Violent incidents occurred in other places as well—Mosul, Al-Najaf, Kirkuk, Basra, Nasiriyah, Tikris, etc.

Provoked by Muqtada al-Sadr, the influential Shia cleric of famous Imam Ali shrine, Shiite militia of 10,000 devotees clashed, persistently, on allied forces. The American onslaught on Najaf claimed more than 300 lives by the early August.

Even such high-handed approach did not help the Anglo-American occupation or its puppet government. Chalabi, their first protégé on Iraq's Governing Council, proved an utterly corrupt head of its finance committee. He stashed away millions of dollars meant for Iraqi people. He had to be removed and punished. It was chiefly on his advice that Paul Bremer, the US pro-consul in Iraq, disbanded the Iraqi army and police while also dismissing tens of thousands of employees on the pretext of 'de-Baathification' of Iraq (making the country free from the structures of order and administration under Saddam). This one move cost jobs to hundreds of thousands, inflicted economic hardships on their families and fuelled mass anger, while leaving the occupying authorities no personnel with which to tackle law and order" ("Empire's Nightmare" by Aijaz Ahmad in *Hindu on Net*, June 6, 2004).

Commented Hans Blinx from Stockholm, the former UN nuclear investigator, "It is our complete ignorance about the PMD of Iraq—the people of mass destruction, suicide bombers—and the environment that nurtures them. The intelligence failure was not just about the chemicals Saddam was mixing; it was about the emotions he was brewing in Iraqi society.

There have been some 125 suicide bomb attacks against US forces in Iraq in the last 16 months, carried out most likely by Sunni Muslims. What is even more unnerving is that, unlike the Hamas, who produce videos of themselves, explain their rationale and say goodbye to families, virtually all the bombers in Iraq have blown themselves up without even telling us their names."

On other front also, the problem is getting enormous. As John Podesta, former chief of the staff of President Clinton said, near Times Square in New York, an electronic 'cost clock' on an unusual bill board counts the total amount spent on the Iraq war. "The figure is astonishing: Ticking upwards at more than $137 billion, it increases at a rate of $177 million per day, $7.4 million per hour and $122,820 per minute." So far $144 billion are already dedicated to Iraq. A news report by a think tank analyzes a range of projects that could have been undertaken for the cost of war in Iraq, demonstrating exactly how the $144 billion could have funded no fewer than 18 major projects to make America safer at home and in the world (*Atlanta Journal-Constitution*, September 21, 2004). In a more serious study (*Foreign Affairs*), the economist Peter Peterson has cautioned against the astronomical the end result should not be trading a dictator for a chaos. Again, without becoming a second Vietnam, Iraq has partly become a political wedge that has divided America. The contentious Iraq issue created a wide divide between George Bush and John Kerry in the presidential elections of November 2004 and polarized the nation. The dreaded Vietnam-effect without a second Vietnam!

Sums up Jonathan Freeland in *The Guardian*, London (August 11, 2004), "Bit by bit, the intellectual foundations of this war are crumbling to dust. No WMD; no outright end to human rights abuses; no democratic breakthrough. Even the most basic facts of the war are now in dispute—including the continued American-British attempt to pretend it's over." As Professor Juah Cole puts it, "And the Arabs, who resent Iraqi democracy as a model since it will have a 'made in America' tag on it. January 2005 elections, with a very poor voter turn out, will not give legitimacy to the new 'elected' Iraqi government—that, too, with a continuous stamp of USA and Britain."

Asks *The Economist* (September 25, 2004), "Can a 'credible' Iraqi election be held in such circumstances? Or should the Americans mount a powerful pacification effort first? These are fine judgments.... The lesson of the occupation so far is that filling the political vacuum is part and parcel of filling the security vacuum. But to fill Iraq's security vacuum, America needs to fill the country's political vacuum."

Adds Freeland, what the early August "proves is a bleak truth: this war is not over—nor has it achieved any but the baldest of its stated aims". Meanwhile, National Intelligence Estimate (made public in September 2004) portends a civil war and chaos brewing toward the end of 2005. Iraq has proved to be 'a profound diversion' from the war on terrorism. And, most seriously, the post-Saddam Iraq has already succeeded in strengthening of a monster and that too, on a wider spectrum—the contrary to what Bush-Blair have claimed: to make the world free from terrorism and its operators.

The year 2005 has raised more questions than answers to this claim. Despite threats of attacks on those Iraqis with voting intentions on January 30, 2005, the US and allies could succeed in conducting Iraq's first democratic elections in 50 years. Turn out of 60 percent was surprisingly strong. At least 44 died in suicide and mortar attacks on polling stations including nine suicide bombers. It was a precedent that could shake-up the autocratic Arab world. As Cairo-based author Raymond Stock commented, "The Iraqi election was a total shock to the militant *jehadi* forces in the Arab-Muslim world." Added Friedman, "And the thing they are deciding on is not to be pro-American, not to be pro-Western, but to try to build their own Arab society in a way that will be open to modernism and interpretation of Islam that encourage innovation, adaptation and progress."

But it is not over-not by long shot. Abu Zarqawi, the Jordian-born jehadist has effectfully countered such a process for democracy is based on "right to choose your religion" and that is "against the rule of God". Inspired by him, the Sunni-jehadists have become suicide bombers at the rate of three and four a day. The Shia-Sunni-Kurds triangular ethnic tug-of-war disturbed the formation of a coalition cabinet for three months. When the Prime Minister Ibrahim al-Jaafari, a devout but liberal Muslim formed a partial cabinet, it was greeted by everyday killing of Arabs and Americans that amounted to 500 deaths within three weeks in April.

The future of Iraq—and perhaps, of the Middle East—points to two polar icons: Al Zarqawi and the Shia leader Grand Ayatollah Ali Sistani. Al Zarqawi is the catalyst of new religious conflict. Sistani stands for a democratic constitution in line with Islamic principles with Islam as Iraq's national religion. On whose lines will Iraq finally course its troubled journey?

VII

Perspectives

19

Review: "Al Qaeda 2.0"?

America and Israel are becoming soft. You keep on killing their people; and they would not be able to see their people being killed. That is why, they will reply with counter-attack; constantly fight against you, and would send suicide bombers in response too. This is the line against America that Osama has taken (for his Jihadi war of nerves) and this is also the principle applied against Israel.

One cannot believe that even when Muslim, Jews, and other religions also may have faded from earth, terrorism would vanish totally. It has made a small yet unconquerable niche in the innermost corners of the psyche of mankind by now.

However, it may turn irrelevant or effective, one can hope. Those who love women, books and their own lives, and so are not entangled in the thought of considering death (by suicide) for religion, will find religion itself irrelevant.

After 9/11 also the Nobel Prize winners have contended, while remaining beyond any particular society, culture or force:

The war against terror is not a great war among religions and cultures. The need of the time is not any conflict of cultures but a state of harmony among them.

> The real war that people of the world needs to fight is a war against poverty and backwardness, and it should aim at the throwing away of all the weapons that kill millions of human beings. Only real cooperative efforts of all the religions and nations of the world can be farsighted and result-oriented for development of the mankind.
>
> — Extracted from sources of perceptive views

Islamic *jehad* under al Qaeda morphed into a movement. The objectives of the movement can be seen to be spreading in interlinked phases: *One*, to drive the people and influences of the West-dominated international community out of the Middle East—the Arab core of the Muslim *Umma. Two*, to throw away all the Arab regimes and Pakistan that work under the tutelage of the US and other western powers. *Three*, to acquire a definitive space and entrench in Muslim-dominated countries/regions such as South Asia, Southeast Asia, North and sub-Saharan Africa and Central Asia. *Four*, to destroy Israel. *Five*, to proliferate inside the western world—to start with, in Europe, where Muslim population is on visible increase. *Six*, to replace, in the process, the present state system of democracy and liberal regimes and US-dominated international system by a unified theocratic Islamic system. *Seven*, to use pro-Islamic state and non-state players, with use of *jehadi* fundamentalist ideology and terrorism equipped with the modern-most weapons including the nuclear missiles, technology and traditional as well as sophisticated communication. *Eight*, to indoctrinate, train and use the young generation and even women, as suicide bombers, to ruthlessly carry out their strategies, plans and ultimate goals.

Three years on from its most deadly attacks, al Qaeda has evolved. There is a tendency to see it as a monolithic foe directed by an all-powerful leader pulling the strings. But analysts believe there is a danger in laying too much emphasis

bin Laden and His Top Aide, al-Zawahari

on al Qaeda and Osama bin Laden alone when the reality is more complex—perhaps, more dangerous.

There is no doubt that the core of al Qaeda has been disrupted. It has lost its secure sanctuary and training camps in Afghanistan and is finding it harder to organize and communicate under pressure.

The core of hardened veterans has been hit hard in the past three years.

In his New York convention speech on September 2, 2004, President Bush declared that American strategy was succeeding and that "more than three-quarters of al Qaeda's key members and associates have been detained or killed". He is right, but only partially.

Underestimated

For body counts are not necessarily the most useful way of judging progress because al Qaeda is not a 'normal' military entity and the war that the US is engaged in is not a 'normal' military struggle.

Interpreting the removal of al Qaeda's key operatives as a sign of 'winning' risks misunderstanding both the aims of al Qaeda and its nature as an organization. For instance, one key question is whether the organization is recruiting new personnel faster than its current members are hunted down and whether its broader base of support is being eroded or is growing.

The focus on the core of al Qaeda also ignores the extent to which the baton has largely passed from al Qaeda's historic core to a broader, looser network of radical groups. In some cases, existing insurgent groups have been radicalized through contacts with al Qaeda and drawn into a wider network. One example is Jemiaah Islamiah in Indonesia which has increasingly attacked international targets but is relatively independent of al Qaeda.

As *BBC.com* (September 22, 2004) gives an informed review of the status of al Qaeda and its clones: Other local insurgencies which were sometimes nationalist or ethnic in character have been pulled into the broader rhetoric of the war on terrorism either because of groups themselves buying into the al Qaeda discourse of an international struggle, or because governments cracking down on them have found it useful to cast their own struggles in that wider context.

Sometimes both occur—for instance the growing Islamization, radicalization and internationalization of the Chechen conflict and Russia's efforts to emphasize this trend. It is the local groups and affiliates, not the al Qaeda core itself, which have undertaken most of the post-9/11 attacks.

More significantly, the new, younger generation of militants may only have tenuous, if any, link to the al Qaeda core.

The group that carried out the Madrid bombing in March 2004 did not include people who had been selected, trained and were carrying out direct orders from Osama bin Laden in the way the 9/11 hijackers had.

None of them appear to have been to Afghanistan. Instead, they were inspired by al Qaeda and its rhetoric and statements but seem to have operated as part of a relatively autonomous grouping of European cells.

And, the more dispersed the network is—and the more it relies on local cells rather than people travelling into a country to commit an act—the harder it becomes to counter the threat because these independent actors can be harder to locate and keep track of.

After a neat and quick military victory in Afghanistan in November 2002, Laurence Pope who ran war games concerning assaults in Afghanistan and Iraq stated, "We should have focussed like a laser on bin Laden and taking down al Qaeda, breaking crockery in the neighborhood, if necessary".

The crockery he was referring to included the government of Pakistan, which viewed the Pashtun tribal areas along the Afghan border as ungovernable. The US should have gone into these areas right away, either with Pakistani troops or on its own, Pope says. This might have caused some regional and international disruption—but less than later invading Iraq. Comments, James Fallows, "Failure to do that helped bin Laden to escape from Tora Bora and terrorist groups to reconstitute themselves. And at Tora Bora, bin Laden was confined to several dozen square miles. If he is now in Pakistan's North West Frontier Province, the area involved is the size of Virginia".

Any way, as it happened, as in Afghanistan, after winning a quick military victory in Iraq, Collin Powell declared that a notable victory in curbing terrorism had occurred. The head of anti-terrorist set-up in America also claimed that "the terrorists are now on the run". Since President Bush proudly declared on the ship SS Cole in May 2003 that the US-led ally's "mission was accomplished", by mid-September, 2004, an estimated

12,000-14,00C Iraqis and more than 1,000 American troops were killed.

However, at that very time, on May 12, 2003, two bombs exploded in Riyadh, the capital of Saudi Arabia. On May 16, the bases of allies of America were attacked in Casablanca in Morocco. The limitations of such opinions became obvious as "al Qaeda is on deathbed" and that "al Qaeda is alive and kicking".

Within minutes of the suicidal bomb explosions, and in miles and miles surrounding it, nine suicidal bomber terrorists, seven Americans and seven Saudis besides 29 persons were killed. This was the next great terrorist violence committed after Bali and Mombassa bombings in 2002. By its activities in Iraq, America created somewhat fearsome image in the world and its effect was obvious on the institutions that are run legally. However, those beyond states, non-state kind of terrorist organizations totally ignored this great power working against terrorism. They have not eschewed their chosen path as it was clear from such incidents. Only before six days of the Riyadh bombings, the Saudi security forces had captured a big haul of dangerous weapons. In that raid 19 suspects were captured, out of whom some were Saudis, others Kuwaitis and Canadians. B. Raman believes that they were receiving orders directly from bin Laden.

In the Casablanca bombings the suicidal bombers attacked Spanish and Jew establishments. In these bombings 12 bombers and other 29 citizens of Spain had taken contract from al Qaeda and were connected with organizations prepared to take on great suicidal destruction as well. In the backward area of Casablanca and elements living in rags made up the rightist fundamentalists named 'Jihad Salafists', a militant Sunni Islamic group, who carried out for this massacre, according to the analysis of *The Economist* (London).

The Spanish establishment became a target for the militants, in this case, because Spain had declared its support to America in its war with Iraq. Even then, the ministers of

Morocco who are going ahead on the road to democratic system as compared to other Muslim nations may also be a reason for this attack as analyzed by some papers.

Under these circumstances, in mid-May, the clouds of terrorism were getting darker. The alert against terrorism in America went one notch higher, and the television and the newspapers exhibited orange strips for this. In Saudi Arabia and some other places the American, British and German consulates and missions were closed down. Britain sounded the siren of this danger in East Africa, and some other nations also followed it.

A message in the voice of the right hand man of bin Laden, one al Zawahiri was heard on an audiotape. It gave a call for attacks on consulates and interests of America, Britain, Australia, and surprisingly, even of Norway. Also, those who had helped America in its war against Iraq were harshly reprimanded.

It must be noted, at the same time, that the terrorists had to retreat on certain front in the face of grave defeat. *US News and World Report* (June 2, 2002) stated in its overall report of anti-terrorist steps/policy: Half of the active al Qaeda leaders were either captured or killed. "The top leaders were isolated and were busy seeking secret places to take shelter. Their main army commanders were dead; their main management members were in jails. In the whole world the same story is true for their 3,000 terrorist colleagues." Whatever communications they are doing (phone, chatting or wireless messages that are exchanged) are becoming more and more dangerous for them. This is because, such messages can be interrupted and discovered and decoded by the anti-terrorist set-up through their powerful satellite communication equipments, and accurately and effectively captures those who are carrying on such communications. (No wonder, as the reports say, bin Laden no longer uses equipments like the telephone or cell phone.) Besides, organizations like al Qaeda had a great deal of money with them earlier, but this is no longer the case.

According to a message captured by an American spy system, one terrorist was begging his 'boss' to send only 80 dollars! By early March 2002 itself, America and its allies had captured more than a thousand members and supporters of al Qaeda.

The well-known investigative journalist Bob Woodward, in his books *Bush at War* (2001) (based on interviews with the President) and *Plan of Attack* (2004), has shown that Bush had set up a team for a war against terror within a few days of 9/11. This set-up called 'Worldwide Attack Matrix' has already begun a campaign to uproot al Qaeda and similar terrorist organizations from 80 nations.

In the last part of 2001 raids were carried out on main bases and camps of al Qaeda and thousands of their workers were killed. These raids were conducted with such unusual speed that the workers of bin Laden while fleeing had not been able to take away their address books, videos, computers, etc. "Like the Nazis, they used to keep very detailed information about their plans and activities." The CIA's Counter-Terrorism Center has collected as many as 3,000 such thick files, providing very important details and links. In one estimate they believe that by now the close associates and dangerous disciples with bin Laden are reduced to the number of 180 only. (Of course, such highly trained '180 only' terrorists too can possibly do a lot to shake the peace and security in the world, inject fear and create violence, and the possibility cannot be ignored for such developments.) These people are still ready to give up their lives for their *jehadi* aims and turn 'martyrs' (*shuhada* or *mujahideen*), a term used in place of '*fidayeen*' (or freedom fighters) and determined to act for terrorism of total destruction. Their ultimate aim is "to completely destroy America as we know it".

From the deep investigations of CIA, certain information has come out that has shaken up the analysts. The chief of the CIA's Counter-Terrorist Center, Coffer Black says, "We believed that we had worse secret information than them: in the air attacks by America and its allies on Afghanistan, among the militants of al Qaeda were persons with 'blond hair and blue eyes and with variety of skin colours: Chechens, Uzbeks, Indonesians and Chinese!' " Black adds, "These belonged to an international community, with greater loyalty not for their own nations but beyond it to the Pan-Islamic religion and were really connected with very good network."

As the files grew on them giving secret information, they began to analyze and classify the various terrorist groups, their nature and activities. The *Time* magazine cites one highly experienced scholar of such matters as strategies and management for the same, "Ultimately, two al Qaedas are working. In Arabic, al Qaeda means 'base', the foundation for Islam.

One, 'al Qaeda' is the one providing the philosophy, and taking inspiration from bin Laden, lights up a very wide network of radical Islamists, but they are not direct followers of bin Laden. The insides of this network are what the analysts call is like 'franchisee' and these organizations are either allies or joined with al Qaeda. They are radical organizations, and partners in the dream of bin Laden to carve out an Islamic world that would spread from Indonesia to Uzbekistan. Of the 42 countries that have recruits in al Qaeda, after Saudi, Pakistan is the most prominent one.

Second, al Qaeda is a much disciplined organization. It is a definite, disciplined and determined organization of mafia kind. It has its own rules. A very complex arrangement is set up to use its large secret treasure. It agrees to admit anyone to become its 'member' only after checking out certain elements. The infrastructures linked with it (Madrassas, Maulavis, persons in charge of Masjids, etc.) have prepared thousands and thousands of Muslims in their training camps. However, out of these, very few are selected for active 'membership'.

Rohan Gunaratna, the scholarly author of *Inside Al Qaeda* says, "As al Qaeda is an elite organization takes very few elements (in spite of being trained) as its members. America's intelligence agencies believe that there may be only few trusted terrorists who have taken the oath of 'bayat' i.e. loyalty to bin Laden."

Al Qaeda has more hierarchical structure than the belief of CIA. Unlike what was believed earlier, bin Laden is not a mere figurehead and informal head of this organization. He is the leader who holds the authority to evaluate the plans for terrorist activities and sanction them if he wants. Laden had approved of the plan of 9/11 and similar ambitious terrorist actions. From the internal set-up and method of working, his orthodox 'Wahabi' principles and the blind faith in the leader—all make it seem as if it is a 'religion' in itself while bin Laden is its charismatic messiah. "Even more than Napoleon, bin Laden seems like a 'cult guru' for whom followers of a closed mentality are ready to sacrifice their souls."

There is no agreement about the amount of money al Qaeda possesses. Immediately after 9/11 it had 300 million dollars is an estimate that proved wrong. Still, everyone agrees that from the members of the royal family of Saudi down to certain Muslim citizens of Britain and America and the various groups from all over the world provide financial help in different ways. The main financial base of al Qaeda is the collection of funds made in various religious programs, charity gatherings and mosques and merchants during the armed movement for removing Soviet domination in Afghanistan. With the help of the US Treasury and FBI, the CIA has discovered the methods of al Qaeda for exchange of money and flowing of its funds. It collects its money through international banks, '*hawala*', and 'underground bankers', dealing in gold and gems and such channels. The distribution is made all the way to its active members or suicide bomber squad members. Thus, an underground system prevails. The captured amounts are, still, probably only the tip of an iceberg. The organizations that nurture terrorism probably pull wool over the eyes of ordinary people by using very innocent and value based names and aims. For example, the Saudi-based Harmei Islamic Foundation, and a Saudi group working in Afghanistan as Vafa

Humanitarian Foundation, and many fraudulent groups allegedly working for human welfare based in Pakistan and yet in reality working to encourage and support the terrorist elements of Kashmir, Pakistan and Afghanistan in their intrusions and attacks across the border into Kashmir and India. In the spring of 2002, about 100 spies of FBI and CIA themselves came to Pakistan and they have set up secret associations with the local intelligence agencies too.

Many well-known terrorist leaders have been captured from the area of Pakistan bordering Afghanistan, which is suggestive. From Faizalabad CIA captured Saudi Palestinian Abu Zubbaidah and this is very significant catch. Certain terrorists have provided much important information about many links. Such persons possessed CDs, diaries of addresses, and even satellite phones at times. Then, one Ramzi Binalshibh was captured. Ramzi had provided funds to the hijackers of 9/11. A team of American and Pakistani officers captured him along with laptop computers, satellite phones, funds and weapons.

On the whole, after the retreat of the Taliban rulers in Afghanistan, al Qaeda had remained dormant for a while. But, as US turned the noose tighter, it began to retaliate in the fall of 2002. An oil tanker in Yemen was bombed in October; within the week a hotel in Bali was devastated in a bomb attack and this was a serious incident. After 9/11 more than 200 people were killed in car bombs of the terrorists. In the Bali incident the largest number of tourists killed or injured was from Australia.

In 2003, CIA worked hard to curb the terrorist activities and leaders of al Qaeda. Its Director, George Tenet said, "In recent months we have been successful in our efforts to capture the senior members of al Qaeda." In March 2003, the US-Pakistan team found a prize-catch in the capture of Khalid Sheikh Muhammad (KSM). A highly capable man, KSM was the master mind behind the attacks of 9/11. It was his intellect that had conceived and shaped 9/11 and other half-a-dozen terrorist attacks.

As observed by Coffer Black, the head of US State Department's Counter Terrorism Office, "To capture KSM means to capture the 'Chief of Operations' of al Qaeda." The next big fish to be netted was Mustafa Hosvi. He used to control the moneybag to pay cash by wire to the hijackers of 9/11. Bank ledgers, names and addresses of couriers and financiers, additional phone numbers, secret places of safekeeping, etc., were obtained from him. Many of these brought to light some important networks in Spain, America and Switzerland. One American official said, "In these successful operations we have received much help from our associates in Pakistan. The high-tech communication equipments of America also came in useful in intercepting the messages of the terrorists. Three top leaders of al Qaeda, namely, KSM, Zubbaidah and Binlasheebh, were captured with the help of satellite phones. Thus, the latest technology has helped America a great deal in the wars (against Afghanistan and Iraq), and also in intelligence work to be ahead of the enemies." However, Black says, "Even then, al Qaeda is a force that can pose a dangerous threat for stability and security in the world. There are a large number of workers who are ready to give up their lives as martyrs and suicide bombers and who are spread all over, eager to act."

Suicide attacks have become the contemporary terrorism's weapon with the most audio-visual effects. Says University of Australia Professor of Sociology Riaz Hasan, "Suicide attacks—the targeted use of self-destructing humans against a perceived enemy for political ends—are modern methods with ancient roots" (*ISIM Newsletter* 14, June 2004). In modern times, Japanese employed kamikaze pilots to attack American marines during World War II. In October 1983, the Hezbollah, or a Party of God, a Lebanese Shiite militant group, carried out suicide attacks on a US army base in Beirut, which killed 300 American and French servicemen. This led to the withdrawal of the American and French multinational peacekeeping force in Lebanon that proved it an effective strategic political weapon. This was also underlined in 1985, when Israeli forces had to leave Lebanon and to quit the Gaza Strip and the West Bank in 1994 and 1995. Though during 2003-04, Ariel Sharon has again resorted to deal with Palestinian suicide strategy, grown in number and frequency, with iron-handed reactive violence. The Tamil Tigers in Sri Lanka—a radical nationalist group—first used it effectively against the Sri Lankan government. In fact, one Tamil Tiger woman suicide bomber killed India's Prime Minister Rajiv Gandhi in 1991 for helping Sri Lankan government. The Palestinian radical groups like Hamas, Palestinian Islamic Jihad and al-Aqsa Martyrs' Brigades have used religion to recruit and use suicide attackers and raise operational funds. Citing 'a groundbreaking study of University of Chicago political scientist Robert Papp Hassan shows that "there is little connection between religious fundamentalism and suicide attacks". Even when the suicide bombers are, perhaps, fanatical, the leadership that recruits them may not be so. In his study, University of Michigan's Scott Atran has concluded that suicide attackers have no appreciable psychological pathologies and are educated and economically well-off individuals. In the context of the Middle East, the suicide bombers are driven by "a collective sense of historical injustice, political subservience and a pervasive sense of social humiliations vis-à-vis global powers and allies". At the same time, the fact that they become easy targets of the Maulavis and fanatic leaders for fundamentalist indoctrination and sensitized to martyrdom cannot be underplayed. After her interviews with 250 aspiring suicide bombers and their recruiters, Nasra Hassan, a UN relief worker in Gaza, found that none of them were uneducated or simple-minded. But potential suicide bombers "empowered themselves in the face of powerlessness".

Pew Global Attitudes Survey of March 2004 showed that in several Muslim countries such as Pakistan, Jordan, Morocco, etc., a majority of respondents said that the US government was overreacting to terrorism. They also supported suicide bombings against Israel, Americans and other westerners. The International Institute of Strategic Studies, London has also reported that the war in Iraq has led to an increase in global recruitment for anti-American *jehad*."

An expert of such matters uses a definition from management parlance to explain 'al Qaeda 2.0'. Al Qaeda, he says, "is an organization that learns more and more, day after day from its own work-field. It collects information and knowledge about a nation, group and its political and military strength, develops new skills and to adjust to new climes constantly sharpens the edge of its own techniques and endeavours." This is not good news, but a fact.

Peter Bergen, the author of *Holy War Inc.: Inside the Secret World of Osama bin Laden* (2001), calls today's al Qaeda as 'al Qaeda 2.0'. Today, we shall not see the form and shape of that al Qaeda, which conducted military training camps and used million of dollars, but now it is taking the shape of a more decentralized infrastructures and movements. The terrorist network is now growing with greater linking among various local violent groups as one body. Right from Bali to Casablanca and West Coast-Tel Aviv suicide bombing attacks favoring Palestine are clear examples of this new trend.

Instead of the making big and prestigious centers like the WTC, Pentagon and Indian Parliament as targets of widespread and deep blasts, they are now aiming at 'soft targets'. For example, the streets of Casablanca, non-Arab settlements of Riyadh, Akshardham in Gandhinagar, or tourists centers as in Bali, Jakarta, Casablanca, Mombasa, and Mumbai's Taj Hotels, etc., aiming to cut down their tourist business and breakdown the economy. Bomb blasts on trains in Madrid to school massacre in Beslan, Russia; bomb blasts in Ankara; attacks on schools and security forces in southern Thailand; continuous killing and blasts on American-British troops, Iraqi police, civilians, and employees of foreign contractors (French, Nepalis, Italians, etc.) in Baghdad, Fallujah, Najaf and other cities of Iraq generated deep political impact on politics and thinking in the public in the US, Muslim nations and the world over.

The forward march of the war against terrorism and the successful violent attacks seem to be occurring simultaneously. However, these trends are not contradictory for each other. Al Qaeda is an extremist thought at one end; just as it is also an Islamic movement and campaign too. Also, basically, it is a very well-linked and well-arranged organization. Therefore, to conclude anything or predict about its future is a complex and uncertain exercise. "In spite of many a retreats it possesses a leadership that can guide and conduct violent attacks with the help of its workers." The simultaneous and devastating attacks in Riyadh on different targets are a proof of this. Before their spreading out in the world, with the help of Saudis, millions of *jehadists* have been trained in Afghanistan. This is such a huge 'cadre' or an army of terrorist workers that the number of some thousands of suspected terrorists seem to be a very tiny one among those who have accepted the 'cause' advocated by bin Laden.

Besides, the top leaders of al Qaeda join similar groups and forces aiming at restoring orthodox and fundamentalist beliefs and traditions similar to its own (Wahabi or Deobandi), in order to carry out its terrorist activities and thrust them on the local Islamic communities of different nations. As the International Institute for Strategic Studies, London reported, al Qaeda "was galvanized by the wars in Afghanistan and Iraq. As of mid-2004 it had at least 18,000 operatives in sixty countries". It ominously states, "al Qaeda has fully reconstituted (and) set its sights firmly on the USA and its close western allies in Europe."

On the other hand, local organizations do not receive any orders or suggestions in any measure, small or big, from al Qaeda and bin Laden about their local plans for terrorist activities. They are independent organizations. They address the local issues of dispute and recruit the young people for its network. The local orthodox Muslim inhabitants in Bali disapproved of the modern night clubs, hotels and such westernized centers of entertainment. That is why, they killed off the foreigners (from Dutch to Australians and New Zealanders also) by car bomb blasts. Similar car bombs blasts were also made against the Jews in Mombassa, Casablanca and Kampala, etc. in selected hotel areas.

On May 16, 2003, within 48 hours at five different places in Morocco, the suicide bombers made successful attacks. A total of 29 persons lost their lives in these attacks including some Spanish, Jews and local Moroccans. The Morocco government declared that this inhuman action was a work of the rightist group of Islamic fundamentalists who were trained locally. The security personnel captured two Moroccan terrorists in this matter. *The Economist* (May 24, 2003) has concluded that the local groups were given 'sub-contracts' for acts involving self-destruction by suicidal bombing that would bring great damage in its wake. One such organization, 'Jihad Salafist' keeping their holy book of Koran as their main base, distributes the sermons of bin Laden in recorded form. If someone is found drinking liquor, he is stoned to death. Thus, a very different kind of terrorist activity has appeared since 9/11 that must be differentiated.

21 Months after 9/11

In the early half of 2002, mobile phones or what the American agencies call 'chatters', and e-mails and MSN messages were waylaid and much information was gathered. Also, the terrorists, who were arrested, were also interrogated deeply and gradually the information and links were found out. On the other hand, the suicide bombings or martyr-type terrorist activities in Casablanca, Tel Aviv and the Israeli settlements in the West Coast also have provided much information about the terrorists.

In their files, we find important explanations of their central and small, secret leadership of al Qaeda and the local and autonomous groups, and these can be found in the *US News and World Report* (June 2, 2003). Besides, even at the micro level, there is no dearth of unemployed young men (and now even women) in Palestine who are personally provoked by the speeches or teachings of bin Laden or *jehadi* Maulavis, or excited by the asperity of Israel, or inspired by the desire to protect the 'holy culture' of their own belief structure from encroachments of American one, and they become suicide bombers for that 'cause'. Thus, it must be noted that autonomous and local, i.e., the second level groups as well as very fundamentalist individuals also turn to terrorist action.

According to the message allegedly attributed to bin Laden and telecast in February, now Jordan, Nigeria, Pakistan, Saudi Arabia and Yemen have arrived at a stage when it has become imperative to free them from (modern and corrupt) system and culture: After 9/11 the presence of al Qaeda is increasing gradually in Pakistan, and this is suggestive. In two of its neighboring countries on the western borders extremist Islamic parties are in power, and this is also suggestive. President Musharraf may want to stop the infiltrations of Muslim fundamentalist and terrorist elements into Pakistan and across the LoC into Azad Kashmir (PoK), but it remains a question if he can do so. Once again, at this time, the newly re-gathering Taliban and al Qaeda's *jehadi* attacks have begun in Afghanistan and Lashkar-e-Toiba (LeT) in Kashmir and local organizations in south Philippines have also shown that they too can inflict such attacks.

With a relatively quick and casualty-free military attack in Afghanistan in October 2001 (such neat operation was also to mark the US-led allies' action in Iraq in March 2003), the violent skirmishes restarted in Afghanistan. The military bill for peacekeeping and security of the Karzai administration in Afghanistan, where tribal militia and local warlords rule the roost, reached to a staggering $50 billion by the end of 2003. Even Karzai's car and residence were attacked in September 2004 that revealed the deep penetration reach of the remnants of the Taliban.

As the official claim of the end to hostilities in Iraq was followed there by mayhem and killings, Afghanistan also experienced on the same pattern. "There are other similarities. Attacks in Afghanistan have begun to emulate those in Iraq: suicide bombings, which is not the traditional Afghan approach; similar types of explosive devices set off by remote control; missile attacks from longer range; and targeting foreign aid organisations and the UN" (Deborah Stroggins has given a poignant account of the plight of some foreign aid-centric welfare workers in Afghanistan in *Emma's War*). "Just as Iraqi guerrillas attacked the Rashid Hotel when the US Deputy Defense Secretary, Paul Wolfowitz, was staying there, so Afghan guerrillas fired rockets into the American embassy in Kabul during the visit of Wolfowitz's boss, Donald Rumsfeld, less than two weeks ago" (*The Independent*, London, December 14, 2003). Colonel Mike Griffith, commander of the British troops there told *The Independent*: "There is no doubt. There are now indications of methodology transfer from Iraq. Some of the things we have witnessed in Iraq, we are beginning to see here."

Modern communications and technology are skillfully used by the terrorists whose leaders are educated and trained in the West. They use broadcast servers, vodaphones, laptop video links; satellite and private website; 'embedded' journalists. Communications are an essential armor in al Qaeda's strategy and in recent years the Internet and e-mail have acquired an added usefulness. "They have provided the terror network with new possibilities—but as the case of Khan illustrates, fresh vulnerabilities too" (*BBC Online*, October 6, 2004). Sajjan Gohel of Asia-Pacific Foundation says, the al Qaeda ideology can, probably, be better served on the Internet than by any other means. "Small cells can act very big and pose a serious danger to world order—without the instruments of a state."

Again, the Internet suits the increasingly decentralized structure of al Qaeda. The web offers a channel for like-minded *jehadists* located in different regions and communities to chat and interact, especially when operatives, under the pressure of the US and the like, may be isolated and having to lie low (*BBC Online*). Thus, a virtual community of 'franchised' al Qaeda and terrorist networks through chat rooms and website and operates to spread its message and keep its morale. In sum, the awesome mix of new communications, lethal technology and suicide bombers with catalysis of a fundamentalist ideology presents a deadly challenge to the leaders of the worldwide war on terrorism.

Terrorism is like the bacteria that brings on the disease of dysentery. It can be curbed by military and intelligence power, but if it has taken root deep into the intestine, it is like the left over amoeba/bacteria. This cannot be removed well enough even by antibiotic medicines. Only by proper habits of eating and drinking can it be kept dormant. Similarly, in body of human society too, if the policy of tolerance and liberal mentality with a proper educational system is adopted and practiced, a healthy climate that does not nourish terrorism can be prepared and everyone may breathe freely.

It would be pertinent to cite two different bases here:

The Economist notes the new form of al Qaeda and the movement of terrorism towards decentralization, and then states, "In spite of all this, the leaders of al Qaeda have not left to attack their 'distant enemy' America, or have not accepted that they are no longer able to attack it collectively. The terrorists captured so far and interrogated deeply by the intelligence agencies project a very different picture. This war will prove much longer and less decisive or of any final shape than the war against Iraq."

And, the *US News and World Report* comes to this conclusion, "... (Terrorism) has concentrated on 'soft targets'; but the original creation of bin Laden may still survive. In that case, it may also happen that young Jihadis may occupy leadership positions faster than America and its allies can find them."

It is clear at any rate that America has waited too long in joining the war against terrorism. And this war still remains to be won. This paper cites one senior American intelligence official, "I have not seen anything that you can celebrate so far. I do not know if we would ever be able to declare our 'victory' in this war."

As concluding remarks we may recount some issues. The 'ecology' of the terrorists is complex and so there are certain limits to generalizations about these. However, from the current trends and episodes, two or three aspects are clear.

First aspect is with regard to the strategies of al Qaeda. Along with its linked organizations, al Qaeda seems to have changed from 'hard' targets of the 1990s like Pentagon, political leaders or strategic establishments, and now appear to be looking for 'soft' targets such as citizens, tourist centers, etc., that are providing economic resources in developing nations (e.g., Bali, Kenya, Casablanca, Mumbai). These actions also adversely affect the ruling elite in these nations.

Besides, even with large-scale destruction of their own people, the suicidal attacks bring in martyrdom or '*shaheedi*' even in rich Muslim nations when they attack or hurt the unpalatable foreigners of America or other nations, in addition to individual publicity to the terrorists. Their families are provided with considerable monetary and other kinds of help as well. The family of a suicide bomber gets 200 to 250 thousand dollars from Arafat or Hamas for killing Israeli citizens. *The Economist* puts this in one apt line thus, "Suicide remains a preferred technology."

Another issue is of geographical extent. In countries of Southeast Asia like Bali and Malaysia there were serious and fatal attacks in the latter half of 2002. In these countries the Islamic extremist or fundamentalist forces are not powerful. The Muslim population in both Bali and Singapore is also very small. Also, these countries are under liberal rule. In countries where the Muslim population is in majority (Indonesia, Malaysia) also, social liberal trends prevail. Islam here is not as orthodox or rigid as in the Arab countries of the Middle East;

and yet the Bali episode has shown that in the country of majority Muslim population, even with liberal and moderate social atmosphere, orthodox and fundamentalist forces can implement terrorist plans successfully.

However, the other side of the coin is also significant. It is not only in the liberal and moderate Bali and Morocco, but also in Saudi Arabia which is believed to nourish radical Islamic forces and the very place of origin of the rigid and highly traditional minded sect of Wahabi, too, a number of bomb blasts occurred in May. The royal family of Saudi Arabia has provided al Qaeda and other fundamentalist forces with plentiful funds. The *jehadi* workers from Saudi Arabia have been found actively working from Washington to Pakistan. In the 9/11 episode the majority of the hijackers that took the American planes against the WTC towers to destroy them and died with them were from Saudi Arabia! That is why, these terrorists cursed the ruling group of Saudi Arabia who took help of America and gave help to it in return as 'American backers' or America dependents, etc., in contempt. However, in comparison to their criticism, they had kept away from spreading terrorism within that nation. This situation now changed. As on 9/11, as on the airport of Jeddah, an attempt to hijack a plane was made but unsuccessfully, it was reported by unofficial sources.

The experience of Turkey—the most modern and reformed of all Muslim countries—needs special mention as it helps joining some missing links in understanding the recent face of international terrorism. In the end of 2003, Turkey twice became the target of terrorists—on two synagogues and outside the British Consulate. In these two coordinated attacks 61 people died. It appeared to have all the fingerprints of al Qaeda and Turkish Hizbollah—pieces of two Pakistani passports, video tapes showing killing of Russian soldiers, and shooting down helicopters in Chechnya, and the like. The key suspects had travelled in recent years to Quetta in Pakistan to Kandhar in Afghanistan. Quetta and Kandhar emerged as "two key stops on the terror trail that often served as gateways to al Qaeda's training camps" (*Newsweek*, December 15, 2003).

The link is stretched to the southeast region as well. In January 2004, al Qaeda-linked terrorists helped a Muslim insurgency carry out attacks on schools and security forces in southern Thailand (*CNN.com*, January 8, 2004). As told to Associated Press by the new security advisor of the country, "The attackers are foreign trained extremists. These groups, as a part of a network, know each other well. They were comrades-in-arms in Afghanistan."

But, the May bomb blasts indicate that all types of Muslim governments are also on the map of the terrorists. This type of alarm that such attacks may occur in their own nations too, must be obvious to Musharraf and others who have been nourishing, supporting and helping these elements. As it is, within Pakistan, the American citizens and political establishments, religious places of the Christian as well as the Shias and establishments of other western countries have often been targets of violent attacks. Saudi rulers had adopted a loose policy for such attacks against Riyadh bombers to allow them to run off; but now Saudi has abandoned it and is providing cooperation to America instead, against terrorism, keeping an eye on it and trying to tighten the noose. Musharraf too has also followed this policy—perhaps due to pressures or by recognizing the reality may be—and willy-nilly begin to help the American intelligence and anti-terrorist agencies to capture the active elements of al Qaeda within Pakistan; and the American intelligence agencies and the Secretary of Defense duly appreciated this.

Up to mid-October after 22 months since 9/11 there has been considerable progress in the war against terrorism. The sources of strength, equipments and leaders of al Qaeda have been weakened a great deal; though bin Laden has not yet been captured, many substantial linkmen, close to top al Qaeda leadership have been nabbed in the UK, Pakistan and USA. The basic mental stamina of al Qaeda has not broken yet, and it suddenly appears at unlikely places by decentralized actions at different regions as 'al Qaeda 2.0'.

Even then, the growing nature of coordination and networking among the region-based and regionalized structures of terrorist action and their high level of preparedness and equipments need to be underlined. For example, as *Newsweek* (December 15, 2003) shows, "Attacks in Turkey were better coordinated and financed with more extensive international connections than previously thought—a clear sign that the broader terror network overseen by bin Laden remains alive and viable despite more than two years of relentless pressures by the western counter-terrorism agencies." In a sense, some US officials said, the Turkish bombing represents the new face of international terror. In stead of planning direct, spectacular attacks such as 9/11, "peripatetic al Qaeda operatives, perhaps inspired if not directly guided by leaders such as al-Zawahiqi, essentially piggyback" on the activities of the local militants, provide training, skills and financing that allows the indigenous groups to carry out attacks that are more deadly and sophisticated than would otherwise possible. The model appears to have been used in Turkey's secular Muslim country where until now there has been scant evidence of Islamic fundamentalist presence.

According to the strategic analyst B. Raman, the first half of 2003 indicated two clearly separate trends. One, after main leaders of al Qaeda were captured from Pakistan, its centralized command and control system is broken up. But, as a result, the trained al Qaeda cadres have turned into widespread numerous small cells based elsewhere. Those who are saved from the American onslaught still possess the same will-power as before. There is no dearth of volunteers for suicide bombers for them. Like a boil on skin that is not disappearing, many incidents like those against Israelis, or against western citizens in the Muslim countries or killing 12 soldiers by attacking an Indian Army camp in Jammu (June 12, 2003), keep on occurring every now and then.

Secondly, in the nations that have become victims of terrorism and their government agencies have not so far built any network or are not operating it if there is any, as compared to the network among various terrorist groups. Such groups, under the leadership of America or in their own ways, have proved far more effective in dealing with terrorism than their governments. That is why, it is imperative to have greater international cooperation in tightening the noose against al Qaeda as well as its supporting organizations like International Islamic Front, Hizub Islami and Lashkar-e-Toiba (LeT) mainly operating in Kashmir and Pakistan in their original names or new names and weaken them, and if possible uproot them altogether. Ironically, as *Guardian Unlimited-Online* reports, "South Waziristan (in Pakistan) is becoming Pakistan's mini-Iraq." In Washington itself CIA has captured in end of June 2003 seven dangerous terrorists. They were all trained in Pakistan, and one is of Pakistan origin too. It is significant that these are all members of LeT. They were found possessing lethal weapons and had been preparing for terrorist attacks on Kashmir and America. For the first time, CIA clearly mentioned the pending danger from the terrorists to India in its report. This report can put Musharraf in an anxious mood, for he had claimed on American soil that there are no training camps for terrorists in Pakistan and that terrorism is almost absent from Kashmir. When America also knowingly ignores such a situation, then we can discern hypocrisy in its policy and strategies of fighting terrorism, or cunning for serving only self-interests through them. This has become clear once more. Pakistan is a patron and platform of terrorism. Not only for India but also for the world including America this is a cause of worry. By understanding and accepting this obvious truth, it is necessary to build an overall international strategy for countering it. Dr. Reuben Paz, an expert on the counter-strategy for terrorism in Israel, says, "The terrorist infrastructure has taken deep roots in the Muslims living in the western countries" ('The Future of Global Terrorism is going to be in the West', *Rediff.com Online,* December 6, 2001). Peter Bergen who has met a doctor, two prestigious journalists (and the like) in Pakistan and Afghanistan, who have direct contact with bin Laden and have published their interviews with him sees "a possibility that bin Laden is somewhere in the mountains of Pakistani Kashmir—home to numerous Kashmiri militants, some of which are deeply intertwined with al Qaeda" (*The Atlantic*, October, 2004). He also mentions a significant fact about the multiple relationship between the terrorist groups and al Qaeda or "overlapping networks of nasty people". Citing Pakistani terrorism analysts, he states, "Several of the most militant Pakistani groups have recently gathered under an umbrella organization called Brigade 313, named for the number of men who stood with the Prophet Muhammad at the key battle of Badr, in the 7th century. Also, the Kashmiri militants are genuinely popular in Pakistan. Until January 2002, when it was officially banned, LeT maintained 2,200 offices around the country and hundreds of thousands of followers to its annual gatherings. It operates under a different name and with a lower profile."

Similarly, the highly strict governance of Saudi Arabia also has nurtured terrorism in a variety of ways, is a well-known fact. Raman says, "Afghanistan, Pakistan and Saudi Arabia make a 'Triangle of Terrorism'. Billions of dollars are spent in the name of charity support in a number of areas of the world including a large number of Madrassas and paramilitary Jihadi forces. It provides funds for their training and weapons etc. Some citizens of Pakistani origin, Muslim waqfs and private organizations in America are also doing this type of activities. Pakistan has become a sanctuary for them to get training and refuge if needed. That was the role of Afghanistan for the Taliban. After October 2001, the terrorist infrastructure based in Afghanistan shifted to Pakistan. So long as the world's spotlight is not fixed on this triangle, no great progress would be noted in the war against terrorism" (*Outlook India.com*, May 14, 2003). The world shall have to get used to the idea of facing frequent and violent terrorist upsurges and small or big episodes at unexpected public places so long as such terrorist triangles exist, even if bin Laden does not, and raise their own funds, weapons and think of issues at local level for their strategic attacks with the help of local *jehadi* terrorist groups. Just as *jehad* has become global, it has also become decentralized! The exchange of funds, petrodollar, frequent flyer, e-mail, chattering Al Jazeera, other modern technical means of communication and propaganda, video, audio cassettes, and means of transport—all these have globalized the minds of *jehadi* Muslims and added new force in them. It is not a development that initiated and implemented the processes of globalization; but 'political Islam' has shown that due to these means, even when Islam has different hues in various countries, four 'Ms'—Madrassa-Maulavi-Mullah-Masjids'—have now brought about a semblance of similarities and oneness of form to the definitions of 'Islam' and 'Islamic' terms. As John Esposito observes, "Islam's power and idealistic concepts of *jehad* have spun to become the primary idiom of Muslim politics, used by rulers and ruled, by reformers, political opposition and terrorists." On the other hand, "Globalization has more than one direction—not only from the West to the Rest."

The prestigious critic of American ruling elite and its corporate democratic system, the world renowned scholar Noam Chomsky had given a speech in burning words in June 2003 at the University of Washington DC about the foreign policy of Bush. He said, "President Bush has more than satisfied one of the most impossible dreams of bin Laden. Bush has made America the most disliked, most disgusting and most hated nation in many parts of the world."

Bush needs to appreciate how relevant is the statement of William Shakespeare. One of the characters of this great dramatist says, "A peace is of the nature of conquest; for them both parties nobly are subdued, and neither party is a loser."

History has witnessed some walls that have been dividing human society, or putting up barriers for marking borders.

- The Great Wall of China is so long and huge that even an astronaut can see it. Tens of thousands of laborers had been used for decades by the rulers of China to try and keep the Mongols at bay, away from their empire.
- Between North Korea and South Korea, early in the decade of 1950s, what Thomas Friedman termed as 'Green Wall' was actually a demilitarized zone on the 'Thirty-eighth Parallel'. The 38th latitude separated both Koreas, at the throat of each other since decades, and this non-weapon zone was turned into a green belt with trees and grass. Intervention by UNO brought about a ceasefire between the two Koreas, and at that time new arrangements were made with the 38th Parallel right in the middle, keeping the square central hall and the table on which the negotiations were taking place between representatives of South Korea sitting on the south side and those of North Korea on the north side. (When this author saw after three decades thereafter, the armed guards keeping security, due to mutual fear and distrust, on this very house and hall and the table as well, this episode seemed metaphorically ironic.)
- The third was the Berlin Wall. After the Cold War polarity of differences between western democracy and communist world was reflected in West and East Germany, and a wall was erected in Berlin separating the West Berlin and East Berlin as a symbol of two polarized nations within one. This wall existed up to 1989. After four decades of this artificial division of a nation as symbolized in its physical structure, was torn down by the people of Berlin themselves. Small parts of this wall were sold as souvenirs and these decorated the drawing rooms across Europe in the showcases, now known as 'museum pieces!'

- The Wailing Wall of Jerusalem creates a curious religious-cultural triangle of the world. Here are the symbols of the original founders of the world's great religions—Judaism, Christianity and Islam. The Jew devotees put their heads on the wall and weep. The Christians have to pass here through a strip of land under Muslim ownership to reach their Church. Here, we find echoes and shadows of the crusades of the Middle Age characterized by their various mass annihilations, caused by the Israelis vs. Palestinians and in those who want to become '*shuhada*' or the more recently current word '*istishhadi*' as suicide bombers. We shall not know if this wall is a triangle, triad or a junction of three cross roads, until the initiative of peace taken by the US and the response for its support from Israel Prime Minister and Palestine Prime Minister to it is clear.
- Recently, Israeli Prime Minister Sharon has started building the 'defense fence' as he calls it or the 'Apartheid Wall' as the Palestinian protesters and their supportive people worldwide have charged it. It has deepened the perception gap of ethnic/religious cleavages on both sides of the chronic divide. It has provoked violent attacks of Palestinians' suicide bombers including women and the pre-emptive and reactive air attacks by Israel. Arun Gandhi, grandson of Mahatma Gandhi, visited this area in August 2004 to persuade the Palestinians to persuade the militant intefada toward the non-violent path and force the Israelis to remove the wall. But, the Israeli media and the government highlighted his pro-Palestine statements. Rues Pinhas Inbari, "Indeed, the expanding wall between two peoples in this region is more than just a physical reality" (*Outlookindia.com*, September 5, 2004).
- In April 2003, Indian Prime Minister also has taken an initiative for peace with Pakistan and that has received encouragement from America and other nations. However, Pakistan continues to deny accepting the

present LoC as the international border. Kashmir is the lifeline for Pakistan, its Prime Minister admits. President Musharraf has stated in Europe that any Pakistani who revises the nuclear policy of Pakistan or accepts a compromise on Kashmir issue would be considered a traitor of the country. Infiltrations into Jammu & Kashmir with help of Pakistan continue unabated; some soldiers were killed right in the military camp by these terrorists. When one looks at all these signals together, a peace process that is peaceful or result-oriented seems to be a mirage. That is why, everyone would have to live with the reality of a long-term political instability and insecurity that prevails today rather than believe that terrorist danger or nightmare shall recede from Kashmir or other parts of India or South Asia. Not only this. On July 4, 2004, when Shia Muslims were doing '*namaz*' prayers in Pakistan, the Sunnis massacred 44 of them; and such an incident occurred once again within the month, under the military dictatorship of Musharraf. This merely makes one more anxious about the uncontrolled terrorism taking weird methods of violent expression.

- Pakistan specifically needs to monitored and managed, particularly by the US, before it is too late. In his forthright article, Mark Trehant, *Seattle Post-Intelligence's* editorial page editor cautions the US with its title, 'Ignore Pakistan at our Peril,' extensively quoting his arguments on the bases of National Bipartisan 9/11 Commission report which observes, "Pakistan's endemic poverty, widespread corruption and often ineffective government create opportunities for Islamic recruitment. Poor education is a particular concern. Millions of families, especially those with little money, send their children to religious schools or madrassahs." The Commission goes on to state, "It is hard to overstate Pakistan in the struggle against Islamic terrorism. Within Pakistan's borders are 150 million Muslims, scores of al Qaeda terrorists, and many Taliban fighters and, perhaps, Osama bin Laden." The Commission also is cynical about many of the Pakistani army and intelligence officials who remain at least 'ambivalent' about confronting extremists.

Trehant comments, "The future generation of Pakistan is being taught Islamic fundamentalism. The 9/11 Commission said, in Karachi alone, 200,000 young people are enrolled in nearly 900 madrassahs." And if religious schools are not enough, last year the North West Frontier Province and its Islamic Party government adopted Islam's *sharia* code—including a Taliban-like morality ministry complete with limits on television programs and posters that show women.

"Make no mistake: This group and the political coalition that runs part of Pakistan promote the merits of a new Taliban state. They see the West as evil and dismiss their leaders when they call for a moderate Islam." He sounds the US government to respond with prudence and alertness. The US should be doing more than using Pakistan as a military base and ally, even as the Commission notes, "Musharraf's government represents the best hope for stability in Pakistan and Afghanistan." In fine, the US must be "willing to make hard choices, too, and make the difficult long-term commitment to the future of (terrorism-free, moderate) Pakistan".

- Al Zarqawi who is carrying out widespread bloody attacks from suicide bombings to be headings received blessings to bin Laden to change the name of his group to al Qaeda. Under Zarqawi with fast spreading network to Europe, al Queda has turned into something into a movement. "Bin Laden is primarily inspirational; Zarqawi is primarily operational. They are the two most dangerous terrorists in the world." (British journalist Paul Eedle, trackingterror@CNN.com)
- The greatest wall is of bipolar mental set-up. The Huntington model of the clash of civilizations may not come about fully; but even then the clashes between orthodox Christian forces and *jehadi* Muslim forces,

unchanging traditionalists and modern societies will continue constantly due to terrorist activities. *Jehadi* violence will take any form, any shape at any level. Pakistan along with 57 other countries, having a big Muslim presence but with an 'enclave mentality' and fundamentalist outlook, thinking of hyper power America as their object of distaste and even hate—a situation that reminds one of living 'human volcanoes'. We do not see any leader who has the vision or capacity to bridge such deep perceptual gaps and ideological divide to help remove the religious-cultural wall.

Spread over a very large area in the world, internalized dualism, and with a status quo of Islamic community, the fresh challenges of terrorism after 9/11 must be comprehended in its entirety. The superpower of the world has failed to do this, or accordingly adopt a liberal, farsighted attitude—and so, ever growing in the two extremes of this polarized world. And *jehadi* fundamentalists have hardened their purist (Wahabi) sense of Islam and resolve to further penetrate the Muslim *Umma* with stronger dose of selective amnesia for a humane, liberal world. And skillfully but ruthlessly harness the lethal technology and infrastructure of the West and democracies to force the world to the 'fourth' world war (the third war was of the Cold War variety). In the process, terrorism has already emerged the greatest challenge and a polarizing issue of imminent global concern of the 21st century. A continuous, constant and an enduring challenge at that!

20

44 Months of 9/11

"We are at war. We have struggled with what we have called terrorism for a long time, without quite realising the nature of the threat," stated George P. Shultz, former U.S. Secretary of State before Commonwealth Club members in San Francisco in May 2004. Bin Laden and al Qaeda began to be well-known in the 1990s, but neither the nature of the threat they potentially posed was comprehended, nor pre-emptive or prophylactic steps planned by the U.S.

Meanwhile, terrorism evolved as a phenomenon of choice of a surreptious but ever extending Islam-based ideological movement. It became a movement succeeding as an effectively coordinated loose global network. Assassination of the Egyptian President Sadat (1981), the World Trade Center bombing (1993), assassination of Israeli Prime Minister Barak, killing of 36 Sikhs in Kaluchak, Kashmir (2000) and the 9/11 attacks along with countless terrorist attacks spanning the all the latitudes and longitudes of the globe—were the bloody acts of some part of this movement. The movement nurses as its goal, the destruction of the prevalent international system of accepted norms, cooperation and development scenario of a secular, modern world order. The war on terrorism by the U.S. and its

> allies, India, Indonesia, and others is against this movement; not just against their structures, channels and weapons of terror.
>
> — Extracted from varied sources

The 9/11 attack was the first-ever attack on the American land. Pearl Harbour attacked by Japan in 1941 was not the part of the American nation though it was its military base. The first attack was successfully carried out in the very heart of America powerfully striking at the two proud symbols of its prowess in the world.

America received spontaneous sympathy and support for its agony; so also, Bush's subsequent military steps in building alliance to carry war on terrorism. In an opinion survey of 275 opinion leaders in 24 countries conducted by *International Herald Tribune*, Pew Research Centre (USA) and the press, 79 percent of both US and non-US leaders considered the attacks "a new chapter in world history". However, 70 percent of non-US leaders stated that "it is good that Americans now know what it is like to be vulnerable". A sudden burst of spontaneous nationalist fervor was noticed in America. Some flag factories recorded the biggest-ever demand of American national flag in their history, not even seen during attack on Pearl Harbour or during the Second World War. Gun sales for the months following 9/11 rose from 9 to 22 percent. American mood was to change around the first anniversary of the terrorist attack.

Commenting on the American psyche on that day, Stanford University Professor David Kennedy wrote: "Terrorist attacks have generated a climate of fear and doubt in the American people about their safety. We should assess the real costs of terrorism not in terms of material damage or number of people killed, but keeping in view of the wound afflicting our national conscience, and moral and psychological agonies." The Indian American Professor Bharati Mukherjee told *Mercury News* (September 11, 2002) that Americans have, now, got awakened to their illiteracy and naiveté in not understanding the complexities of the world we live in.

Some explosive events such as assassinations of Mahatma Gandhi, J.F. Kennedy and Martin Luther King, become an enduring, sad part of our collective and human memory. But very few events make a history. With 9/11 a new critical phase in the history of India and a trying period of world history have begun. With the end of Cold War and the disintegration of the communist system and ideology, Historian Francis Fukuyama had heralded the ultimate triumph of economic liberalism and capitalist democracy in his work, *The End of History*. But, within a decade of the end of bipolarism in 1991, bin Laden and forces like al Qaeda have shocked such complacent unifocal worldview. They have also strengthened the challenges to liberal trends and globalization.

The war on terrorism seemed to be making headway till November 2001 when the US-led coalition trounced the Taliban, and forced bin Laden and his militant band to retreat to the tribal northwestern region on Pakistan's border. The volcano, a little cooled down, begun to be live thereafter. Meanwhile, terrorism with modern form and style began to spread worldwide and also take deep roots. It was not merely Afghanistan but the whole geopolitically cohesive block from Morocco to Pakistan dotted its map. Along with this bloc, terrorist organizations have shadowed South and Southeast Asia that together straddle 57 countries. Its presence was increasingly felt in the western countries. *National Geographic* magazine (November 2001) noted a Muslim cleric spreading the hate poison against the whites in a mosque in Brooklyn, New York. In his book *American Jihad* (2002) Steve Emerson has documented on empirical grounds how the Islamic zealots in America were inciting the American Muslims to kill the "white, Christian and Jew dogs". Terrorist operatives take advantage of open polity, liberty, market economy and means of communication to disseminate their fanatic ideology and help terrorist activities outside by staying in the secular democracies of the West.

On the other hand, such democracies as India geared up with stringent security measures and harsh legislations that curtailed the civil liberties that traditionally are the hallmarks of democracy. China took harsh executive measures to contain Islamic fundamentalists in its far-flung western region. It is executing strict rule and the practice of one's religion like Islam remains confined to praying in mosques and no propagation or activity of Islam entertained in public.

Second *Intefada* started in November igniting the cycle of violent action-reaction between Palestinians and Israel. In one gruesome case, Israelis killed 50 percent of the civilians in Jenin—the Arab town of the West Bank—in 2002. Almost all the houses of this Palestinian town were razed to ground. No foreign media persons or the UN observer were allowed to visit Jenin despite international pressures on Israel. At the same time, India-Pakistan region emerged as the second theater of conflict on the issue of increased terrorist incidents and cross-border infiltration in Jammu & Kashmir. Pakistan continued to experience intermittent events of violent explosion in which foreigners and Shias were major targets. Bomb explosions on Shia mosques in Sindh are reported from time to time. On October 1, 2004 suicide bombing on a mosque in Sialkot resulted in death of 30 Shia believers. In the past, General Musharraf himself escaped two major attacks by the extremists. The death in a gun battle of its top Islamist extremist and al Qaeda linchpin, Amjad Farooqi, considered to have planned attacks on Musharraf and, earlier, the acts of kidnapping and murdering American journalist Daniel Pearl came as a great relief to that country's security and intelligence agencies.

For a while, after the precision missile strikes of the US-led allies on Iraq on March 19, 2003 and the pulling down of the statue of Saddam in Baghdad on April 9, the world seemed to have been awe-struck with the might of America. "But this is not a war that can be ended by toppling a statue."

In Spain, on the eve of national elections, terrorist bombs exploded a train near Madrid that killed hundred of civilians.

The public furore against the government that was supporting the US in war on terrorism was clearly reflected in the voting that displaced the ruling party and brought a socialist party in power. The new government announced withdrawal of its support to American occupation in Iraq. For the first time, the Madrid incident demonstrated the power of the terrorists to affect the electoral—political process of a western democracy. Zapatero came to power on the back of the train bombings and quickly fulfilled his election pledge to withdraw Spanish troops from Iraq. Non-state players like terrorist organizations were least impressed. On May 12, 2003, simultaneous car assaults were carried out in Riyadh leaving 34 dead and 200 more were wounded. Four days later, five suicide bombers hit within 20 minutes of one another, spreading 41 death and destruction affecting western communities. Those events gave a blow to the big picture drawn after the visual impression spread by that falling statue of Saddam. "The most qualified regions for liberation" as called by bin Laden on an audiotape played on Al Jazeera TV in February were dealt a blow!

A different pattern of terrorism drew the attention of the world that requires a little detailed examination. Russia became the theater of conflict with unexpected ferocity. International Islamic Front (IIF) struck in Russia. In 2003, Chechen insurgents have taken hundreds of people in a theater in a Moscow as hostages. In the commando action most of the insurgents were killed along with more than a hundred civilians as well. In the four terrorist strikes in Russia on August 24, 2004, 450 civilians were killed. Of these strikes, three were carried out in Moscow and the fourth, in early September, directed at non-Muslim children, their parents and teachers in a school in Beslan near Russia's border with Chechen. In all, 340 people were killed in this deadly incident. First three happened as:

1. An explosion at a bus stop on one of the roads joining the local airport.
2. Two other explosions took place near Moscow airport on board of two air crafts a few hours thereafter which led to disintegration of planes and death of 90 persons.

3. The third was occurred outside the entrance of a metro station on August 31.

It was significant that of the three incidents in Moscow, two involved women suicide bombers. Considered to be widows of Chechens killed at the hands of Russian soldiers, they took arms in revenge. 'Black Widow' is a new phenomenon in this region.

Analysts consider Beslan as Russia's 9/11. That is rather an inadequate description of the horror. Hundreds of children were made to sit in the school premises, huddled and terrorized, without food and water for 53 hours. *The Guardian*, London wrote: "It is etched on every face in small town of Beslan. That helpless gut-churning flash of panic that seized every parent near that middle school." Beslan killing also revealed the link of the Chechen rebels with Arab militants and al Qaeda. John Kampfuer, political editor of *New Statesman* (Britain) noted that Chechnya till long was Russia's domestic issue, now underlined "the international nature of the terrorist threat". Beslan is now officially listed as part of the same Islamist assault on 'civilized' values that led to attacks on Twin Towers in New York and Atocha station in Madrid". (September 5, 2004). Madrid and Moscow incidents that occurred within six months underlined that both the eastern and the western ends of Europe were stalked by the spectre of terrorism.

Meanwhile, on the West Bank-Israel front, the violent cycle of Palestinian suicide bombing killing Israelis and Israeli retaliation carried out greater ferocity continued to roll on that provoked a more venomous climate of religious hatred and anti-Israel, anti-America rage in the Muslim world. Another major development of global implications of the post-September era is al-Aqsa *Intefada* (uprising) that erupted after the highly charged September 2001. By the second anniversary of 9/11, Iraq had joined to put an extra energy to the process of terrorists' escalator. Before its third anniversary, Iraq still continued to hit the media headlines in the Middle

East, US and the rest of the world. Madrid, Moscow and Iraq created an air of doubt and demoralization in the camp that is carrying the war on terrorism. Critics of Bush-Blair war on Iraq pointed out that during March 19, 2003 thru September 8, 2004 more than 1,004 Americans died in Iraq. "The US troops have died in Iraq in these 18 months were more than the first three years of the Vietnam war." The figure of the US-led troops killed reached 1,133 including 65 British and other allies 66. The corresponding loss for Iraqis was 16,688 and 20,172; for militants between 4,895 and 6,370 and for civilians, between 11,793 and 13,802. Kerry called over 1,000 causalties as "a tragic milestone".

The Bipartisan Commission on 9/11, in its official report, stated that Saddam Hussein had little to do with al Qaeda. "No credible evidence of a link between Iraq and al Qaeda attacks against the US." It was the US that lost the credibility in the Middle East and the world. In the process, Bush and his colleagues succeeded only in uniting the Iraqis—Sunnis and Shias alike—in their hatred of Americans. Observed Bhaskar Ghose, "That hatred is far more intense than it was when Saddam Hussein was in power, and it is from fierceness of this hatred that an organised resistance will grow and continue to harry Americans as long as they are there...It is this vulnerability, and consequent onset of an era of fear, that George W. Bush has gifted to his fellow citizens" (*Frontline*, May 22-June 4, 2004). He had perceived correctly. (Significantly, the fact that at least 40,000 lives were lost in J&K during 15 years of militancy and later-day terrorism was ignored by the western governments and media.) Events on the ground—the mounting insecurity, violence and kidnappings of aid and construction workers and taking foreign troops as hostage and their ghastly beheading by the insurgents—meant that reconstruction of Iraq was paralyzed. Rather, the US cash intended for reconstruction has been diverted to security spending. Terrorists have succeeded in paralyzing the US plans for reconstruction of post-Saddam Iraq.

The US was increasingly isolated. Even Kofi Annan, Secretary-General of the UN slammed the US, calling that Iraq attack was illegal. The same "gang of three"—France, Germany and Belgium—that had opposed invasion of Iraq, also was divided about the post-war situation. Now, Spain has joined this 'gang'. The so-called 'Old Europe' that Rumsfeld called derogatively, now was joined by Spain. Significantly, such phrases as 'Eurabia' and 'Euro-jihadists' paint the lengthening shadow of Islam and terrorism in the West Europe. So also, at the level of public opinion in West Europe. A survey of an American and an Italian think tank showed that some 58 percent of Europeans seek a more independent role from the US leadership in the world was undesirable, an increase of nine percentage points from a similar poll in 2003. Only in Britain and Netherlands do a majority desire strong American leadership.

A total of 80 percent of the Europeans did not believe the invasion was worth the loss of life and cost. Another 73 percent believed the war increased the risk of terrorism as do 49 percent of Americans. "Trans-Atlantic disagreement over Iraq is accompanied by continuing EU-US splits over the Middle East where Bush is now seen to be acquiescing to the ruling Likud party's hard line approach to Israeli settlements, as well the wider question of tackling the root causes of terrorism." When, during a meeting in London with Ayad Allawi, President of Iraq's interim government, Tony Blair commented that Iraq was now the crucible in which global terrorism would either succeed or founder, Jacques Chirac stated that it was like opening a Pandora's Box which no one can close. Chris Patten, the EU External Relations Commissioner, asked the European Parliament in September: Is global terrorism in retreat? Are we closer to building bridges between Islam and the West? Is the world's only superpower more respected? I simply pose the questions. The answers are well-known. He put it well. "We all have stakes in rebuilding Iraq and closing the gates of hell."

French terrorism experts like Roland Jacquard and Alexis Debat have documented in their studies the growing menace of terrorists spreading in Europe. Al Qaeda's leadership has asked Zarqawi to expand his grisly terror campaign to Europe and the US. In his provocative study Washington's think-tank expert shows that of "373 radical Muslim terrorists arrested or killed in Europe and the US from 1993 through 2004, 87 percent are from immigration background, but 41 percent are Western nationals, either naturalized, second generation or converts to Islam." In Europe, they virtually recruit themselves. Zarqawi has proceeded to build a new network to North Africa and Western Europe.

Recent disclosures also are worrisome. The official data in a report, "Patterns of Global Terrorism" that the Bush administration gave to the US Congress in mid-April, 2005 revealed that the terrorists staged 198 attacks in 2004 vs. 22 attacks in 2003. 650 terror attacks occurred worldwide in 2004. 300 attacks reported in Indian-controlled Kashmir by Pakistan-backed Muslim militants was the highest figure for a region.

In fact, terror attacks worldwide more than tripled in 2004, with much of the increase traced to incidents in Iraq. (This figure significantly went up with more than 600 killings occurred in Iraq till May 2005).

The number of even Muslims killed by Zarqawi's car-bombs and suicide bombers in Iraq reached around 500 within three weeks of the formation of the partial cabinet. Meanwhile, American toll since the attack on Iraq reached around 1,500.

Change in the leadership equation in the early 2005 is also discerned by observers. Beyond Iraq, al Zarqawi is emerging as a global player on par with, or even eclipsing Osama bin Laden. Says French anti-terrorism expert Debat, "with operational control of terrorist network laid down in Europe, his ambitions very clearly are global." He is on the rise as an international terrorist as the old guard bin Laden is descending in large part because of the continued Pakistan-supported US operations in Afghanistan-Waziristan and the continued post-war insurgency in Iraq under the former.

The achievements of the US-led war on terrorism need not be underestimated, though. Bin Laden or the likes have not been able to strike in America on America that can be comparable to 9/11. Not even any other minor inland attack, despite frequent threats of Laden, al Jawahiri or the like that were released through Al Jazeera TV channel or through video/audio cassettes. President Bush's confidence that the war on terrorism will be finally won is not without some bases. The war on the Taliban drove out al Qaeda from its sanctuary. By September-end, more than two-thirds of its known senior leadership was killed or captured. As the Bush administration claimed, globally, more than 3,000 al Qaeda operatives were 'incapacitated'. Terrorists' cells are disrupted in Pakistan and across Europe.

Some pro-democracy analysts were nursing the fear that shocked by the 9/11 events and as a reaction to the phenomenon of hostile anti-America demonstrations worldwide, the US would withdraw itself from the outside world, become cool to them. But America has not become isolationist. Instead of abandoning its role in widening the space of liberal ideology and become an introvert, it became active in forging a broad coalition of nations to fight the scourge of terrorism.

As Michael Doran stated in *Foreign Affairs*, bin Laden might have expected that such events will widen the distance between the *Umma* (Islamic trans-national community) and the authoritarian rulers who are patronized by America. Laden hoped that the Arab people would dethrone the US-patronized rulers and spread radical Islam in the Middle East. Such a scenario did not become a reality. The Arab Street did come out from Libya to Pakistan, but that could not cause the so-called revolutionary change of regime in Saudi Arabia, Jordan, Indonesia or Pakistan.

In a way, bin Laden's attack was as much against America as against the polluted 'un-Islamic' Arab regimes. The ultimate goal of al Qaeda and its likes is to make the Muslim *Umma* a *jehadist* and ultra-conservative society liberated from the evil influence of the western culture and America. The war on America was a means and a political route. To the extent

America grasps this fast and fashion its soft educational-cultural approach to help the Muslim society, its war on terrorism will become productive. But before it could effectively trounce the structures such as al Qaeda and leadership becoming widespread across the world, or relieving Pakistan from the entrenched and well-protected *jehadist* forces, it opened the new front in Iraq. In a way, it outsourced its combat arsenal, military and attention in Afghanistan to the local warlords, and diverted its multiple resources from Afghanistan to Iraq with disastrous consequences. Blunders of Bush-Blair alliance in managing the post-Saddam Iraq subjected them to sharp criticism even in their own countries. About 50 of the most senior former British Ambassadors and High Commissioners, steeped in the ethos of working behind the scenes and speaking with great restraint, came together to address their Prime Minister publicly. They called the announcement by Ariel Sharon and President Bush of new policies (and endorsed by Blair) to promote peace in the Holy Land as one-sided and illegal... The conduct of war in Iraq has made it clear that there was no effective plan for the post-Saddam settlement. Writes Aijaz Ahmad, "Their severe indictment, itself extraordinary, indicates a vast sea of discontent among officials still serving in the diplomatic services" (*Flonnet.com*, June 6, 2004). Friedman criticizes Bush at other level—for "politicizing 9/11 that put a wedge between us (America) and our history...I want a president who can one day restore September 11 to its rightful place in the calendar: as the day after September 10 and before September 12. I do not want it to become a day that defines: because ultimately September 11 is about them—the bad guys—not about us. We're about the Fourth of July" (*Atlanta Journal—Constitution*, October 14, 2004).

Opinion poll in some western countries taken in October 2004 also reveals, in the same mould, the mood of the people whose leaders are with USA. Leaders of those countries—Tony Blair of Britain, John Howard of Australia and Silvo Berlusconi of Italy—all get low marks from their people for their handling of the war on terrorism, shows an Associated Press-Ipsos poll.

More than half of those in the United States, 52 percent believe the Iraq war has increased the threat of terrorism, while three in 10 in the United States think it has decreased threat—a view promoted President Bush. In a poll conducted by major newspapers in respective countries in October 2004, more people (on average 57%) in Canada, France, Britain, Spain, Japan, South Korea, Australia and Mexico said that they had a worse opinion of the US than two to three years ago. Only in Israel, more people said that view of the US had improved. "It must be underlined here that the survey also found that despite widespread animosity toward President Bush, huge majorities said that they have a good opinion of Americans."

At another level, the US can take solace for the fact that its ports and borders are better protected than they were, though no foolproof arrangement can be claimed by any country in such cases. Since September 11, 2001, terrorist organizations have exploded repeatedly the soft or civilian targets in Bali, Morocco, Turkey, Saudi Arabia, Pakistan, New Delhi, Kenya, Spain, Russia and so on. But not on the daring scale of the WTC. Civilians in democracies have, by and large, condescendingly adjusted to the realities of the erosion of a few civil liberties for relative safety and tranquillity. However, Laden "may be incapacitated and sometimes incommunicado, but has remained a powerful totem of *jehadist* resistance" (*The Economist*, October 1, 2004).

The Economist also envisions, "Perhaps skulking in a cave on the Afghan-Pakistan border, Laden also reflects that al Qaeda enjoys two strategic advantages over its enemies. One is its diffuseness. Even before the loss of its Afghan base, al Qaeda was not an organization in a conventional sense: bin Laden operated more like a venture capitalist than a CEO, sponsoring operations with varying degrees of control. Since then, the alumni of his Afghan camps—perhaps numbering in tens of thousands—have dispersed across the globe, forming their own more or less autonomous units. Some of the bombings committed under the al Qaeda banner may take little more than inspiration from bin Laden himself. Nobody really knows how large that loose network is, nor whether it is growing or shrinking." It adds, "al Qaeda's other strategic advantage is its philosophy of time...bin Laden and his sort take a long view of history...They plan meticulously and nurture their aspirations for years. Given that, the world should draw little comfort that it has so far been spared another September 11. Since al Qaeda is less a concrete adversary than a movement or an ideology, any war waged against it must be equally subtle. 'Incapacitation' has its place, but so do public diplomacy in the Muslim world and conflict resolution in the Middle East and beyond—both less in evidence."

A ray of hope, dim one but significant, must be noted in this context. Moderate opinion in the Muslim world came out clearly in the wake of Beslan incident when images of terrified young survivors and dead children carried from the scene aired repeatedly on Arab TV stations and newspapers. Al Rashed of Al-Arabiya TV lamented, "Our terrorist sons are an end-product of our corrupted culture," with the headline, "The Painful Truth: All the World Terrorists are Muslims!" Hasan Al-Batal in Palestine daily *Al-Ayyam* wrote, "The day of horror in the school in Beslan, September 1, should be designed as an international day for the condemnation of terror." Al-Watan in Saudi Arabia commented, "The acts of barbarism occurring at present are nothing but the natural consequences of generations of Muslims having been force-fed speeches (filled with) hatred for others...which deepened the backwardness and the ignorance in the Islamic world." Such critiques were fundamentally different from the 9/11 glee expressed by the anti-American forces that said as well as unsaid element of "Americans had it coming". Comments Aniruddha Bahal, "Beslan might be a catalyst for introspection—on both sides."

In this context, *The Economist* has relevant piece of sagacious advice. "Another part of the anti-al Qaeda strategy ought to be the education of western publics. Talk of a 'war' itself encourages people to believe in a clear and none-too-distant a victory, whereas the apocalyptic spirit of al Qaeda may be around for decades. 'Terror', which is after all, a technique and a movement rather than an army—will stalk the world for ever.... The public will be able to cope better with such dangers if it understood that al Qaeda-like peril is one with which it will have to learn to live for the foreseeable future—and which, unfortunately, will occasionally inflict more than just inconvenience."

If suicide bombers continue to emerge in greater number at more places, or the zealot militants can manage to conceal lethal bombs in their suitcase, the much trumpeted state-of-the-art missiles of great powers also will become ineffective. Historian Lewis admits, "We may, perhaps, be all powerful. But we are not omniscient—especially in the matter of the Muslim society and the Third World."

In the latter half of 2004, feud between the US and Iran on the issue of the latter's plan of developing atomic weapons was reaching crisis proportions. In August, Iran had test-fired its Shahab-3 ballistic missile with a range of 1,200 miles. Sensing that it could endanger the existence of the Jewish state, Israel acquired 5,000 smart bombs, including 5,000 one-ton bunker-busters that can destroy 6-foot-thick concrete walls protecting Iran's nuclear facilities. In defiance of the UN's atomic watchdog agency to freeze its uranium enrichment program, Iran added a 'strategic missile' to its military arsenal. Its defense minister said that his country was ready to confront any external threat. Israeli foreign minister remarked that Iran was a worldwide threat whose missiles can reach London, Paris and southern Russia. Israel is the only nation in the Middle East that possesses nuclear weapons, although it refuses to confirm this. This has made the problem of arresting nuclear proliferation and its black marketing or passing into the hands of terrorist elements all the more complex and the one that requires imminent, firm and coordinated action.

Pakistan is the most complex case in this context. The surreptious way in which Pakistan has acquired and developed its nuclear bomb and missiles has been fully exposed by different agencies including CIA and atomic inspection agencies. Pakistani government under Musharraf itself has confirmed that the father of its nuclear bomb program, A.Q. Khan was an instrument in passing its nuclear technique and know-how to other countries like Libya, Iran and North Korea. Khan was questioned in connection with 'debriefing' of several scientists working at his Khan Research Laboratories. That such a dangerous deal was black marketed without the knowledge or connivance of an authoritarian regime ruled by a Military General and its powerful top army and intelligence agencies will not fool any government like the US worth the name. *The New York Times* reported about the information Iran had turned over to International Atomic Energy Agency in October 2003. That report strengthened suspicions that Pakistan sold key nuclear secrets to Iran.

The Times (London) reported, "American and European investigators are interested in what they describe as Iran's purchase of nuclear centrifuge from Pakistan 16 years ago, largely to force the Pakistani government to face up to a pattern of clandestine sales by its nuclear engineers and to investigate much more recent transfers including ones to North Korea in late 1990s." The US remained unconvinced about Pakistan's claims in such deals that some of its scientists may have been motivated by "personal ambition and greed". Thereafter, the paper further commented, "Pakistan has emerged as the intellectual and trading hub of a loose network of hidden nuclear proliferators" (January 3, 2004). For example, Libya rulers admitted that "Nuke plans came (to Libya) from Pakistan" (*India Abroad*, January 4, 2004). For this, it quoted experts and referring to "the most conspicuous of evidence: A.Q. Khan Research Laboratory's own sales brochure quietly circulated to aspiring weapons states, and a network of nuclear middlemen around the world." *The Times* cryptically said, "In other nations, such sales would be strictly controlled. But Pakistan has always played by its own rules." After posing questions with experts on nuclear terrorism, Daniel Sneider says,

"Pakistan's cooperation is highly limited—US officials have not been allowed to directly question Khan." Also, frightening scenarios are already drawn by strategic analysts about Pakistan. What if President Musharraf is removed from power or assassinated and nuclear installations pass in the hands of the extremists/terrorists. Though number 2 in Pakistani army is pro-US, calamitous implications for the US, India and the world, of a fanatic rule in Pakistan and Iran are already seriously deliberated upon in Washington, DC, New Delhi, Moscow, Tel Aviv, etc. The US is said to have worked on the pro-active plan to keep the terrorists from the eventuality of getting control over nuclear power.

Harvard's Graham Allison, in his book, *Nuclear Terrorism: The Ultimate Preventable Catastrophe* (2004), states, "Pakistan is a shaky state in which a substantial number of people in the army and intelligence services have serious ideological ties to al Qaeda." Experts, some of whom had served in senior government posts, told Sneider that in case of terrorists set off a nuclear weapon in a some western city, "two suspects topped all lists—Russia and Pakistan" (*Atlanta Journal-Constitution*). Russia's vast arsenal of nuclear weapons and its stores of bomb quality uranium and plutonium are vulnerable to theft and terrorist assault. Sneider, in his investigation in 2002, found that it had an arsenal of thousands of tactical nuclear weapons and smaller bombs that were portable enough to fit in the trunk of a compact car. He then adds, "Pakistan represents a different challenge. A.Q. Khan, the man who built Pakistan's bomb, turned out to be the leading black marketeer, selling warheads and equipments to Libya, Iran,

North Korea and who knows who else." That else could be al Qaeda. The most vulnerable nuclear-equipped nations are former Soviet republics. Bin Laden had stated to Hamid Mir, the Pakistani journalist, who had met the former two months after 9/11, "openly discussed his willingness to use nuclear weapons" (quoted by Peter Bergen, "The Long Hunt for Osama" The *Atlantic*, October, 2004). Al Qaeda's desire to get a hold of enriched uranium is well-documented. If they succeed, "we have significantly underestimated the ease of manufacturing a crude but effective nuclear weapon," warns William Potter, co-author of a new book, *The Four Faces of Nuclear Terrorism.* Ominous reports need be noted here. In March 2005, the Germans arrested an Iraqi identified only as Ibrahim Mahamed K. who was accused of trying to obtain 48 grams of enriched uranium through a middleman in Luxembourg so he could make a radiological "dirty bomb" (*Newsweek*, March 25, 2005).

Ze'ev Schiff's terse comment is relevant here. "Nuclear danger is without an address; without even the threat of a phone number by which it is possible to negotiate with nuclear terrorist(s)." 'Atomic terror' or 'an American Hiroshima' is not an impossible eventuality (*Haaretz.com*, September 28, 2004). An analyst also fears in this case, about what he calls, "Cyclops-like nature of President Bush's perception of nuclear proliferation." In case, the US or other powerful country sees an imminent danger of a nuclear attack on it, it is bound to take pro-active or pre-emptive action against its perceived enemy—state or a non-state actor like a terrorist group hiding to operate from an Islamic country. The US or Russia, Israel or India may try to resort to put into practice its blueprint of smashing the nuclear installations located in that country. If the Cold War was the Third World War that did not actually happen on the ground because of the balance of power as well as balance of terror, the fourth war, set forth by the fundamentalism of Islamic and American varieties and the nuclear-powered terrorists, will become the shortest world war, but the one that would combine the untold sufferings of mankind of all the previous wars, and the one ending with the destruction of human civilization that different peoples have enriched at different points of time of the mankind's progress. In a way, this time then, it will be the final 'end of history'!

Unfinished business

AMERICA RESPONDS

America's successes on the battlefield in Afghanistan mask the hard work that remains to be done before the war on terrorism is won.

21

Overview: In Perspective of Paradigms

Due to powerful pulls and pushes of globalization, the leaders of all countries must make and use a number of ethical and cultural 'sieves' at more than one level so that a country's heritage, cultural and historical, does not get mixed up and obliterated. If this does not happen, the atmospherics will undergo great changes and those who fail to make adjustments to them would (like the large number of species such as too delicate yet important vegetation species and the dinosaurs, etc.) perish from the world.

GLOBALIZATION: The most effective 'sieve' for this process is *'glocalisation'* (i.e., a discretionary cultural differentiation process between 'global' and 'local' identities). A healthy 'glocalism' is like an experiment by 'trial and error'.

If a nation or culture is unaware of this '*glocalisation*' process or is too weak to undertake it, in such a vacuum we find reactions like the 'Taliban', or as in some of the Muslim countries a greater section retreating into fundamentalism, etc. These fundamentalists believe that by 'experimenting' only mistakes can be made and globalization will take over their religion-culture. That is why, like their women, they cover their entire nation under a veil (just as their women, to cover themselves, wear the 'burkha') against the Western thought.

> Such an atmosphere only makes the roots of *Talibanisation* stronger.
>
> Again, these countries must arrange their public policies and planning in such a way that in the great flow of globalization their own cultural and economic foundations are not wiped off. Israel, Japan, China, South France etc. are illustrations of the nations that have achieved such success. Even their political leaders are protective nets to save their special arrangements and culture, and the public is educated in that manner. Without basic environment for it, one cannot have a 'sustainable' culture; and without a sustainable culture, one cannot have a sustainable society; and without sustainable societies globalization is not possible. Therefore, only the thought process of *'glocalisation'* has the capacity to nourish equilibrium and peace.
>
> **— Thomas Friedman**

After the end of the Cold War, "what would be the new global order" was a topic of some deep studies done with different perspectives. Among the most read, and the most discussed by professors, journalists, sociologists and others concerned with the developments, the works of Francis Fukuyama, Paul M. Kennedy, Robert Kaplan, Samuel Huntington, Benjamin Barber and Thomas Friedman are truly insightful. They have collected a great amount of data based on experience in order to understand terrorism and other trends of conflict in the world. They have presented us with original worldviews, paradigms or conceptual frameworks. It will be relevant for this study also the presentation as well as analysis of this focal issue. Besides, they have revisited their worldview or paradigm first developed in their books published before 2001 in the light of 9/11 and rewritten them with the new perspective. Their original paradigms and observations and their relevance in the light of the events of 9/11 are examined in the following sections.

The Vision of Fukuyama

Historian Francis Fukuyama has given a lucid exposition in his landmark work, *The End of History and the Last Man* (1993), about the end of Cold War that ushered in the victory of political-economic liberalism and market-oriented capitalism (as against statism). He propounds that for effectively building up a global society, the only ideology relevant to the present times is that of liberalism-capitalism. He says in this book, "Now in history no more than two or so main concepts or supportive ideologies would remain." Although, the title of his book does suggest that this is the last ever event in the world, he implies that capitalism as the fixed destination of the developing process. His analysis is very useful, but Fukuyama does not support the real world and real dealings with real world. He says: "The one main culture in the world that has to deal with its very basic questions to adjust with modernity and secular policies is that of Islam. One section of Muslim society may possess sophisticated and urbane features, but except for Turkey no Muslim country can claim to have a working democracy or a liberal social life."

The renowned historian examines the reason why Islamic culture differs from the others, and searches for the historical roots. Islam also has a complex structure, like other great world religions as Christianity, Hinduism and Confucianism. Establishing this, he says that Islam differs from others in one point. In modern times, Islam is the only religion that has bred rebellious movements time and again that protest and oppose not just the policies of the western nations but also the basic principles of modernism, such as secularism. "They were the groups that celebrated the events of 9/11. For, they shamed the society that some Islamic fundamentalists believe to be corrupt. They believe that the West is corrupt not only because of its indecent sexual behavioral patterns, such as homosexuality and lesbianism, and freedom for women, but also because of its secular ideals. The object of the hatred of Islamic fundamentalists is such a westernized state. For, such a state (and this is applicable to India, Japan and Israel) does not put forward the religious truth but religious tolerance and plurality. That is the one reason for Fukuyama to believe that 'the present war' is not just a war against terrorists; nor is it, as the fundamentalists believe, a war about the foreign policies of America with Palestine and Iraq. Unfortunately, this basic conflict spread over a much wider canvas. It is not merely limited to small groups of terrorists, but is concerned with the radical Islamic groups that consider their own religious identity so much more important than any other political values. If bin Laden has been able to get active sympathy from the slum dwellers of Jakarta and military officers of Pakistan and also the Algerian inhabitants of France, it is all due to this cultural reality. On this point, both Fukuyama and Huntington have some similarity in their worldview. Fukuyama even goes to the extent of using the term 'Islamo-Fascism'. "To speak frankly, the modern conflict is not just against terrorism or against Islam as one religion-culture; but it is against rebelliously intolerant, anti-modernism principles of Wahabi sect and the pure Islam that have been received well in Muslim world."

Secondly, most of the sociologists and thinkers with a broader worldview believe that the main elements that have given nourishment to such extremist and fundamentalist trends are the deep poverty that spread after 1980 in the Middle East, and suspended and authoritarian political systems. "For political extremism these elements have proved to be inflammatory agents." Once a dictator and an effective ruler of Singapore, Lee Kuan Yu had upheld 'Asian values', different from western democratic political values. Nations like Singapore, South Korea, Taiwan, and even China, Brazil, India, Chile and Mexico have adopted, more or less, democracy, or free trade and liberal economic reforms, and begun to keep pace with the world trends and sustainable progress. On the other hand, the oil-rich Arab rulers have used their wealth to rear an extremist generation of Islam rather than to give them modern education and an industrial society.

How does the historian Fukuyama view the world after 9/11? He says, like fascism and monarchy before it, communism also was defeated by democracy. In all parts of the world it seemed that economy based on the American model besides democratic institutions were progressing. It seemed as if technology was making nation-state irrelevant and was integrating everybody into a global village.

But today, things seem to have changed. Nations with large Muslim populations and billions of Muslims seem to have turned away from America. History is witnessing the progress of human societies, after the experiences with a variety of political structures, and lastly was looking at the modern liberal democratic market-centered capitalism as the stage of progress.

But, in today's context, what has been happening? Fukuyama asks. Are we looking at the beginning of a 'cultural war' of about a decade that turns into a war of the West vs. Islam? He raises other questions too:

- Would the technology that gave us freedom, aircrafts, skyscrapers and great progress in the biology laboratory be used against us? And would we be able to survive that onslaught?
- Or, would the forces like bin Laden and the Taliban be drowned and the terrorist networks destroyed? Would the present conflict end and a new global economy that can accommodate everyone well be coming up?

Fukuyama says that his own earlier hypothesis still holds: We have come to the end of history, but it does not mean that historical incidents will not occur now; rather it means that history has become the last milestone of political and economic liberal democracy and modernity. America, their symbol and representative, and other developed democracies would become effective forces in world politics; and the institutions embodying the western values of freedom and equality would spread more and more in the world. The attacks of September 11 are a desperate backlash against this.

Such Islamic backlash or counter-action really raises the questions of the sustainability of our culture. The answer would depend on how far in their 'war' against terrorism America and its allies are successful.

- How deep is this challenge? To meet it, what kind of allies does and can America really get? What can be really done to counter this threat?

Benjamin Barber keeps the question open when he says, "History is not over". Nor are we arrived in the wondrous land of technoscape promised by the futurologists.

Cultural Conflict

Among the worldviews that are considered for understanding the contemporary world and its great challenges, the views of Samuel Huntington seem to be the most thought provoking.

Huntington calls the contemporary world politics as "an age of Muslim battles". In comparison with other civilizations, the Muslims have fought more battles with non-Muslims and among their own different sects. The place of Cold War has been taken over by a much deeper and more complex of 'Muslim wars'. These are wars against terrorism, guerrilla wars (Indonesia, Malaysia, etc.), and war across borders (Kashmir), wars of border disputes (African Muslim countries), wars for separatism (Chechnya), civil wars and wars among states.

After 9/11 Huntington re-examined his thesis, but he holds its base as correct, needing only some minor changes: In the mid-1990s nearly half the ethnic and racial wars had Muslims as one party in them. According to the analysis of *The Economist* (London), of the 16 big events of terrorism between 1983 and 2000, Muslims were responsible for 12 of them. In the list of the seven nations that patronize terrorism prepared by the US State Department, five are Muslims. (It is a different matter that Pakistan has not been included in this list!) Similarly, it has also named the terrorist organizations.

International Institute of Strategic Studies, London shows that in the year 2000, 32 armed conflicts were occurred, and in two-thirds of these Muslims were involved, although theirs is only one-fifth of the world population.

Huntington says, "In the present-day Muslim wars, the root cause seems to be political, and not the 17th century religious principles." He gives the following causes for his thesis:

- Whatever social, cultural and political trends we have seen in the last few decades, nearly everywhere a high tide of Muslim consciousness, movements and identity are seen clearly, and it is the most important development. In such orthodox and traditional Islamic societies as Egypt, Malaysia, Indonesia, etc., the militant Muslims have emerged as major opposition.
- In Muslim world, especially among the Arabs, strong sentiments against the West and its wealth, power and culture are prevalent. Intense protests are found in the fierce feelings of annoyances, opposition, jealousy and enmity. To some extent the western imperialism that had dominated the Muslim countries is also responsible for such mentality.
- Since 1991 America has taken hard steps against Iraq, and maintained close relations with Israel (at the cost of Palestinian 'cause'), and with Britain, etc., has extended to the oppressive rule to Arab rulers—all these factors are also responsible for the anger of the Muslims and their opposition to West.
- Among the Muslims themselves conflicts continue owing to differences in tribes, sects/religion, and race/ethnicity at political or cultural levels. For instance, Saudi Arabia (Wahabi) and Iran (Shia) support their brands of Islam. They support their co-sect Muslims spread over the vast spectrum from Bosnia to Philippines in their quarrels and conflicts with non-Muslims.
- Most of the Muslim societies have a high rate of population growth. And, among them youth of age group

of 16 to 35 are found in great numbers, giving the population curve a 'youth bulge'. Lack of proper education and lack of employment prompt these young to join Madrassas and further down the sectarian-political organizations. The guerrilla groups and terrorist networks also co-opt them. Thus, they are like a live volcano.

Huntington asks, "Until now, such organizations and the violent acts they perform are confined to local, scattered and limited nature. But, would they grow into a war of Islam vs. the West and possibly into wars among civilizations? The statements and strategies of Osama bin Laden clearly indicate the developments on these lines. By declaring a 'holy war' against America, he has given a call to the Muslims to kill Americans without thinking ahead. President Bush, however, unwittingly and unintendedly reinforced this theory of polarity. In mid-December 2001, President Bush "showed his deftness in managing domestic and international symbols by hosting an end-of-Ramadan ceremony at the White House, even as battle raged in Tora Bora region of Afghanistan". But, after the overthrow of Saddam, the first thing Rumsfeld said is "We'll accept any government as long as it is not Islamic". Bergen rues, "He proved Laden's argument that the U.S. is leading the West to annihilate Islam." Robert Kaplan notes other ironical paradox. The insurgents in Iraq used Baghdad's mosques to plan for the butchering and burning of four Americans in the city. (As the militants hide weapons and themselves in the mosques in Kashmir to force Indian guards to attack them in mosques.) So, the American army had to snuff them out from their hidings in the mosques. In one such situation, "the chaplain of the U.S. Christian Marines compared their entry into Fallujah with Jesus Christ's entry into Jerusalem," and impending destruction of much of the city as "a spiritual battle". With its about 80 mosques, Fallujah is known as Medina al-Masjid and the very conservative Salafi brand of Sunni Islam. This incident became more than symbolic; rather catastrophic for propagating the paradigm of 'the clash of civilizations' with telling effects. Comments Fallows, "The administration had come a long way from the end-of-Ramadan ceremony at the White House."

The same phenomenon is evolutionarily viewed by Alexis Debat, a French consultant on terrorism, in his article "Vivisecting the Jihad" appeared in *National Interest* (summer, 2004): "Al Qaeda has taken terrorism beyond its initial function as a vehicle of resistance. It has turned into a global instrument by which to challenge not only the Western influence in the Muslim world but the West itself. This is new and global clash of uniqueness."

Huntington believes that now the ground has been prepared for a common and large-scale conflict among civilizations. The reactions to 9/11 and response of America reinforce this line of thought. Britain, Canada, Australia and other cultures with western (Anglican) cultures immediately sent army units in support of American position, as did Germany, France and other European powers declare their support to America in the war against Laden-Taliban. The French daily *La Monde* printed the famous headline: "We are all Americans!" (One needs to remember here that this headline was printed in bold letters in a leading daily of France that is known for its cultural independence and which is critical of American culture). It's another matter that the relations of France and America turned bitter on the issue of war with Iraq. Many Americans and restaurants also boycotted 'French fries' and French wines during the phase of strained relations!

Would the Muslim enmity towards the West diminish? Huntington says that it is possible to happen, but it needs certain conditions fulfilled first.

- America accepts a significant change in its policy of indiscriminate support to Israel.
- Arrangements are made for achieving remarkable reforms in political, economic and social conditions and for modern education in Muslim society everywhere. Arab governments should satisfy economic and welfare-based

needs of their people. The developed western countries and international financial institutions extend their aid and help in these fields.

- Similarly, the governments of India, Russia and other non-Muslim countries give space for their Muslim populations and by examples and experiences convince the people of the Muslim countries the significance of an environment of democracy and social liberalism.

America and liberal democracies have to face the challenge on such a large scale from the Muslim world that is spread on vast land, population and oil resources. "In some ways, this challenge is much more fundamental than what even communism had posed." America has become aware of everything its (universal) civilization stands for. Says Tunku Varadrajan, "It is not merely a question of shutting the gates on the marauders; it's a realisation that it is prudent now, even imperative, to take the battle to their lands, to pursue war as prophylactic."

Peace-loving leaders have, thus, to arrange/plan and have approaches that would open the Muslim societies, enable them to have diversity of thought and cultural variations of mankind, and to look at them with empathy at heart.

Secondly, if the initiative for change and the process for change come from Muslim society itself, it would be purposive and effective. How much and in what manner does it want to adjust with modernity? Specially, how to adjust to key principles and ideals of a secular state and religious tolerance, and if not adopt them, how to respect them? Religious politics, very often, not only creates conflicts between the Muslims and the non-Muslims, but also within the Muslim societies themselves. Resorting to bombing during conflicts between Shias and Sunnis in Pakistan, the decade-long war between Iran and Iraq, rebellions and uprisings in Indonesia and the Philippines etc. come to mind here. In the present times of biological, chemical and atomic weapons proliferation, such trends can really be extremely destructive, that bring intolerable experience for all. "Turkey and reformist Islam or Iran that gives out some indications."

On this point, what Samuel Huntington has to say after 9/11? He says, "This war is not of the West vs. Islam; but against terrorists. The Bush Administration emphatically does so. This is a correct understanding. Yet, it cannot be ignored that cultural views are also involved in it." Americans believe that their values like affluence derived on the bases of democratic freedoms and economic liberties represent universal aspirations, and that the peoples of the world over shall embrace them. They also believe that all people of different cultures welcome the appeal of the American society. But, the incident of 9/11 has given their beliefs a great shock indeed. Muhammad Atta, who led the attacks on World Trade Center (WTC) and some of his colleagues, who hijacked the aircrafts, had taken their education in the West and lived there too; even then, they had not been enraptured by the West. In fact, so disgusted they were with it that they turned anti-West and blew up the two towers of WTC. Thus, it is quite easy to see the cracks in its cultural structure. Does this mean that the belief that western values are universal is a cultural myopic view that we, westerners nourish?

On one hand, we have information technology, semi-conductor or bio-medicinal technologies that are no different for the westerners than they are for the Chinese or Muslims. But, the use one can make of it needs certain types of economic institutions, the rule of law and the individual freedom to take certain economic decisions and dealings, etc.,—all imperatives for economic progress of a high standard.

In this process, the economic progress nurtures liberal democracy. Among some of the universally accepted 'laws' of political science, one is that economic progress and democracy are interconnected. This helps develop a vibrant and broad-based middle class. Such a class, in the process, nurtures modernity that is potent enough to evolve in a universal developmental phenomenon.

On the other hand, religious beliefs, social habits, and cultures based on long traditions make these societies play obstructive role of moss-like vegetation in a flowing concentric, uni-directional stream. It may seem strange, but owing to increasing popularity of McDonald's and Hollywood etc. among the elite and wealthy classes of the Third World, a good amount of '*swadeshi*' (protectionist movement for 'use our own products') type economic-emotional backlash has taken shape among the masses, and that too creates questions about the future of globalization.

Both the East and the West have to take note of three books with titles that resonate with a variety of dishes like falafal-dosa, chutni—popcorn-salsa, and pizza-curry—enchilada. Among them is the book of political scientist Benjamin Barber, entitled *Jihad vs. MacWorld: How Globalism and Tribalism are Re-shaping the World*. The second one is Samuel Huntington's *The Clash of Civilizations and the Remaking of the World Order*; and the last one is Thomas Friedman's *The Lexus and the Olive Tree*.

Jihad vs. MacWorld

Professor Barber examines the complexity of interrelationship of *Jihad* and *MacWorld*. Although MacWorld is not any definite geographic or physical corporation, it is a virtual corporation. The totality of this imaginary MacWorld is international finance, global markets and high-tech information network that power multi-national corporations. It may be transnational and even anti-national!

Professor Barber says, "Dynamics of relationship of Jihad and MacWorld has been of a deeply dialectic pattern. For example, Japan developed a large number of MacWorld's new technologies (car, television, latest telephone equipments, etc.) and also purchased the products of MacWorld in ever growing number. However, it has studiedly preserved its traditions in cultural fields with great awareness as well. In 1992, the fast-food multinational McDonald outlet in Japan was first in the ranks in terms of number of consumers; and Kentucky Fried Chicken—the KFC chain store was second in rank. On the other hand, social events and cultural festivals were celebrated with the traditional Japanese dresses (such as the Kimono), the courtesy extended by bowing to each other (rather than a shake hand), community and ethnic relations, the tradition of serving the main Japanese dish of 'Sushi', and Japanese dances and music were also continued.

Barber graphically illustrates. Villages that touch the periphery of Mumbai are absolutely poor. The girls are killed in infancy and sometimes wives in India are killed for dowry. But just next to them in the '*Screep Zone*' (The Santa Cruz Electronics Export Processing Zone), we find people speaking Hindi, Marathi and Tamil working as computer programers and who prepare software programs for Swiss Air, AT&T and other multi-nationals employing these skilled workers at a low wage. Thus, "India is the main example of the simultaneous ancient ethnic and religious tensions as well as international level of software industry. To go and work in 'Sceepz' means to cross international boundaries." Though, it does not mean visiting another country; it merely means to visit the imaginary, illusory, virtual land of McWorld that does not belong to anyone."

Barber says that many times MacWorld and Jihad do not put us in a bipolar (or a polarized) scenario where we have to make a compulsory choice between only one of them. However, both these forces are hanging in a common chaos and confuse us so that we have felt some mixed experiences. Barber warns that although MacWorld and Jihad are two diametrically opposite forces, yet for they could be dangerous for those like us who have won civil liberties after great efforts (and in many countries it is not fully achieved even now). They can also spell danger for the future potential of world democracy. Both of them can penetrate nationalist boundaries and weaken the concept and practice of nation-states. We must recall the French intellectual Jean-Marie Guehenno, who gave the suggestive title of his book as *The End of the National State* in 1995.

The forces of Jihad will turn more vocal and violent as well as repressive than the forces of MacWorld in the initial phase, wrote Barber in 1996. As a result of this, local tragedies and regional massacres would also occur. The small-scale wars would continue sustaining the insecure environment, and they also would hinder the better global integration as well. But, in the long run, the forces of MacWorld, slowly but steadily, would spread western culture further and nothing can stop this. In this 21st century, the small wars of Jihad would occupy the headings of the media and silence the prophecies of 'the end of history'. Barber believes that ultimately whatever uniformity MacWorld may usher in, this would determine the trends in the fields of trade and commerce, transport, controls on media and entertainment, and affect the destiny of man. In his work *Giligan Unbound* (2001), Paul A. Canter has studied the cultural dimensions of the media growth, and he analyzes the last two decades beginning with 'The Star Track' and up to 'The Simpsons' television show, the subjects they deal with in their programs. He explains that the American symbols of entertainment and other fields have had great impact and the world has turned a global village; yet we cannot term this development as a really complete or unmixed blessing.

The Lexus and the Olive Tree

We are in the second round of globalization now. The first round—from the end of the First World War (1918) till the breaking of the Berlin Wall (1989)—was not so universal or comprehensive as it is today. And yet the world is not made up of only microchips, free markets, MacDonald and electronics media; it also contains communities and regions with their own religions, gods, traditions, languages, geographies, unimagined expectations and cultures who want to co-exist. Therefore, "the world and its dealings have become an area of exchange and interface between new things like the Lexus car or Internet website are novel, an olive tree like jobs in the Middle East or Mediterranean countries." However, if nation-state is to continue its identity for a long time in spite of the extensive pervasion of terrorism and great impact of globalization, it is because of such an olive tree—the sense of identity as to "who are we, of whom we are, from where are we, what are our roots", etc.

Friedman goes further: "But, while it is necessary to have a connection with an olive tree for our primary existence and identity, if it is allowed to grow unchecked, or is exaggerated, it would separate a community or region from other communities and regions, and keep all others, all the wider human groups at a distance. If discretions were not used in this, Nazis would be born in Germany and AUM Shinktikyo and Serbo in Japan, or the Taliban, Ramzi Yusuf, bin Laden and such terrorists in contemporary times." Thus, Friedman sees the Lexus car and olive tree as the meaningful symbols of the new world as shaping after the Cold War.

Friedman has spent a considerable time in the Middle East as a correspondent for *The New York Times*. Based on his observations and experiences there he has published his book, *From Beirut to Jerusalem*. In 1992 he had visited the well-known Toyota city near Tokyo that manufactured the luxury car Lexus. There he saw 66 men and 310 robots producing 300 Lexus Sedan cars everyday. The production process was so completely mechanized that after a car is ready it did not have even a speck of paste such as even a toothpaste tube has when you cap it after pressing some paste for your use. Thereafter, Friedman had sat in the bullet train that took him to Tokyo city at the speed of 180 mph, and in this travel he thought of the contradictory metaphors of the olive tree and Lexus car as well as their interrelationship.

Lexus represents technology, modernization, work efficiency, privatization in economy, and high standard of living and free market—a symbol of globalization. Apart from the western countries, the other countries of the world too adopt, use or want such symbols; while there are other big sections of the world's peoples and regions with large populations are attached to the olive tree. They quarrel over the question—to whom does the olive tree belong? The 'olive tree' is as well-known in Greece and other Mediterranean countries and among the peoples of the Middle East as the trees of *tulsi* and banyan are well known in India or cherry blossom in Japan. "The olive tree is important. Because, it ties those who find it difficult to adjust to a speedily changing world with their roots; it gives them an identity; and it seems to them that in this vast and complex world, they too have a place in the sun. The medium for this may be family, community, caste, race, religion or nation, anything." The olive tree gives them the warmth of their own (in family, race, religion, etc.), it thus provides a sense of belonging, oneness with others and deepens the sentiments of belonging that, altogether, give rise to a sense of security, and a confidence to deal with 'outsiders' as well.

Between the Jews and Palestinians, India and Pakistan, Serbs and Muslims or Armenians and Azerios, and between Kurds and Iraqis, such quarrels and conflicts have occurred for achieving regional-cultural identity—the olive tree. The conflict between Lexus and olive tree, between the Americans and Islamic fundamentalists had begun since last some decades and has now reached a peak. The inner understanding here is something like this: "If I leave my olive tree (its own identity and culture base etc.), I shall be overwhelmed by an alien culture or powerful economic, political and cultural influence of an outside force on me." For this tree of their soil they would write poems and novels, sing songs, kill others and would even sacrifice themselves. This is was what Friedman had observed in his book published before the fateful 9/11.

On the other hand, the attractions of Lexus are not mean. At present, the greater economic stability, prosperity, modernization, trade beyond national borders, and a race for cultural expansion and diffusion, computer and biotechnology, global market, entertainment and latest consumer goods for comfort are becoming available everywhere. The villages in Africa may have water shortage, but the ordinary villagers can see the local elite guys drinking Coca Cola; in India, the hungry and poor people living in slums may not be able to celebrate *Diwali* (Hindu festival of lights) festival, but they can see on the television set in a shop the celebrations of Christmas or the New Millennium in a five-star hotel of Bangalore; a poor woman fetching water daily from a long distance for her domestic use can see in her employer's home an American movie with the bikini-clad women swimming in a private blue-water pool of a rich man. All this generates a jealousy against Lexus, a feeling that they would be left out of all this globalization process, an incipient contempt—and the fundamentalists can easily exploit such a mentality. Thus, the polar distance between the ethnocentric identity and material progress makes the international scene more picturesque.

In this context, for the people on the side of the olive tree, the Coke, as the American multi-national drink with its availability all over the world, has turned unsavory and undesirable.

Again, for his field study, Friedman has travelled India, Bahrain, Syria, Israel, etc., and showed how a balance can also be maintained between the forces of the Lexus and the olive tree. When he travelled by air from Bahrain to London, a television monitor in his business class constantly displayed on one channel with the help of GPS (Global Positioning Satellite) the direction in which the plane was flying from Mecca as the point of reference. This facility provided the Muslim passengers the idea of the direction in which Mecca was placed as they flew, and they could face it when it was time for their *Namaz* prayers, even as they flew so high! Thus, the equipments of globalization provided an aid to their religious identity and necessity. Abu Jihad (the father of Wahabi movement) had set up along with Yasser Arafat the organization called Al Fatah in Palestine. Later on he was in charge of PLO. He also was in charge of the Palestine army in Lebanon and West Bank. Friedman knew him well personally since he was a correspondent of *The New York Times* at Beirut and Israel. Abu was known as the most dangerous terrorist, but his killer team assassinated him in his own drawing room in 1988 at Tunis as it shot innumerable shots at him. In 1995, at the Middle East Economic Summit, Friedman met Abu's son. That young man gave Friedman his business card that read:

Jihad-al-Vizier,
Managing Director, World Trade Center, Gaza, Palestine.

That the Jihad-al-Vizier, connected as he is with WTO in his own country, is an example Friedman puts forth to point out that a balance can be struck between Lexus (globalization) and olive tree (religious incline) among other such picturesque illustrations. He wants to establish that for achieving economic progress, Lexus approach needs to be pursued, but it may not be at the cost of one's own cultural root or identity. A worldwide acceptance is given to a healthy globalization only when in the countries/communities concerned the olive tree is still fresh and strong. Only such communities can help keep up an open mind for the outside world. By merely holding on to the root of the olive tree (as the Islamic fundamentalists are indicating in greater degree), then without Lexus we cannot progress much; and in such an atmosphere only terrorist mentality would keep on growing. Thus, "keeping a balance between the two would be like a constant movement".

However, even such a keen observer does not neglect the viewpoint of cultural conflict. After six months of 9/11 Friedman writes (*San Jose Mercury News*, March 12, 2002), "An Egyptian official informed me in February that when he was recently giving a lecture to some Arab students on 'Peace in Middle East', one student interrupted him and said, 'Only eight small suitcase sized atom bombs are needed and only then the entire problem with Israel can solved'." Friedman then quotes the Middle East expert, Professor Stephen Cohen: "The question is that what bin Laden could not do, would the Palestine extremists be able to do? If you and thousands of your brethren were prepared to sacrifice yourselves then even the unlimited powers of America and Israel would not be able to stop you. We have now arrived at this borderline. Before our (Arab) and Muslim majority could be prepared for another objective (for peace), the Jihadis would arm themselves with their destructive powers. That is why the Israel-Palestine war is not a mere local, ethnocentric conflict that could be ignored. It is connected with not only a number of satellite televisions and dangerous weapons but also the life of billions of people as well."

On the basis of his extensive travels and wide contacts with different kinds of people, Friedman believes that "Israelis and Palestinians, American as well as Muslims, do not want such a war". Accepting, however, the deep cultural divides and its great impact, he says, "This conflict of Israel-Palestine has reached such a level of intense violence that it seems that it may turn into a fuse to ignite great wars of civilizations. Musharraf can become an architect of a more liberal political system, the originator and guardian of this issue of change." If even the verbal version of Musharraf also steps in the direction of a modern society and liberal political reconstruction, it can become a model for a new Muslim world. It is important that on this issue the liberal Muslims living in America and elsewhere should play the role of a stimulant and a catalyst.

Anyway, as Varadrajan states, the medieval forces have struck at culture and civilization itself. 'Civilization'—mankind's most valued gift in peril—has taken a central place in our political discourse (*India Today International*, December 31, 2001).

It is in this perspective that two developments gives a breather and reasons for hope to mankind. In the wake of his historic joint statement with Manmohan Singh, President Musharraf stated that the new geo-political realities have marginalized borders, and made interdependence between the two South Asian neighbors deeper. "It is a fact that militant attacks on innocent citizens (in Kashmir) will alienate them."

The wrath of the people of the Valley (of Kashmir) against the terrorist attack on the passengers of Srinagar-Muzffarabad (April 2005) is a telling reminder of the new phenomenon. They show that the gun-trotting terrorists are totally on the wrong path. The people of the state came out on the streets as one to spontaneously welcome this gesture of reconciliation.

Singh said at that time that the border (LoC) cannot be redrawn, but was ready to discuss any other option. Responding, Musharraf said that "the propositions floating around—that LoC cannot be redrawn; it cannot be permanent; the border must be made irrelevant—can all be taken together to workout some out of box solution." Singh offered then that the border can be "softened" over a period of time. They indicated that the two countries meanwhile, could go on improving contacts between people on both side of LoC, step up trade and transport and *the flow of ideas across the border that will melt that way.*

Conflict Avoidance and Resolution

Like some other fierce conflicts (centered on caste/community/religion), for resolving this conflict of terror, both conflict avoidance and its resolution need to be adopted. The edited work of famous sociologists like Roman Herzog, Amitai Etzioni and others entitled *Preventing a Clash of Civilizations: A Peace Strategy for the 21st Century* throws much light on the subject. But even here, not adequate attention is given to checkmate factors that give nourishment to terrorism. Dousing the fire of religious hostility between peoples is given greater importance rather than those to entirely prevent the fire right from building. It is imperative that every nation would now have to adopt, individually and collectively, a policy to promote among all groups many long-term programs and plans for education and awareness, with imaginative use of audio-visual technology, which would create in them a sense of equanimity, impartiality and an open mind for the various cultures of the world, various lifestyles of various peoples and their viewpoints.

The policy to promote or encourage mono-religion teaching in the style of Madrassa-like centers must be given up. Similarly, how destructive can be not only about the terrorist organizations but even the practice of encouraging propaganda of only one religion or community, its symbols, interests or value-priorities and keeping out all other religions/communities, is now well illustrated by the communal violence that erupted from Karachi, Gujarat to Bradford, UK. In March 2002, in spite of the dangerous terrorist threat on the Indian Parliament itself still looming large, Vishwa Hindu Parishad (which, alongwith the Babri Masjid Action Committee) had taken an intransigent stand about reconstruction of the Ram Temple at Ayodhya) had themselves basically played the ISI-abetted game of terrorists against India through the Godhra incident. Looking at the role played by organizations like SIMI and Sangh Parivar (respectively, fundamentalist Muslim and Hindu organizations) in thoughtlessly sacrificing peace in India, obstructing the process of development, and shaking the socio-cultural foundations of security of the nation, it seems that steps to curb and limit activities of such forces and organizations as a part of conflict avoidance and resolution need to be considered well. The same applies to fundamentalist Islamic outfits in other countries.

Another long-term approach also must be adopted in countries where a democratic form of government and practices are not in operation. Drawing attention to the 'bloody borders' of Islam, Huntington says that in the last quarter of the 20th century and especially "in the decade of the 1990s the militant attitude and violence of Muslims are facts and these cannot be denied either by Muslims or non-Muslims".

Jonathan Fox too notes in *Journal of Peace Research* (2000) that in all the inter-cultural conflicts that occurred from 1945 to 1989, Islam was involved. From 1990 to 1998 the role of Islam in such conflicts was of 24.7 percent. On this issue, Professor

M. Shahid Alam (North Eastern University, USA) argues, "Taking note of the high figure of Muslim population of the world, this percentage is not significant. Again, the borders of Muslim nations touch those of African, Western, Hindu and Buddhist nations. The borders of nations with non-Muslim cultures jointly are much less than borders of nations in the Muslim world. That is why it is easy to understand if it gets the lion's share for the percentage on 'bloody borders' resulting from such conflicts!" However, why do these conflicts occur mostly between Muslim and non-Muslim nations only? And why does Alam observe silence on this point? Also, as Professor Alam himself accepts, what about those 'internal borders' that 'pockets' of Muslim majorities create within many non-Muslim nations also?

On the whole, we may say that in all religions we find elements of extremism, violence and *jehad*, and they are responsible for the environment of violence and religious fanaticism across the world. However, by the empirical and sense-of-proportion measures, the greatest concern is created by the Muslim society. According to a Gallup Poll survey (February 2002) in nine big Muslim nations, majority of Muslims have anti-American feelings. The Muslims consider America 'aggressive and unruly'. Similarly, after a lapse of six months of 9/11, Edward Said had written that the Arabs and Muslims feel discriminated against in US and suffer from an alienation complex; and even when living in America they have a dislike for it. Journalist-writer Stephen Emerson, connected with the leading media and author of *American Jihad*, presents very shocking details to tell us about how literature was being distributed among Muslim children showing them methods to kill the 'dogs'—the Jews and the Christians. He has also collected provocative video, etc., that encourage killing of Americans in the fairs at Chicago.

Friedman, already having lived in the Middle East, once again went there in the winter of 2002 after 9/11 and met the people. He says, "Wherever you go—Egypt, Saudi Arabia, and

Pakistan—you will be able to see a tall, mentally dividing wall between them and America even today." He adds, "Last week's (the last week of February) Gallup Poll indicates that (even now) 61 percent Muslims believe that in the 9/11 attacks Muslims were not involved and 51 percent are critical of Americans...but after the travel experience of mine I find that these figures are not yet too bad and that is surprising in itself."

Friedman says that after the Berlin Wall was broken in 1989, we came to know that there were thousands of people (on the other side, East Germany) who were accepting the American thinking and vision. "That may be so, but today we see another wall, and it is not erected on the ground; it is built in the minds of the Muslims, and it separates America from Arab-Muslim world." He further makes a significant comment, "But unlike the Berlin Wall, this wall is built from both sides; and only the two societies on both sides can break it."

Just like the metaphor of a wall, Huntington uses another: that of a 'fault line'. There have been great and deep underground splits that originally join the earth at surface. When conditions change in such 'fault lines' the underground earth plates move and thus an earthquake occurs. The culture, community, religion, ethics, etc., are like these deep underground splits among mankind. When the attachment to one's own religion/culture crosses limits and the contempt for other religion/culture runs sharp and pointed, then these fault lines in the concerned society become active. They result in conflicts and riots—a kind of social earthquake. Such fault lines may be more or less deep and wide in every society/region. But, in order to fill them up or for plotting the coming changes in them in time and taking immediate pre-emptive steps, the leaders must adopt policies as sort of 'seismographic' notes. Social leaders also must take up such cultural projects as to make people properly aware of such splits and dangers within. If this kind of economic-cultural-religious 're-engineering' is not done, then mankind will have to be prepared for suffering hardships and devastation caused by violent conflicts and social earthquakes.

Globalization Approach

On issues of an environment of world peace and ecology, everyone will have to develop a humanitarian worldwide view. For example, the gigantic multi-nationals ushering in this globalization result in sense of human degradation and relative deprivation among many large communities. A number of movements against the structural violence of global market and consumerism are supported by many peoples based on cultural diversities. Not just the plethora of NGOs thriving in other parts G-8 and World Economic Forum nations, many of the rich nations also, in their last conference, expressed their acceptance of the imbalance among the worldviews that are considered for understanding the contemporary world and its great challenges. America and liberal democracy have to face the challenge on such a large scale from the results from globalization and consequent feelings of anger, discontent and frustrations among various sections.

As Vandana Shiva, eminent environmental anti-globalist says, "If (and when) we shall understand the ecology of terror, we shall be able to see the road-map to peace. We shall attain peace only by nurturing democracy, partnership of communities and cultural diversity."

The 'fault line' metaphor is also applicable to the area of globalization and the underground gaps among various regions and communities of every nation. The political system that globalization ushers in allows open markets to its economy. Freedom in system gives greater freedom of individual choice (as a consumer) and new opportunities for progress. Such arguments are logical. With growing momentum in globalization, the nations accepting its policy and principles would develop new infrastructure (as Shanghai and Bangalore turning into the Silicon Valley of China and India respectively). With new broad roads, electrification, communication equipments, etc., new space would be available to new entrepreneurship. The emergence of entrepreneurs with the role model of Narayan Murthy of Infosys and the broad basing of the middle class would help fill in the gaps. These are indeed logical consequences experienced in reality at some places, but it is also true that those who live at the bottom of the society and have not yet received benefit out of it feel alienated from globalization process.

Such communities do not have the base of necessary technology for participating in the competition of the open system. Many a time the lack of a work culture or opposition to whatever 'new' is introduced may also be present in them. Among the Arab/Muslim communities there a lack of a critical mass that is imperative to bring in such change. In many Third World countries there is a small class of people that adopts the equipments of technology and free market and use them skillfully for ushering in globalization. But, there is also a greater section of the masses that is ignorant and unequipped to keep pace with these trends as well. These 'haves' and have nots' both have vastly different vocabulary and symbols of progress. This psycho-cultural distance gives an idea of the 'fault line' yawning between them. Thus, there is a distance not just between North and South worlds, or between East and West, but also within the South (or Third World) itself. We find the presence of such North World (the 'haves') and so within the South World also there is a wide distance among classes. The psycho-political effects result in a conflict situation.

Globalization has helped the giant multi-national companies like McDonald, Taco Bell, KFC, Coca Cola, Pizza Hut, etc., to make it in the interior villages of the Third World. Some of them interfere with the traditional patterns of food and drink in these nations, and create a sense of 'relative deprivation' among the poor. Besides, the golden arches built up by McDonald's at one sight create an illusion about the prevalent high standard of living there, while the lower and poor classes still remain deprived. Certain anthropologists term this as 'systematic misunderstanding'. Fundamentalists and the Left utilize it for spreading misunderstanding and contempt against the West that is wealthy—the 'haves' among the traditional and orthodox forces of these vast 'deprived' masses. Taking advantage of religious symbols and the fear (or a sense of insecurity) of their culture, the discontent or a sense of deprivation actually produced by the failures of their own rulers and inherent limitations of economy and society in the Muslim countries are demonstrated instead as a result of globalization and its leading force, America, that are advancing on an alleged 'wrong map'.

After about a decade of movements against globalization, even the wealthy nations themselves have begun to accept this. Claus Schwab, President of World Economic Forum, admitted, "The rich and powerful will not be able to ignore the voice of those who are deprived, in rags and deprived of rights to progress. Due to globalization, the world has shrunk and a situation has arisen when one has to understand the perception of gap between the 'haves' and 'have nots'. Thus, a need for a dialogue between the two polar entities to listen to the problems of the poor countries and population is increasingly felt. If we can do this, only then can we avoid the future possibilities of such conflicts as occurred in the latter half of the 20th century in Africa, Latin America and South East Asia." Then, he concludes with a significant observation: "Moments such as the world wars and terrorist attacks on New York-Washington that we can term as turning points in human history, make us aware of the truth that the world in which we live is today much more complex—and fragile than what we had thought...Drawing from all these lessons, we have to be clear on this point: in a world where the voice of the poor is ignored, where the economic growth is advantageous only to the rich and where clashes occur in a culture of misunderstandings, now we shall not be able to live at all. Those who are in an advantageous situation to use power and wealth would have to see, in their own enlightened self-interest, that such distances do not increase and does not give rise to conflicts" (*Newsweek*, December 17, 2001). (Before this, this same Schwab had raised a huge fund of $82 billion in New Delhi and Davos, to be used for the refurbishment of the army, for American Congress for the year 2002. This figure is twice that of the figure given in its latest report by the UNO for removal of poverty from the world! If America is not ready to fight the new humanistic war for the 4 billion people wallowing in poverty in this world, then would it be possible for it to find a lasting peace at home or in this world at all? Earlier, in such forums led by Schwab India was tendered an advice for speeding up globalization!)

Gandhi had proclaimed this truth in very brief and telling words: "Poverty is the lowest form of violence."

Gandhi's Worldview

Fareed Zakaria says that two facts made the attacks of 9/11 possible: one, globalization; and two, human nature. (We have already analyzed globalization in detail.) Human nature indicates a highly subtle and complex process and phenomenon. Culture and human nature play important roles in creating a situation of backwardness or community's development. When the world, along with America, determines to wage a war to remove this poverty and the terror of backwardness from roots—or, at least keep it at the minimum level—only then, as a result of such a new kind of war the chances of a sustained and lasting peace can come up.

And, that is why, one cannot easily ignore, in context of conflicts of cultures, globalization, Talibanization and economic class upheavals (as examined in preceding relevant chapters), that ultimately the task of making the mind of the humans a healthy space is the hardest of all. Gandhi used to say that non-violence could become the greatest weapon against violence; and non-violence arises from fearlessness and firm commitment to peace. He had also said that non-violence of the fearless would prove much stronger than the violence and terror born of power. In 1934, he also had said (no doubt the context, form and style of terror were different then than what it is today, but the basic element was the same): "The infallible weapon against the violence of terror is the non-violence nurtured by inner peace." On the other hand, he also said, "I would prefer violence over cowardice anytime."

Are the trends and contexts emerging in the 21st century making the philosophy of Gandhi (who is considered as the most exemplary man and the greatest person of the 20th century), more relevant?

Mahatma Gandhi did not occupy any political position or office. He commanded no terrorist organization or a guerrilla army behind him. Yet, he developed and used the effective 'weapon' of non-violence against the beastly and violent power and physical might. This weapon had, as its elemental strength, the value of non-violence, peaceful non-cooperation, *satyagraha*, and civil disobedience. In other nations the struggle for freedom or movements for other proper issues had turned violent. But Gandhi was able to uproot the long nourished belief of the world that there is no alternative to violence to face violence. By his thinking, by his behavior and his performance he was able to inspire millions of unarmed persons for a struggle for freedom of their country. Thus, he has challenged many earlier deep-rooted and fundamental assumptions of politics, power, violence and terrorism. History witnessed a new intellectual 'paradigm shift', and experienced it too.

Gandhi called terrorism as "an effervescence of an excited emotion on the surface of the mind of man". (Of course, in those days, the intellectual base or 'praxis' for action—and form, structure and style were not as complex as they are now.) He supported the power of truth and a civil non-cooperation based on ethics as his tools. When the British authorities took violent steps to curb the *satyagrahis*, he protested successfully against it by his non-violent *satyagraha* again. This is his unique contribution to this field. Here, the observations of McSwiny seem apt: "Those who can suffer the most will win at the end." However, the limitations of McSwiny's observations are also obvious in light of the success of Gandhi. As such, Gandhi, and later on some of his followers, have shown that to suffer or to survive thus does not mean 'violence'.

Against political violence and other types of violence also, many ethical leaders of the world have effectively used Gandhi's weapon of non-violence with its basic idea and practice as he espoused it. Reverend Tutu, Nelson Mandela, James Farmer, Martin Luther King, and the leaders of 'new social movements' for such causes as peace, ecology, human rights and development with justice are cases in point.

From the thoughts of Gandhi and King, we get our answers how terrorism can never be considered proper or be justified. On practical grounds too, terrorism can never be justified. Terrorists have achieved their tactical aims by kidnapping important personalities and keeping them as prisoners, or by hijacking airplanes, killing the persons for demonstration effect, etc., but they have never been successful in bringing about any fundamental change or achieving strategic goals, such as a revolution in their own societies. The purist and orthodox Islam of Deoband sect, as represented by bin Laden-Wahabis, has not proportionately spread far and wide in the world. Nor has any terrorist leader been able to create a state on the basis of such a form of Islam. No terrorist has obtained such an acclaim that can be comparable to that of Gandhi or King's success.

From the viewpoints of Jesus Christ, Gandhi, King, Vinoba, Mandela and the like, terrorism and other forms of violence actually fail in their objectives and may even achieve results that are totally opposite to the aims of such actions. Even to Hitler, the 'supreme terrorist', Gandhi wrote in clear terms against use of violence. Echoing his sentiments, King had warned his Black brethren: "Returning violence for violence multiplies violence." He said that if we answer the injustice of the White rulers by violence, our future generations will have to suffer from their negligence. As Thomas Raymore says in his book *Terrorism: Past, Present and Future*, wherever violence has been resorted to, including in America, each society has experienced the truth of his warnings. It is not easy to internalize 'fearlessness' of Gandhi by his methods, though. In an opinion poll in October 2001 of *Newsweek*, most of the Americans considered the question of their security as the greatest problem. After six months of 9/11, in early March also, the Americans were worried about security issue. In the MSN-NBC Media Internet survey, only 35 percent were able to say that of the 22,288 travellers those who travelled by airplane were 'safe'. Only 26 percent considered it 'safe' to gather in huge public meetings. Only 18 percent believed it 'safe' to work in high buildings. Only 25 percent believed that it was safer than before to open postal covers. In a country where the public demand is to reduce taxes, now, more than half (52%) of the people believe that they are ready to pay more taxes if the state is to provide greater security and related services. This is two times the figure of willing taxpayers as a poll in the decade of 1990s indicated.

It is in such an age of insanity and insecurity that we need to revisit Gandhi whose influence is traced in 'far and wide' places by Jack DuVall of Washington-based International Center on Non-violent Conflict. DuVall wrote: "Solidarity in Poland, the 'people power' movement in the Philippines, the people's movement that defeated General Pinochet in Chile, the Velvet Revolution in Czechoslovakia, the non-violent campaign in Serbia in 2000 against Slobodan Milosevic, the Rose Revolution against Shevardnadze in Georgia (2004)—all deliberately used the kind of non-violent strategies that Gandhi pioneered."

In response to his column in *The Guardian* (August 23, 2004), Brian Whitaker wrote about a few rarely-heard people in the Middle East who advocate Islamic non-violence, or 'civil Jihad'. He asked, "Why the techniques used by Gandhi against the British in India had not been more widely used by Arabs and Muslims, and wondered what Gandhi would have done in Najaf." He received an unusually large number of emails from readers, "many of them suggesting that non-violent action in the Middle East was an idea whose time had come. Others claimed that Muslims are incapable of anything but violence." Adds Whitaker, "My question about Gandhi and Najaf was answered rather dramatically on Thursday when Grand Ayatollah Ali al-Sistani, who had returned to Iraq from Medina accompanied by thousands of unarmed supporters (*The Guardian*, August 31, 2004).

Such a widely respected figure that he was, Sistani was "able to achieve by his presence and persuasive powers, what Americans and Iraqi governments had failed to achieve by force of arms. It was most Gandhi-like act we have seen in Iraq since the conflict began". Whitaker thinks that it was what Sistani had urged Iraqis to engage in 'civil Jihad'. "Sistani brings to Arab politics a legitimate, pragmatic interpretation of Islam, one that says Islam should inform politics and the constitution, but clerics should not rule." Friedman wishes him a Nobel Prize (for peace).

Nor Gandhi principle was unknown to Palestinians. "In the first intefada (uprising) against the Israel", says Palestinian educator Terry Boulata, "we did it all without shooting one bullet and succeeded in putting the Palestinian people on the map of world nations." Calling the construction of the fence, a separation wall, by Israel a 'violent action,' he said, "It cannot be countered by violence." He refers to the non-violent resistance being carried out by the peasants and farmers against the confiscation of their land by Israeli authority.

The peaceful movement gathered some momentum in August 2004 when Dr. Arun Gandhi, Gandhi's 70-year old son, an American citizen, visited Israel-Palestine to persuade Palestinians to adopt a non-violent form of struggle to persuade Israel to allow them elections, to organize mass protests against the 26-feet tall barrier of separation (fence) of concrete, etc. During his visit of this troubled land, Dr. Gandhi held a protest meeting at Abu Dis, attended by 2,000 Palestinians and Israelis in the shadow of illegally constructed barrier. The veteran

Israeli peace activist, Uri Avnery commented: "This may indeed be what Mahatma Gandhi have advised in a situation like this...An open non-violence act of defiance shows the oppressor the futility of his measures."

Brian Whitaker, in his column in *Guardian Unlimited* (August 31, 2004), brings back the question of "whether the Middle East really is fertile ground for Gandhian activity". On this point, he quotes a Brussels-based Khaled Diab, an Arab journalist, who wrote: "I don't think Arab culture is less-equipped than any other culture to take on a Gandhi mantle. In my own native Egypt, you see peaceful conflict resolution in action..." Giving then his own view, Whitaker states: "One key difference between 1940s India and 21st century Arab world is that no Gandhi has emerged to galvanise popular support for such means. This is further complicated by the fact that an Arab Gandhi would not only have to battle against a foreign oppressor but the home-grown variety would chop him down before he could mature." But he discerns that the common refrain among the Arabs is "force is not repelled except by force". The governor of Ramallah city, Mustafa Liftawi openly disagreed with Arun Gandhi saying, "We tried to apply non-violent techniques of resistance. But the Israeli occupation has given us no choice but to use force" (*Outlookindia.com*, September 5, 2004). He thinks that "the need is the charisma of Nasser in the mould of Gandhi to make the political and cultural case for peaceful resistance, that being a pacifist does not mean that you have been pacified..... Unfortunately, the only people who have so far made that case are some Arab intellectuals and outsiders" (*Guardian Unlimited Online*, August 31, 2004).

The Gandhian praxis in America is reinterpreted through "a whole range of non-violent protests, to letter writing, making phone calls, prayer vigils, and sit downs," observes Bill Dobbs of an anti-war group, United for Peace and Justice. A life-long student of Gandhi, Kalle Lasn says, "I think Gandhi would have found something even better to do; he would have found some ways to inspire billions. We need a new Gandhi, some one to mobilize that lousy feeling inside us and give the planet a new voice" (reported by Suleman Din in *India Abroad*).

Security-Freedom Balance

Fareed Zakaria makes a telling statement about this issue: In the last decade the importance the state was lost in the streams of globalization and liberalization. Economy, instead of politics, was in the driver's seat, and the state had taken a back seat. But, after 9/11, suddenly, the state has come to the forefront once again. Leaving trade and commerce, entertainment and other industries, it is now widely accepted that the state should perform its original role to relieve from the minds of the people all the anxieties of personal and national securities.

Although, America and other Western European countries have a 'system' and tradition to be sensitive about values of individualism and individual freedom and keep the field of action of the state to the minimum, and although there are societies that insist that the state has no rights to interfere with 'latest' things like the 'Internet', now have mostly begun to accept such state regulatory laws as 'Patriotic Act' and all the way to 'POTO' (repealed in India in 2004).

Before 9/11, the global capitalism had made free economy, limited role of the state, unlimited individual activity and movement, etc., to be accepted widely all over the world. After the Cold War, the alternatives of statism and communism were no longer available or operational. After 9/11, we have begun to view the world with a new paradigm. "The state has again come to the forefront; culture has returned; ideologies are given new importance; and among all this the government has made a comeback." If such a 'paradigm' has become a reality for America, the citadel and place of pilgrimage of individualism, then it would be no surprise if it becomes acceptable and real for many other societies as well. However, we shall have to carefully maintain a proper balance between the new paradigm of government and security and the paradigm of freedom of the individual and open economy.

This 'paradigm' will have to adjust with a variety of issues: to provide safety from terrorism on individual basis; to uplift the 'deprived' during the process of globalization applied without discretion; to fill up the distances between classes and hearts; to widen the field of modern thought and education; and to create an environment of cultural tolerance by bringing various cultures near each other.

With a view to understand the qualitative change worldwide after 9/11 and to understand the newly shaping world, we have taken a collective overview of the reality of all the 'paradigms' or conceptual frameworks here. We find some paradigms taking diagonally opposite directions, or sometimes even running parallel. But, as all are basically complementary to each other, it is possible to develop a holistic worldview on their basis.

All the societies of the world, all communities, followers of all religions, and all countries of North-South/East-West/First-Third Worlds have to face the present challenge not just individually, but more importantly, collectively and together. The 'paradigm shift' ensuing 9/11 and 12/13 requires not a 'polar', but a 'plural', multi-angled and multi-centered approach. This, again, needs to be tackled in a collective manner; for this is indeed the imperative of the present challenge and change anticipated. Only through such an approach, based on values of freedom, equality and justice, can the peace and progress of the world be achieved and sustained.

The New York Times stated that there are two 'superpowers' in the world—America and the world (public) opinion. But, the latter is still dormant. One can add a third superpower—*Ladenism*, which will persist even in the absence of bin Laden. Can the world opinion mediate between the other two polar superpowers? In his insightful piece, "Why Terror?" (*Prospect*, April 2004), Professor Bhikhu Parekh has formulated an imaginary exchange between Gandhi and bin Laden. He comprehends at least part of the "twisted worldview that

Why terror?

OSAMA BIN LADEN *is a Saudi-born businessman and al Qaeda leader. He is believed to be responsible for a number of attacks on the US and its allies*

MAHATMA GANDHI *was the celebrated Indian leader who led a campaign of non-violent civil disobedience against India's British rulers. He was assassinated in 1948*

inspires bin Laden, for we cannot defeat it without understanding it". Parekh's Gandhi argues with bin Laden, "If you are serious about creating a good society, you must stop measuring yourself against the West." His Gandhi emphasizes, "There is not a single example in history of terrorists creating a humane and healthy society" (in Anna Lannstrom (ed.), *The Stranger's Religion: Fascination and Fear*, 2004).

Man can regulate the spacecraft and its trajectory. He can monitor every movement on earth or detect an oil source beneath from the satellite floating in the space. Sitting at NASA, one can gauge the nature of crops coming up in a farm near Nairobi or the size of the green patch in an oasis near Dubai. But, only when he is able to view the other human beings, societies and cultures with empathy and in totality, he would be able to have a sustainable peace on this earth.

In the 21st century, the man, travelling on the path of 'his' civilization, has now to be decultured. He needs to strike and maintain a balance between the misplaced polarities of Islam vs. the Rest, the West vs. Islam, the West vs. the Rest, and the perceived polarities of globalization and Talibanization, McWorld and Jihad, and the Lexus and the olive tree—at the same time, promoting an open-minded dialogue between the forces positioned at two ends of the fear-terror and non-violence-peace syndrome. Let the borders turn into rivers and the walls into bridges.

Annexures

APPENDIX 1
Appraisal of the War/Military Options with India

For the field of South Asia peace is so necessary that the two neighbouring countries must not sacrifice it for their short-term tactical moves. In spite of having promised to curb infiltrations across the border, President Musharraf has not taken the necessary steps in that direction. The Chief Minister of Jammu & Kashmir, Muhammad Mufti, has been requesting New Delhi for a change of stance. The Indian Government thus needs to take a fresh look at the issue.

Pakistan must give up its half-concealed war in Kashmir that is actually ruining its own country. If Musharraf is ready to take the risk of going on the path of peace, he would be surprised to know how a large number of Pakistani people are ready to welcome the step to drop this seemingly endless conflict with India!

But this is a riddle like some mental disease. Both the countries are caught up in the whirlpools of motion created by them. We (both of us) believe that it is a weakness to grant any concession to the rival/opposite country, and the people of the two countries also believe the same. But nothing is father than the truth. And yet both believe that the other is just buying time, and therefore they make the mistake of not bringing any major change in their policies or even critically evaluate them.

India, with a complex of being a greater power, is unable to show the necessary courage for this. On the other hand, the people of Kashmir have to suffer a great deal due to the presence of Indian Army, and it must be fully aware of this. And, Pakistan too must have no doubt on this that the Kashmiris are weary of terrorist Islamic forces fighting in the name of their freedom. To the Kashmiri Muslims with moderate traditions the excesses committed in the name of Islam seem a headache. There is only one avenue to get out of this maze: both the nations will have to change their viewpoints drastically.

– **Prof. Parvez Hudbhoy**, *The Daily Times Pakistan Daily*

Joshua Kucera, a staff reporter in the prestigious *Jane's Defense Weekly*, Washington DC (October 4, 2004) gives a report about Pakistan's show of the latest deadly, India-oriented weapons that provides an appropriate introduction to this scenario.

As delegations from a veritable biggest arms show, IDEAS 2004, ironically, has a slogan "Arms for Peace". As delegations from a veritable who's who of pariah states—North Korea, Myanmar, Iran, Zimbabwe, Sudan—make the rounds, a Pakistani company shows off its new cluster bombs (which, the company press release notes, "can be used against soft targets"). A Bangladeshi delegation looks approvingly at a display of Pakistani tanks. Pakistan's missiles, including the nuclear-capable Shaheen II, are displayed outside, behind a sign reading "Technological Demonstration—Not for Sale". It seems to be an oblique reference to the most notorious past IDEAS exhibitor—A.Q. Khan, the father of Pakistan's nuclear program and now the apparent mastermind of a global nuclear smuggling network. Four years ago, his company, Khan Research Laboratories, was at IDEAS handing out glossy brochures advertising specialized equipment for making a nuclear bomb...Pakistan is requesting the US that the

F-16s be armed with top-of-the-line air-to-air missiles that would be of little use against targets like the Islamists it's fighting on the ground. So also, navy surveillance planes it is getting from the US. They would, of course, be useful in a war against India. But the big news at the show is the US presence. This is the first time that American companies have exhibited at IDEAS.

1. Air Raids on the Terrorist Camps inside Pakistan

The Indian Air Force's Mirage, MiG-27 and Jaguar warplanes carry out raids on the hidden camps/centers of the terrorists in Pakistan territory near Azad Kashmir/PoK, and during these raids helicopters send land soldiers and heavy vehicles like tanks in that area is very dangerous (because on the LoC both the nations have laid down land mines in great numbers). Also, both the nations must also stop the forward march policy during the rainy months.

Targets

All the training centers and hiding camps of terrorists in Azad Kashmir.

Dangers

The enemy (Pakistan) ready to attack India. Can find out the Indian airplanes by its radars. By its surface to air missiles and other fighter planes can interrupt the Indian planes in their flight and by these flying weapons destroy Indian airplanes. Thus, it does not get any advantage of a surprise or sudden attack.

In the meantime, if India resorts to this strategy, America, UK, UNO, etc., are informed at once that the purpose of this is 'for a limited military manoeuver', so that it is clear that the purpose is not for a war on wide scale.

2. Missile Attacks on Terrorist Camps

'Prithvi' missiles, armed with traditional bombing shells or exploding devices, aimed on such enemy camps, then they would achieve their purpose within hours.

Targets

All the terrorist camps can be the targets. If it seems necessary, the camps across the border and into the Pakistan territory that are being used as 'launching pad' for the infiltrators form that side into Kashmir, can also be destroyed.

Dangers

Pakistan also may answer the attack with one of its own to crack the missiles and/or attack another part of India altogether. In such attacks, India army may have to lose its precious 'Prithvi' missiles. If 'Prithvi' were used against a land army of Pakistan advancing with heavy artillery and tanks, it would suit Indian strategy better.

Advantage

In that situation the possibility of losses to India would be small.

3. Simultaneous Air/Land Attacks in PoK

In order to destroy Pakistan's security arrangements beyond the LoC and the camps of terrorist activities, air attacks by bombing airplanes can clear the way for sending armed infantry into that territory, while giving it an air protection by air bombers. It would be something like the 'Kargil' war but this time from India.

Targets

The air strips and bases in Azad Kashmir, helipads surrounded by high mountains, dense forests and snow-clad areas of Skardu, Gilgit and Uri, besides Poonch, and the army camps of Muzzafarabad, the capital of Azad Kashmir to be destroyed and also ruin the protection centers behind them. The topography and terrain of Poonch, Skardu, Uri area are highly suitable for armed infiltrators into the valley of Jammu and Kashmir, so these areas must be conquered at the speed of lightening; such areas be taken over from Azad Kashmir as to achieve the aims of 'salami slicing operation'.

Dangers

There are a number of dangers in sustaining military steps that stretch long into the mountainous area. Besides, India has to be prepared for being blamed for waging a 'Kargil' type war of 1999 on Pakistan this time. Also, it would be criticized for crossing over the international Line of Control (LoC).

In the meantime, India can provoke the armed separatist forces within Azad Kashmir. Thus, when there is a lot of war-like chaos in this region, Pakistan would openly provide military and political support on a large scale to its Independent Kashmir Movement. This may stop the military, political and diplomatic planning of India, as thus Pakistan opens a totally new sensitive strategy of using non-state or stateless elements. By that counter-strategy, it is possible that any of the above-mentioned scenarios may take shape.

Advantage

If this plan is successful in Kashmir, India gets regional advantage. India can claim that after the 'Instrument of Accession' of 1947, India has the legal/constitutional right over all of Kashmir region, and this is what it gets back here.

Alternately, when international pressure (and it is likely to begin from the first week of the conflict) builds up against the two nations, mostly a compromise would be agreed upon with America or UNO or such bigger nation as the arbiter, the two nations can meet at one table and for the purpose of negotiations, India can insist on keeping with it certain strategically important regions, or keep such areas that may stop infiltration, and insist that a new LoC be drawn. (Undoubtedly, a similar strategy would also be with Pakistan by conquering Kashmir valley and Poonch-Uri region under India and get the new LoC drawn in its own favour.)

4. All-Embracing Traditional War

This would be an all-out war to attack and destroy the atomic refineries and other centers; air base; heavy artillery centers and infantry lines, command-control structures; communication structures, bridges and roads and other transport facilities with missiles and bombings by Mirage and attacks by other bombing squads. From Rajasthan and Punjab areas take out, at a lightening speed, land army for attack in enemy territory with armed infantry and tanks prevent similar attack of Pakistan in the region of Punjab in India. Pakistan would resort to strangulate the oceanic routes for oil supplies by its naval strategy along the Arabian Sea, steps be taken to stop it. Bombing Karachi and unleashing chaos there would come in handy. (This is what Pakistan aims to do with Kandla and Mumbai ports.)

Targets

All air bases of Pakistan, army headquarters (Karachi, Bahavalpur, Multan, Lahore, Gujranwala, Mangala and Rawalpindi) and its sub-structures at Saraghoda, Gujaranwala Okara, Multan, Jang Dera-nawab Shah and the ports of Karachi and Gadar must be attacked heavily.

Dangers

After so many months have passed since December, the mobilization and other readiness of the army the attack would come as no surprise now. The enemy is also aware and ready for such strategies. He is also ready for not just defensive but even offensive war and eager or taking the initiative strategy if need be. This would mean that India may have to suffer great losses in men and material, and even some military losses would accrue. The other countries may label India as an aggressor and even intervene. There would be great, and may be harmful, political and diplomatic repercussions too. Pakistan would experience great setback and discomfiture or suffer loss of large land portion, and then may not hesitate to use the 'atomic alternative'. As it is, the military leaders and even the people advocate quick war policy; and the character as well as the past of General Musharraf and the entire lack of value-based behavior would inspire him to make use of atomic warhead missiles and India must have considered such a possibility without doubt. Thus, such a step carries great dangers.

Advantage

If it is a repeat of the war of 1971, India would get its traditional superior and advantageous position entirely. The whole of Pakistan's military set-up and structure can be destroyed, and it would take years for it to rebuild the same once again. That would make Pakistan a land of total chaos.

After capturing its strategic areas and cities, India could declare a ceasefire (as the international pressure would turn effective by that time) and at the table for negotiations when India offers to return these places to Pakistan it can dictate terms of the treaties so that its own interest are better protected. The situation after the war can thus be exploited for this purpose. To make the new treaties long lasting and free of any loopholes and mistakes, the Indian government will learn its lessons from the experience of the treaties of Tashkent (1965) and Shimla (1972), we may hope.

5. All-Out All-Level War-Atomic War

As India has adopted the policy of not taking initiative of using atomic weapons, it is not going to begin atomic attack on Pakistan; but if the atomic equipments of Pakistan will not be turned inactive or useless at first stage (America may do this in its own way, or India-Israel have their own secret understanding; and still it is impossible to keep such an enemy free from any attack, and even when it may come into play it is a very dangerous development for the military science also has some unimagined results in practical manoeuvers), then Pakistan would not let go of an opportunity to ward off its won big defeat or stop its own disintegration by initiating an atomic attack on India and would throw the first atomic missile against it without hesitation. The strategists, governments as well as the media—all have made this clear. India also is very much aware and equipped for such an eventuality. Against the highly destructive missiles of Pakistan (Gaznavi, Ghori, Abdali, Hatf-2, etc.) India has also developed and acquired 'Mobile Missile Launcher' to withstand their attacks and within no time (only about 143 seconds) it could launch its own attack that can wipe out entire Pakistan.

Targets

The entire states of Pakistan.

Dangers

This carries all the dangers of an atomic war. Like Pakistan, after the war, India also would have to suffer untold tortures and destruction of human and physical resources, obliteration of economy and many other sufferings for a long time. The world would have nothing but contempt for India. America and other nations may even take punitive steps against the nation who uses atomic weapons.

Advantage

On the other hand, for five long decades, the country that has been in thousands of ways harming and worrying India would almost exist no more. This would be a great source of relief for India.

However, the vision of India after the atomic war is very scary. Poverty, lack of all basic necessities, such as education, health, economic infrastructures like communication and transport would create great problems. This would lead to limitations on its sovereignty even; for it would have to depend on foreign help and aid all the time. For a decade or two it can lose its standing as a major power in the world. The removal of its permanent and harmful rival from the Indian subcontinent may, in the long run, yield advantageous results for India.

* * *

Note

With such above-mentioned alternatives before it against Pakistan, India has been preparing for any initiatives and pre-emptive strategies that Pakistan may resort to, through military drills and simulations by military and computer experts. India feels that all the pressure tactics of diplomacy have been already put to use and still have not yielded any desired result; due to the policy of Musharraf—or even ignoring them—the terrorist elements have continued their armed infiltrations and violent attacks across the borders; the anti-Indian people whose names have been submitted for returning to India will never be sent for trial; and Pakistan is creating further instability to obstruct free and fair elections in Jammu & Kashmir; then India may use the final alternative of a war along with pressurizing America to keep Pakistan away from such policies. In the meantime, experts like B. Raman say that India also must now react with a 'psy-war' (psychological warfare) tactics and resist by a long-term strategy of 'counter-terrorism' without delay. The discontent in regions like Sindh and Baluchistan against the Pakistani system being in Punjab-oriented can be utilized to create internal instability within that country too.

Clarification of Ceratin Terms

Terrorism

Any act that harasses and disgusts and terrorizes other/s. This term has its origin in the Latin term 'terrere' (to make another tremble with fear). In its political context, the term 'terrorism' is being used since the last decade of the 18th century, beginning during the French Revolution.

Any philosophy or action that resorts to violent and illegal action or treatment with the aim to shake up an established civil order, legal political arrangement and to make a person/people experience fear and harassment or tremors are known as 'terrorism'.

Jihad (Jehad)

'Muslim' means one who takes refuge of ALLAH. The personal efforts (struggle with self-'manthan') to become a 'better and purer Muslim' are termed as jehad/jihad (literally 'effort'). A diligent student of this subject, Ahmed Rashid, a journalist by profession, believes that for a large number of Muslims the term 'Jihad' indicates "one's own internal struggle for upward lift in spirituality", not a bloody expansionist war. But, in practical life, this idea turned into a (sacred) religious war against non-Muslim peoples, and such diabolical perverted meaning and activities. Gibbs Kappel, in his *Jihad: The Trail of Political Islam* (2000) says, "The defensive sacred war that bin Laden claims to wage is the of the greatest, most powerful and highest danger altogether." Christopher Dicky evaluates the 'Jihad' of Laden thus: The Jihad that bin Laden has declared against America, in the eyes of most of the religious scholars, was never 'a religious war', but merely 'an absolute untruth and fraud' only.

Religions

In his suggestively titled book, *Confluence of Religions*, Dr. S. Radhakrishnan indicates that while it is possible to have different religions but the 'religiosity' may not be different. The religion may be Christianity, Islam, Hindu or Buddhism/Jainism or Jew. The scholar who has deeply studied the sacred books of Bible and Koran, Prof. Kenneth Woodworth says, "The Bible and the Koran both reveal the words of the God. The prophets of both advocate freedom from Sin and the idea of Heaven and Hell. Both the great religions believe in One God; then why is such violence committed by them?" To find an answer, this scholar studies and analyses the two great Books minutely. In Koran the lines to perform Jihad against the non-Muslims or 'napak' people are very few, but these have been 'used' and 'mentioned' over and over. Koran emphasizes on many deeds of compassion, justice and mercy; but in practice its lines have been interpreted differently and used for support of religious fights and quarrels. Such scholars do not fail to point out the difference in the profiles of founder Prophets of the two religions either. Under the title of 'Holy Books', focused on these two great sacred books, in an article in *Newsweek* (February 2002) this matter is presented clearly: "Muhammad was not merely a Prophet, but he was also a military commander to lead his Muslim armies; whereas Jesus Christ even refused to defend himself against the Roman soldiers who arrested him. The Koran and the New Testament have approaches to war and violence different from each other, and by this example we can understand it."

As Vinoba Bhave says, Hinduism is basically a humanistic religion. It does not have any one sacred book, nor one path, nor any one saint or prophet. There is no one-centered organization similar to that of Christianity or Islam. Its nature is not sectarian. 'Islam' means peace. Vinoba analyzes the term 'Hindu' thus: "*Hinsaya duyate chittam sa vai Hinduritiritah*". It means that Hindu is one whose mind-heart is hurt or harassed by violence.

Just as Hinduism is connected with theism, even atheism has a place in it. "We can see the greatest height of freedom of thought in Hinduism. It has a venerable place for six philosophies (khat-darshan) within its fold; and it is a matter of surprise for many as to how so many strains of thought can co-exist in it." Although the Hindus have created certain practical traditions, the Hindu religion is not tied down to it. Its structure is that of a compiler or collective of the whole world thought. That is why there is plenty of space for all thoughts and practices within Hinduism. The original nature of Hinduism is—tolerance of different practices, freedom of thought, pluralism and firm ethical norms. But, in its long history, a number of distortions and defects have crept in the practice of this religion. Otherwise, the emphasis of Hinduism has always been on looking at everybody as human beings first.

Vipul Kalyani, editor of *Opinion* (UK), aptly put this point in these words: "We do not put it thus that 'anyone who is not a Muslim is a Hindu, anyone who is not Christian is a Hindu'; rather it is to be put thus that 'the Hindu is both a Muslim as well as Hindu; and both are human beings and both must have humanity as their religion'."

We have contemporary experiences of World Trade Centre, West Bank, Kashmir-Gujarat, Iraq to show how if the religions turn narrow-minded what havoc they can play by violence, terrorism and savagery, and may destroy all religions and cultures.

Cultures

In this book, the terms 'culture' and 'civilization', although have separate nuances in analytical terminology, used as one or mutual alternatives.

The term 'culture' denotes values, thoughts and lifestyles of social communities. Broadly, the concept of culture is to cover the ethical, intellectual and social values in the background of the concerned society. On the other hand, the term 'civilization' is connected largely with the style of life, its physical and material equipments and techno-progress. The rough definition of K.M. Munshi is handy here: "Culture is 'for what man lives'; Civilization is 'by what man lives'."

Paradigm/Worldview

This term used here is sometimes to indicate 'culture' and in certain contexts to indicate 'worldview', or it refers to conceptual frameworks or thought connections that develop concepts and thought patterns. Also, the term 'worldview' is also often used to indicate 'cultural order', as an alternative of paradigm. The term 'cultural order' includes 'secular' thought—not the negative connotation of non-sectarianism or the neutral content of non-partisanship in religions; but it goes further to give a positive concept of equal respect for all religions (*sarva-dharma-samabhava*) that envelopes concepts of both religion and 'secularism'. Thus, when in a study of terrorism the 'cultural conflicts' have been discussed, to use the terms of 'paradigm' and 'worldview' alternately seemed more opportune and meaningful. In this study of terrorism also for the politico-cultural approach that I have adopted, such an experiment seems more relevant and purposeful.

APPENDIX II
Al Qaeda (AQ) Network

This most dreaded terrorist organization was founded by Osama bin Laden in the 1980s. AQ was supported by the mujahiddin fighting for the Taliban against Soviets in Afghanistan. At present, it carries on its war as *jehad* in the world with America and its allies in focus. AQ's is a 'war by other means', through a global Islamist insurgency.

Its members are 'unknown'.

Main Groups Afficiated with AQ

- Salafist group called COMBAT – Alegria
  Activities: Attacks on government and military
  Members: Several hundred.
  This comparatively new Islamist group targets to pull down Algeria's secular government and eliminate the 'coumpling' foreign influences. Its long-term goal is to spread AQ's influence and advance agenda in Africa and Europe.

- Morroccan Islamic Combatant Group – Morocco
  Activities: Forgery, bombing, arms.
  Members: Unknown
  This Islamist group, allegedly linked to AQ, is believed to have effectively carried out mass casualty bombings in Madrid (March, 2004) and Casablanca (in Summer, 2003).

- Lashkar-e-Toiba (LeT) – Pakistan
  Activities: Bombing, massacres enjoys good funding
  Members: Several hundred
  With training camps run in Afghanistan and in parts of Pakistani territory. LeT is reported for its daredevil terror-missions with dreadful effects. They are directed mainly against Indian troops and civilians in Jammu & Kashmir.

- Jaish-e-Mohammad (JeM) – Pakistan
  Activities: Bombing, massacres
  Members: Several hundred.

This Islamist organization is believed to have bombed the Indian state legislature of Jammu & Kashmir with death toll of 38 persons. It has split into two factions. These groups like LeT, section of Hurriyat and the like, Kashmiri separatist/militant Islamist groups, fight to make predominantly Muslim Kashmir part of Pakistan.

LeT and JeM have been funded, trained, patronised and abetted to carry out their terrorist activities against India and destabilise regions on India's border. President Musharraf has, in public, committed to ban them. They have, however, continued their activities in different guise.

- Lashkar-e-Jhangvi (LeJ) – Pakistan
  Activities: Bombing, massacres
  Members: Fewer than a hundred.

Though small, it is known as a "brutally effective group". LeJ has attacked Shiite mosques and foreigners to destabilise Pakistan. Rabidly anti-American, it is linked to the kidnapping and murder of journalist Daniel Pearl in 2002.

- Moro Islamic Liberation Front – Philippines
  Activities: Bombing
  Members: Around 12,000.

It has unofficial link with the powerful terrorist organization in Southeast Asia, Jemaah Islamiya (JI). It officially disavows having any link to JI. It has led attacks on Philippine cities with the support of JI. At present, it has entered in peace talks with the government with objective to gain ethnic autonomy.

- Asbbat Al Ansar – Lebanon
  Activities: Bombing, Assessination
  Members: More than 300.

Members are linked to AQ. They attack both domestic and international targets located in Lebanon.

- Chechen Separatists – Russia
  Actvities: Kidnapping, murder, bombing and massacres
  Members: Thousands.

They have carried out daredevil activities in Moscow and on the Mosco-Chechenya borders. The insurgents, seeking independence from Russia have killed Russian and even Chechen officials, including Chechenya's President. Despised worldwide and criticised even by moderate Muslims for their massacres of school children in Beslan, they have sensitised the world to what extreme the terrorists can go.

- Islamic Movement of Uzbekistan – Central Asia
  Activities: Bombing, kidnapping
  Members: More than 1,000

This coalition of homegrown Islamist militants aims at replacing the secular regime of Uzbekistan and advance the regional goals of AQ.

Note: There are numerous other terrorists groups like Hamas and Palestine Islamic Jihad, Al Aqsa Martyrsi Brigade (Palestine); Hezbollah (Lebanon); BASQUE (Spain); Abu Sayyaf (Philippines); LTTE (Sri Lanka), etc., but they are not part of AQ official network.

APPENDIX III
Timeline: Al Qaeda

1988: Al Qaeda founded in Afghanistan by Osama bin Laden

As Soviet troops withdraw from Afghanistan, Osama bin Laden and other Arab fighters in the country form al Qaeda which in Arabic means quotthe basequot. The network begins looking for new *jehads* holy wars.

1991: Bin Laden moves to Sudan where he sets up training camps

Sudan becomes al Qaeda's base for business operations and preparations for *jehad*. From here, a number of attacks on Western targets are alleged to have been organised or supported. Bin Laden stays in the African country for five years. During this time, it is believed, he begins a search for nuclear material.

26 February, 1993: Bomb explodes at the World Trade Center in New York

Six people are killed and more than 1,000 injured by a 500 kg bomb. Al Qaeda's involvement is unclear but some analysts believe that after the attack the group sought out the plotter Ramzi Yousef and offered him money. Yousef is serving a life sentence for the attack. His uncle Khalid Sheikh Mohammed currently in custody is thought to have helped plan the 11 September attacks.

4 October, 1993: Eighteen US servicemen killed in Somalia

Members of a Somali militia shoot down two Black Hawk helicopters. The US believes that al Qaeda fighters helped train those responsible for the incident in which 18 American servicemen were killed.

May, 1996: Bin Laden leaves Sudan and returns to Afghanistan

In the mid-1990s, Sudan comes under growing international pressure to expel Osama bin Laden. It is not clear whether he is actually forced to leave the African country but in May 1996 he returns to Afghanistan.

25 June, 1996: US military base in Saudi bombed 19 servicemen killed

A bomb rips through a US military housing complex near Dhahran, Saudi Arabia, killing 19 Americans. The US believes al Qaeda may have been involved in this attack which has been blamed on the militant Hezbollah group.

22 February, 1998: Bin Laden issues fatwa calling for attacks on US citizens

A statement signed by bin Laden and four of his associates calls for the killing of Americans saying it is the quotindividual duty for every Muslim who can do it in any country in which it is possible to do itquot.

7 August, 1998: US embassies in Kenya and Tanzania bombed

More than 220 people are killed when lorries laden with bombs drove into the US embassies in Kenya and Tanzania. On 20 August, the US retaliates with air strikes against alleged training camps in Sudan and Afghanistan. Bin Laden is later indicted by a US court for the bombings in East Africa.

12 October, 2000: Attack on US warship in Yemen kills 17 sailors

Two suicide attackers ram a boat carrying explosives into the USS Cole in Aden port, killing 17 American sailors. In 2004, six suspected al Qaeda militants are charged in connection with the attack by a Yemeni court.

11 September, 2001: The worst attack on US soil kills about 3000 people

Nineteen al Qaeda suspects hijack four planes and fly them into the World Trade Center in New York the Pentagon in Washington and a field in Pennsylvania. Six weeks later, the US launches attacks on Afghanistan from where bin Laden has been operating. After the war, hundreds of suspected al Qaeda fighters are sent to America's base in Guantanamo Bay Cuba where they are held in US custody.

12 December, 2001: First al Qaeda suspect charged over 9/11 in the US

A French citizen of Moroccan origin is charged with conspiring with Osama bin Laden and other suspects to kill thousands of Americans in the 11 September attacks. Zacarias Moussaoui was detained in the US on immigration charges in August after he aroused suspicion at a Minnesota flight school where he sought training. He admits being a member of al Qaeda but denies involvement in the plot to hijack planes and crash them.

14 December, 2001: US releases bin Laden 9/11 video

The US government releases a video which it says proves that Osama bin Laden masterminded the 11 September attacks. In the West, the tape is widely seen as strengthening the case against bin Laden. In the Islamic world, there is widespread scepticism and some claims that it is a fake.

23 December, 2001: Briton held after trying to blow up plane

A British man is arrested on a flight from Paris to Miami after trying to blow up the plane with explosives hidden in his shoes. During his trial in the US Richard Reid pledged allegiance to Osama bin Laden. He is now serving a life sentence.

22 March, 2002: Senior al Qaeda member captured in Pakistan

Abu Zubaydah believed to have served as Osama bin Laden's field commander and chief recruiter is captured during a raid on a house in Pakistan. Number three on America's list of most wanted al Qaeda suspects he is then handed over to the US authorities.

11 April, 2002: Blast at Tunisian synagogue kills 17 people

A fuel tanker is blown up outside a synagogue on the Tunisian island of Djerba, killing 19 people including 14 German tourists. An al Qaeda spokesman later says the organization was behind the suicide attack.

11 June, 2002: Dirty bomb plot foiled says US

The US authorities announce the arrest of an American citizen they accuse of planning to build and detonate a bomb containing radioactive material. Jose Padilla was detained on 8 May at Chicago airport after arriving from Pakistan.

11 September, 2002: 911 plotter captured in Pakistan

Ramzi Binalshibh is arrested in Karachi on the anniversary of the attacks on America. He is accused of being a leading member of al Qaeda and one of the main planners of the 11 September attacks.

12 October, 2002: Bomb attacks on Bali nightclubs kill 202

Two bombs rip through a busy nightclub area in the Balinese town of Kuta, killing 202 people most of them foreign tourists. The Indonesian authorities believe the attacks were carried out by the Southeast Asian militant network Jemaah Islamiah which is said to have links to al Qaeda.

22 October, 2002: First 9/11 trial opens in Germany

Mounir alMotassadek a Moroccan citizen goes on trial in Hamburg accused of membership of a terrorist cell and of being an accessory to the murder of more than 3,000 people. He denies any knowledge of plans to launch the attacks. In 2003, he is found guilty of assisting the hijackers and sentenced to 12 years in jail. Another court later orders a retrial.

28 November, 2002: Israeli targets come under attack in Kenya

Sixteen people including three suicide bombers are killed in a blast at an Israeli owned hotel in Mombasa. A missile fired at an Israeli plane misses its target. A message on a website purporting to come from al Qaeda says the group carried out the attack.

1 March, 2003: Al Qaeda kingpin captured

Khalid Sheikh Mohammed thought to be one of al Qaeda's most senior leaders is arrested in a joint Pakistani CIA operation near Islamabad. The US believes he helped plan the 11 September attacks.

12 May, 2003: Dozens killed in Saudi bombings

At least 34 people are killed in a series of bomb attacks in Saudi Arabia's capital Riyadh. The targets are luxury compounds housing foreign nationals and a US Saudi office. Al Qaeda is the prime suspect, Washington and Riyadh say. It is the first in a string of attacks over successive months in Saudi Arabia.

16 May, 2003: Morocco rocked by suicide attacks

Bomb attacks in Casablanca kill 45 people including 12 attackers. Targets include a Spanish restaurant, a five star hotel, a Jewish community centre and the Belgian consulate. Four men later sentenced to death for the attacks are said by the Moroccan authorities to be members of the Salafia Jihadia widely believed to be linked to al Qaeda.

27 June, 2003: Mastermind of Riyadh attacks arrested

The man suspected of masterminding the series of bombings in Riyadh is detained in Saudi Arabia. The arrest of Ali Abdul Rahman alGhamdi also known as Abu Bakr alAzdi is described as a major blow to al Qaeda's operations in Saudi Arabia. He was number two on the list of most wanted suspects in connection with the 12 May attacks.

15 December, 2003: Suicide bombers hit two Turkish synagogues

At least 23 people are killed and more than 300 injured in two devastating suicide attacks on synagogues in Istanbul. The government blames al Qaeda for the attacks.

20 December, 2003: Two bomb attacks on British interests in Turkey

Attacks on the British Consulate and the HSBC bank offices in Istanbul leave 27 people dead and more than 450 wounded. There are separate claims of responsibility from two allegedly al Qaeda connected groups.

9 February, 2004: US uncovers al Qaeda plans for Iraq violence

US officials say they have uncovered what they believe is a plot by an al Qaeda linked militant Abu Musab al Zarqawi to stir up sectarian violence in Iraq.

11 March, 2004: Madrid rocked by deadly train bombings

Ten bombs explode on four packed early morning commuter trains in Madrid killing 191 people and leaving at least 1,800 injured. Spanish officials later say their investigations are focusing on the Moroccan Islamic Combatant Group which is said to support al Qaeda's war against the West.

15 April, 2004: Bin Laden offers Europe truce

An audio tape purported to be from Osama bin Laden is broadcast. In it, he offers Europe a truce if it quotstops attacking Muslimsquot and withdraws all its troops from Muslim countries.

17 May, 2004: Top Iraqi official killed in suicide attack

Ezzedine Salim head of the Iraqi Governing Council is killed when a bomber blows himself up near the headquarters of the US led coalition in Baghdad. A group linked to al Qaeda suspect Abu Musab al Zarqawi says it carried out the attack. US officials believe Zarqawi is behind a number of attacks in Iraq and was responsible for the beheading of a US hostage.

29 May, 2004: Militant shooting spree and siege kill 22 in Saudi Arabia

Gumen allegedly from a group linked to al Qaeda attack company offices in the eastern city of Khobar killing a number of people. The militants then move to the Oasis housing compound where they seize several dozen people mostly expatriates. The 25 hour crisis ends on 30 May when Saudi commandos storm the housing complex.

18 June, 2004: US engineer beheaded in Saudi Arabia

Suspected al Qaeda militants in Saudi Arabia behead Paul Johnson after holding him hostage for a week. The purported head of al Qaeda in the country Abdul Aziz alMuqrin is later killed by security forces.

30 July, 2004: Embassy bombings suspect arrest announced

The arrest of a key suspect in the bombings of two US embassies in East Africa in 1998 is announced by Pakistani officials. Days after Ahmed Khalfan Ghailani's capture Pakistan confirms the arrest of another man believed to be an al Qaeda computer and communications expert.

26 September, 2004: Pakistan al Qaeda suspect killed

Pakistani police shoot dead suspected al Qaeda militant Amjad Farooqi in a two hour gun battle. Farooqi was wanted in connection with the murder of US journalist Daniel Pearl and attempts to kill Pakistani President Pervez Musharraf. He was said to be a close associate of Abu Faraj alLibbi described as the operational chief of al Qaeda in the region.

29 September, 2004: US warship bombers given death sentence

A Yemeni court sentences Abd alRahim alNashiri and Jamal Mohammed alBadawi to death over the bomb attack on the USS Cole which killed 17 people in 2000. Four others are given between five and 10 years in jail for the attack.

29 October, 2004: Bin Laden video threatens US

Four days before presidential elections in the US, Al Jazeera TV airs a videotape in which Osama bin Laden threatens fresh attacks on the US. The al Qaeda leader says the reasons behind the events of 11 September 2001 still exist.

Courtesy: Source: news.bbc.co.uk (Internet)

Note: Countries where al Qaeda cells are known to be operating: North America, Mexico, Columbia, Peru, Brazil, Argentina, Paraguay, Uruguay, Equdor; Mauritania, Algeria, Nigeria, Libya, Egypt, Sudan, Uganda, Kenya, Jan Zamia, Somalia, South Africa; Spain, France, Italy, UK, Germany, Austria, Bosnia, Uzbekistan, Kazakhstan; Turkey, Iraq, Syria, Iran, Lebanon, Saudi Arabia, Yemen; Afghanistan, Pakistan, India, Bangladesh, Malaysia, Indonesia, Philippines; Australia.

Index